THE LAST
NEW WORLD

THE LAST NEW WORLD

The Conquest of the Amazon Frontier

MAC MARGOLIS

W · W · NORTON & COMPANY · NEW YORK   LONDON

Copyright © 1992 by Mac Margolis

The text of this book is composed in Times Roman
with the display set in Neuland
Composition and Manufacturing by
the Maple Vail Book Manufacturing Group
Book design by Jacques Chazaud

Library of Congress Cataloging-in-Publication Data

Margolis, Mac.
    The last new world : the conquest of the Amazon frontier /
  by Mac Margolis.
        p.   cm.
    Includes index.
    1. Man—Influence on nature—Amazon River Region.
  2. Economic development—Environmental aspects.   3. Amazon River
  Region—Economic conditions.   4. Environmental policy—Amazon
  River Region.
  I. Title.
  GF532.A4M37   1992
  333.7′0981′1—dc20   91-37685

ISBN 0-393-03379-1

W.W. Norton & Company, Inc.
500 Fifth Avenue, New York, N.Y. 10110
W.W. Norton & Company Ltd. 10 Coptic Street, London WC1A 1PU

1 2 3 4 5 6 7 8 9 0

For my parents,
and for Paola

CONTENTS

ACKNOWLEDGMENTS

This book could not have been written without the care and comfort of my friends and colleagues. Heartfelt thanks go to Margaret Engel and the Alicia Patterson Foundation for the fellowship that got me started on this Amazon journey. José Murilo de Carvalho generously took the time to read Chapter 3 and offered invaluable insights and comments. Paola Bustamante's incisive criticism, scholarship, and affection helped me through the roughest moments.

Dear friends Michael Kepp and Andrew Posner were untiring in their encouragement and provided crucial technical assistance at the Garota da Urca and other centers of investigation. Walter Tauber, an accomplice on many Amazon travels over the last years, was a constant source of ideas, inspiration, and *caipirinhas*. Special thanks go to Lúcia Guimarães for believing in me.

More than they know it, Jim Miller of Trinity College and Rick Hornung of the *Village Voice* helped me turn raw ideas into pages and chapters. David Levitt's friendship was in many ways what gave me the courage to go to Brazil in the first place.

Earl Foell of the *World Monitor Magazine* gave me the confidence and the space to write articles that would become central to the shaping of this book. Cesar Ottoni, in Rio de Janeiro, was unflagging in his efforts to ferret out the most obscure of texts from the mustiest libraries. Anne Margolis did the same in mustiest Connecticut. George Margolis kept my clip file fat and up-to-date.

Many more people than I could possibly give tribute to here were vital in focusing my vague notions on the Amazon and on Brazil or simply in helping me get through page after page. Some of them are: Jaime Lerner, Amaury de Souza, Marcos Magalhães, Ricardo and Adriana Lessa, David Atkinson, Charles Thurston, Christina Lamb, Alexandre de Barros, Alfredo Homma, Stephen Schwartzman, Juan de Onis, Willem Groeneveld, Jeff Ryser, Jason Clay, Jean Dubois, Anthony Anderson, Judson Valentim, and Mário Romagueira.

Of course, this would not have been a book at all had it not been for the support of my agent, Rollene Saal, the valuable criticism and careful eye of my editor, Starling Lawrence, and the always cheerful assistance of Richard Halstead and everyone at W. W. Norton.

In Brazil, especially in the humble backlands, it is customary to send one's visitors off with a touching *adeus:* "*Desculpa qualquer coisa.*" Forgive me, that is, for anything that may have displeased you. Anything at all. To the dozens of people I met in the Amazon, who were so generous with their time and wisdom, I express my deepest gratitude and can only echo their salute. "*Desculpa qualquer coisa.*"

BRAZIL

VENEZUELA

COLOMBIA

GUYANA

SURINAM

FRENCH GUIANA

Boa Vista

RORAIMA

AMAPÁ

Macapá

Belém

São Luís

RIO GRANDE DO NORTE

Fortaleza

PARAÍBA

Natal

Manaus

A M A Z O N A S

P A R Á

MARANHÃO

CEARÁ

Teresina

João Pessoa

ACRE

Rio Branco

Porto Velho

PIAUÍ

PERNAMBUCO

Recife

Miracema do Norte

TOCANTINS

ALAGOAS

Maceió

RONDÔNIA

MATO GROSSO

BAHIA

Acaraju

SERGIPE

PERU

BOLIVIA

DISTRITO FEDERAL

BRASÍLIA

Cuiabá

Goiânia

GOIÁS

MINAS GERAIS

Salvador

PACIFIC OCEAN

MATO GROSSO DO SUL

Campo Grande

SÃO PAULO

Belo Horizonte

ESPÍRITO SANTO

Vitória

RIO DE JANEIRO

PARAGUAY

PARANÁ

São Paulo

Rio de Janeiro

CHILE

Foz do Iguaçu

Curitiba

SANTA CATARINA

Florianópolis

ATLANTIC OCEAN

ARGENTINA

RIO GRANDE DO SUL

Porto Alegre

URUGUAY

0   100 200 300 400 500 miles

0   200   400   600   800 km

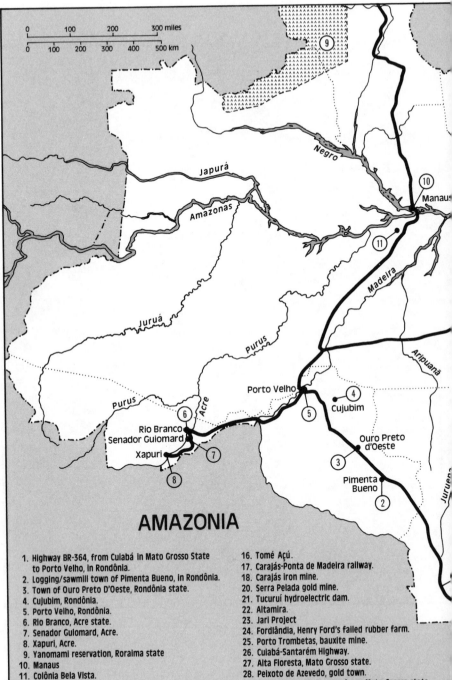

AMAZONIA

1. Highway BR-364, from Cuiabá in Mato Grosso State to Porto Velho, in Rondônia.
2. Logging/sawmill town of Pimenta Bueno, in Rondônia.
3. Town of Ouro Preto D'Oeste, Rondônia state.
4. Cujubim, Rondônia.
5. Porto Velho, Rondônia.
6. Rio Branco, Acre state.
7. Senador Guiomard, Acre.
8. Xapuri, Acre.
9. Yanomami reservation, Roraima state
10. Manaus
11. Colônia Bela Vista.
12. Brasília
13. Belém-Brasília Highway, or Highway of the Jaguar.
14. Transamazônica, or TransAmazon Highway.
15. Açailândia, Maranhão state.
16. Tomé Açú.
17. Carajás-Ponta de Madeira railway.
18. Carajás iron mine.
20. Serra Pelada gold mine.
21. Tucuruí hydroelectric dam.
22. Altamira.
23. Jari Project
24. Fordlândia, Henry Ford's failed rubber farm.
25. Porto Trombetas, bauxite mine.
26. Cuiabá-Santarém Highway.
27. Alta Floresta, Mato Grosso state.
28. Peixoto de Azevedo, gold town.
29. Fazenda Itamaraty, soya farm, Mato Grosso state.
30. Cuiabá, capital of Mato Grosso state.
31. Mimoso, Rondon's birthplace.
32. Michelin rubber plantation.

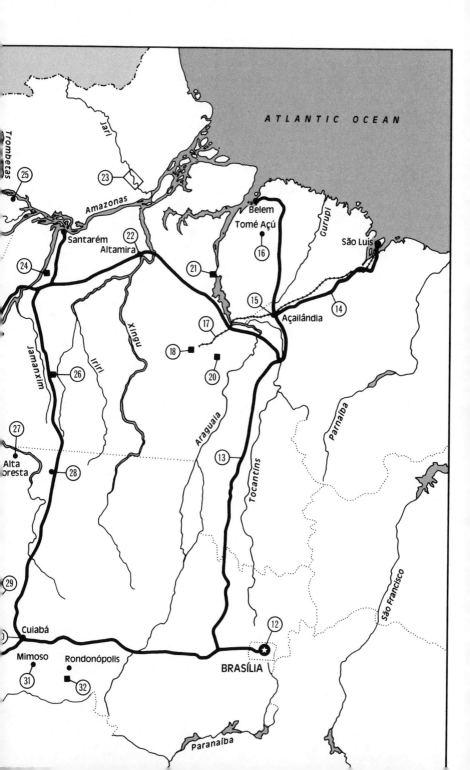

INTRODUCTION

That jungle wasn't just leaves and silent paths and moving sunlight on still pools of water; it was people too.

—Moritz Thomsen, *The Saddest Pleasure*

About a hundred miles north of Manaus, the old rubber barons' town that sits at the crook of the Amazon and the Rio Negro, a two-lane dirt road cuts a winding path through the rain forest. In time the wall of woods gives way to a pleasant parquetry of farms and cattle pastures. Here and there cows forage on knee-high grass, made green and thick from the rains of the wet season. The soil is spongy and sodden after so many days of downpours, and wisps of vapor hang in the air like bits of tissue paper. At the edge of these tidy fields the jungle begins again, dense and dark, rising ten green stories. It was here in the central Amazon, at the frontier where human landscapes meet wilderness, that I got my first real sense of the storied Amazon rain forest.

This was April, the end of the six-month rainy season. My destination was a forest camp, a rugged three-hour drive by jeep over roads that days of downpours had made treacherous with slick reddish mud. Those tending the camp were not cowpunchers or Amazonian colonists but young students of biology, botany, and geology from American and Brazilian universities. They were devoting their vacations to a special experiment in the rain forest, a place most of them were seeing for the first time. For weeks on end they put up with stifling heat and clouds of mosquitoes. They had no beds below them and only a flimsy tarpaulin roof above. Food was no better than army fare. But there was excitement in their words and expectation stamped on their faces.

It was 1984, and these students were taking part in a newly launched research project by the World Wildlife Fund, a twenty-year effort to study the animal and plant life in disturbed areas of the jungle. Brainchild of noted tropical forest ecologist Thomas Lovejoy (now of the Smithsonian Institution), this was one of the boldest experiments of its day. The goal was to discover, in the face of the inevitable assault of man on a dwindling wilderness, just how much punishment this woods could take before the families of species it harbored would deteriorate and die off. I had the opportunity to accompany these researchers for a few days and for the first time to get a feel of the world's greatest tract of tropical forest.

Hours earlier, from the window of a Boeing, I had seen the forest the way I supposed most newcomers did, only as a carpet of ignoble-looking vegetation. Its fabric was full of rents and flaws, spun in haste, it seemed, from threads tinged in a hundred shades of green, ocher, and dun. Here and there rivers, serpentine and brown from their overload of accumulated silt, wound through the forest. Cumulus clouds, dark and flat at the base and rising to cottony domes above, lumbered about the skies. Flying for nearly an hour, I saw no roads, no towns, or farms—no human imprint on the tedious woodscape scrolling below. Such a tenantless wilderness defies the imagination. It numbs the senses with its immensity, try as we may to contain it with our paltry measures and metaphors. The Brazilian explorer Euclydes da Cunha, who was in thrall to the majesty of the Amazon, called it "the last page of Genesis."

If not with pictures, we try to grasp the Amazon with numbers. There is, in fact, a kind of ritual accounting recited to describe the Amazon's vastness. I recalled from textbooks that the lands drained by the Amazon's thousands of rivers sprawl over some 2.8 million square miles, stretching from the foothills of the Andes in the west nearly to the Atlantic in the east; from the marshes of the Pantanal in the south nearly to the Caribbean in the north. It is as large, we are told, as the whole continental United States. Just the Brazilian part of the Amazon could swallow up all of the United States west of the Mississippi. That great American river is less than a tenth as long as the Amazon, which loses out in length only to the Nile, and then by just a few miles. During the wet season the Amazon River dumps some 300,000 cubic meters (10.5 million cubic feet) of water per second into the Atlantic—nearly a fifth of all the waters disgorged into oceans by all the world's rivers. The high, dense forest that dominates the region contains perhaps 1.5 to 2 million species of plants and animals, or nearly 2 to 4 percent of the estimated total of species reckoned to live on the planet.

Once on the ground, I got a different vantage on the Amazon. Its canopy was as tall as skyscrapers and so thick as practically to ink out the burning equatorial sun. Below, giant trunks of Brazil nut, cedar, and *cerejeira* soared, dusky colonnades to this living edifice. Vines hung down in a tangle, like telephone cables torn loose after a storm. The understory of the forest was painted in pastels and halftones, broken only by a dash of electric blue or red when the occasional parrot or macaw flashed across the sky. At night, in the pitch heart of forest, the catalog of Amazonian numbers gave way to subtler information supplied by touch, smell, and hearing. The forest exhaled a musk of decay and played a muffled calliope of sounds.

I was ill prepared for my first night in the Amazon, only by science books, bad movies, and the manufacture of my imagination. So I conjured pictures of cats with wild eyes circling the campfire and snakes coiling down from boughs into my hammock. I listened for disembodied howls. As it turned out, the night was disturbingly uneventful. No great mammals prowled or bellowed, no scorpions bedded in my shoes, and no witless tenderfoot was swallowed by an anaconda.

The most terrible of beasts were the most minute. The mosquitoes took to my bug repellent like flies to doughnut glaze. Remarkably, the caboclos, or mixed-blood Amazonian woodsmen, seemed inured to these attacks. They curled up in their hammocks like armadillos, offering up their bare backs, sleeping soundly while a host of mosquitoes lit, fed, and taxied dizzily away.

I was surprised by the cold of the forest at night. Only hours earlier I had stepped out of a pressurized Varig Airlines jetliner smack into the wall of heat that encastles Manaus. Sweat emptied from every pore. But in the woods, with the sun gone, the humid air clung to me like a clammy overcoat. There was no wind, but the chilly wetness penetrated to the bone. Any article of clothing or equipment left uncovered was soaked with dew by morning. I had come only with the equipment I imagined was required in the tropics: T-shirt, cotton pants, a light nylon hammock, and Lomotil. Envious of the more seasoned campers wrapped in wool blankets, I ended up tossing and trembling all night.

But the discomfort faded before the discoveries of my hosts as they tramped through the forest. These scientists were trying out something never before attempted. Though investigators had already observed natural succession on small tropical islands and in various isolated patches of rain forest in Central America and South Asia, never had there been an attempt to intervene massively in the process and watch for the consequences. The scientists had made over a sixty-square-mile tract of the Amazon into a vast laboratory experiment, systematically altering the natural habitat and measuring the results.

One entomologist spent hours at a time trying to seduce a two-yard-long column of army ants into a twenty-gallon plastic trash bucket. His plan was to transport the regiment to another habitat to see how it would fare. A mammal specialist padded over miles of deep forest trails, craning her neck skyward, visually combing the canopy for spider monkeys. Still another intern pointed giant-stemmed microphones at the muck to record the songs of rare frogs. For the sake of their science, these researchers bore the heat and the bugs and the dampness. Their skin went sallow from the lack of sun, and their wardrobes were laced with a permanent perfume of mildew.

One Harvard junior explained such stamina: "How many people can actually say they got to discover a species?" And that was the magic of this otherwise oppressive jungle. Buried in the woodland chaos were mysteries waiting to be unraveled. Here were new scientists discovering new forms of life, practically tripping over them, in fact, rejoicing in the forest that pioneers knew as a green hell.

Months later, and a thousand miles to the southwest, I watched another community of strangers confront the Amazonian wilderness. This was on a damp winter day in the western Brazilian Amazon. I left the paved highway in a Ford F-1000 pickup, bumping along a dirt road that wound its way due southwest, leading eventually all the way to the Bolivian border. Roads like this one had blossomed all up and down this territory, shooting off from the trunk of the asphalt highway like the tendrils of some indomitable weed. Along these roads came travelers. And wherever they put down their loads, towns erupted, as suddenly and plentifully as earthworms after rain.

After a few hours of driving, I pulled into one of these towns that appeared to have been only recently carved out of the rain forest. This was Alvorada do Oeste (Dawn of the West), in the extreme west of the territory (it had not yet become a state) called Rondônia. The forest had been felled to expose raw earth, as moist and scarlet as a fresh wound. On each side of the muddy track, new houses were going up, ribbed with the blond sideboards of freshly sawed timber and cobbled together with shiny steel nails. Pickup trucks rumbled down the main street, dodging potholes and mule carts. The whine of half a dozen sawmills filled the air.

There I met the keeper of a small hotel. At twelve dollars a night, his inn was easily the priceyest in town. It was also a tidy place with gleaming ceramic tile floors and a girl to sweep up the red mud and dust tracked in from the unpaved street. Predictably his hotel was full up, with farmers, ranchers, loggers, and drifters. My encounter with this man lasted only a few minutes. But before I pushed on, we traded comments about bad weather, bad roads, bad harvests, and the mean way of life on the Rondônia frontier. We watched as the afternoon sun darkened and died over the tree line; its glow was replaced by that of a single hundred-watt bulb gleaming dully on his porch. These were tough times in Alvorada, in all Rondônia, in fact, and this man had something to say about that. Leaning on his stoop, he lifted a chin toward the woods, where the broad dirt road became a clay ribbon and vanished behind the curtain of green.

"If you walk the road there"—he gestured again—"every hundred meters or so you'll find a shack with a roof of straw and coconut palm leaves. Go still farther, and you'll see a *picadinha* [a footpath], where nothing bigger than a mule can pass. Follow it, and way back in the woods you'll find a house, a shack really, a man, his wife, five, six children or more, maybe, living there, in the middle of the forest and the malaria. He works all day every day. If he gets sick, he may die. And if he dies, they'll bury him right there." The innkeeper went quiet, waiting a beat for effect. "Life here," he finished, "is like that."

These were pioneers' words. They were born of fear but also of a respect for the wilderness that began just in back of his outhouse. To this man, and to so many settlers of the Amazon, the forest was an unruly, awe-inspiring place, as implacable as that "vast and howling wilderness" Mary Rowlandson trembled before in untamed Massachusetts three centuries ago. Their Amazon did not inspire joy but an equally strong emotion: dread. But in this way the settlers of Rondônia were environmentalists, in the most basic sense of that word. To them, life was ruled by the contest with the elements, an unequal contest in these niggardly tropics that only electricity, cultivation, and asphalt could make even again.

I left Alvorada the next day but returned to the Amazon a number of times over the next years. I visited dozens of frontier towns like this one, meeting scores of settlers, farmers, and ranchers, rubber tappers, and Indians. All of them struggled in the way the innkeeper had described to make a life in the Amazon. I also met field scientists, agronomists, and rural extension workers, and learned a little about their investigations and the new worlds they were turning up. Both these communities, the scientists and settlers, were steeped in their own colliding visions and truths about the same environment. Both their Amazons seemed to compete for attention. Were these two sets of peoples, settlers and scientists, doomed to be antagonists? Did the fate of the Amazon depend on whichever camp shouted louder? Would the suffering pioneers bull onward, brazenly destroying the environment in order to tame it, while the ecologists mobilized only to embargo them?

Today, some nine years after my first visit to the region, these questions still echo. They resound even louder now that the destruction of the Amazon has become headline news and the target of world protests. Can the forest coexist with the frontier? I found no ready answers then or in the years since. Yet something seemed to bind these two peoples of the Amazon. In separate and seemingly contradictory ways, both were trying to make order and sense out of the opaque tangle of the rain forest. Both the pioneer and the scientist were environmentalists in their contrasting ways. The elements were what inspired them and commanded their lives. Both of them looked to the land for secrets and solutions. Their struggle was to know this region and its requirements and so to conquer the Amazon.

But the struggle over the Amazon has spilled way beyond the borders of South America, and a reporter is drawn inexorably into the larger arena. Since my first visit to the Amazon in the early eighties, halting the destruction of the rain forest has quickly grown from a concern to a campaign. Now that sensibilities have greened almost everywhere on the planet, it is a crusade. My niece's elementary school in the Connecticut suburbs sponsors "rain forest socials," to raise funds to buy up acres of the endangered tropics. The corner grocery markets forest-friendly products, like Brazil nut cookies and copaiba oil soap, whose raw ingredients are culled, instead of cut, from the woods. Rock stars sing for Indians and rubber gatherers. Forest Indians with lip plates and war paint lecture in Toronto and Berlin. The pages of *Cosmopolitan* and spots on MTV decry the vanishing woodlands. Fate and fashion have come together.

These odes to the Amazon are not just noble poetry but warnings about our overburdened earth. If they are not heeded, the environmentalists have schooled us, we may not be around to file our regrets. The trees of the rain forest provide shade, absorb moisture, and stay soil erosion. Their trunks and boughs contain carbon matter that, if toppled and burned, transform into carbon dioxide and methane, the gases of our planet's steamy greenhouse. Societies may contribute only modestly to the total global carbon budget, but some experts now reckon that just their slim addition may be enough to tilt the atmospheric balance, thus changing the slim band of tolerable temperatures and amenable weather that ensure man's tenancy on earth. True, most carbon emissions come from the burning of gasoline and oil. But in the developing world, forest cutting and burning are the chief sources of greenhouse gases, and in Brazil, forest burnings release three times more carbon matter than the burning of fossil fuels.

Most important, perhaps, the rain forest is also home to countless living things. More creatures make their homes on a single Amazonian tree than on an acre of the temperate countries. Locked up in the fabulous "biodiversity" of the tropical woodlands may be cures for maladies ranging from cancer to skin rashes, as well as the raw material for organic fertilizers and pest controls. The genetic resources of the Amazon are goods that societies may acquire not in the usual way, by clearing the land, but by preserving it from cutting and cultivation. Cutting down the forest may be burning our botanical bridges to survival.

Because so many areas of the Amazon are still unexplored and their wealth of species is uncounted, many ecologists argue today for cordoning off as much of the rain forest as possible. This last position is also the most controversial. Total preservation would, of course, mean embargoing the development of such prized natural resources as timber, gold, tin, hydroelectric power, and natural gas buried in or under the forest. The Brazilian government, while acknowledging the need for preservation, has traditionally recoiled at suggestions—particularly suggestions from abroad—that the nation ought to write off any part of its domain to ecological posterity.

But politics is not the only challenge. From the movies or a Boeing, we may think of the rain forest as a uniform leafy ocean, but there are, in fact, many Amazons. The dense, high forests, which Alexander von Humboldt dubbed *hylea,* after the Greek word for "jungle zone," cover about half the Brazilian Legal Amazon, or a little more than one million square miles. Within *hylea* there are also many kinds of forest, ranging from the dense, biologically rich woods of the *várzea,* or floodplains, to the taller upland forests with the most prized timber, like mahogany and cedar. The Tapajós Forest of central Amazonia, for instance, harbors four distinct ecosystems, each with characteristic trees, creepers, insects, reptiles, and mammals. Some parts of the Amazon have virtually no forest at all. One such region is the Cachimbo ridge, lying between the states of Pará and Mato Grosso, a land as arid and sandswept as any desert. Much of the rest of the region is divided into natural savannas, flat and grassy as the plains of central Africa; sparser palm forests, where far fewer species exist; and scrubby bush, called *cerrado.*

Some of these microecoystems, though laden with treasures, are so delicate they would sustain neither people nor the
progress they seem to promise. But the reverse is also true.
There are areas of Amazonia where soils are fertile or rich in
mineral and timber wealth. Embargoing their development
would mean denying the people of Amazon vital resources.

Even a brief passage through the Brazilian frontier is an
immersion in a bramble of questions and quandaries. How to
balance the preservation of vast spaces of the Amazon against
the requirements of the people who, for better or worse, have
settled in the region? Wilderness is what we worship these
days, but it is society we must abide. Here, perhaps, is the link
between the young scientists in the field north of Manaus and
the miserable pioneers I met buried in the entrails of Rondônia. Now they may be antagonists, but they are inextricably
bound together, locked in a separate search on common ground.

It was Chico Mendes, the Acre rubber tapper and union leader
slain by a rancher in 1988, who told the world not only about
the splendid rain forest but also that there were people living
there. He told us that the drama of the Amazon was also about
its residents and their struggle to come to terms with their complex habitat. For the people of the Amazon are poor, desperately poor, and there is nothing so destructive as despair. Despair
is what drives them headlong up the tendrils of dirt roads and
forest trails and ignites the flames of every burning season.
Now, more than ever, the people Mendes championed and died
for also need tending. Mendes's Amazon was a human landscape. It still is today.

See, I have this day set thee over the nations, and over the kingdoms, to root out, and to pull down, and to destroy, and to throw down, to build, and to plant.

—Jeremiah 1:10

Each blade of grass has its spot on earth whence it draws its life, its strength; and so is man rooted to the land from which he draws his faith together with his life.

—Joseph Conrad, *Lord Jim*

What soon became known as the New World was in fact the old world, the oldest world we know, the world the West once had been.

—Frederick Turner, *Beyond Geography: The Western Spirit against the Wilderness*

THE LAST
NEW WORLD

THE CONQUEST OF THE AMAZON FRONTIER

> They were conquerors, and for that you want only brute force—nothing to boast of, when you have it, since your strength is just an accident arising from the weakness of others. They grabbed what they could get for the sake of what was to be got. It was just robbery with violence, aggravated murder on a great scale, and men going at it blind— as is very proper for those who tackle a darkness.
>
> —Joseph Conrad, *Heart of Darkness*

> We know the whole breadth of the habitable world up to the uninhabitable regions which bound it, where habitation ceases on the one side because of cold, on the other because of the heat.
>
> —Aristotle

One day late in September, in 1984, when the rains of winter had not yet come to allay the heat of the Amazon, a construction crew poured and packed the last bit of asphalt on a new highway. João Baptista Figueiredo, the Brazilian president and the last of the generals who ran things in this South American nation for twenty-one years, presided over the inauguration. Known for a sour face and a spirit to match, the general was now in shirt sleeves and even

smiling, relieved, it seemed, to be suddenly in the rough outdoors and so far away from the steel and glass confines of
Brasília and the nagging requirements of ruling. The ceremony
was a simple affair—a ribbon cutting, a speech, a purling of
applause. But the road was to change the story of the Amazon
and, in no small way, of Brazil itself.

The highway was called simply BR-364, and it cut a diag-
onal slash through nearly one thousand miles of the far western
Brazilian countryside, from Cuiabá, at the extreme south of
the region known as the Legal Amazon, to Porto Velho, the
old river town in the densely forested federal territory of Rondônia. Before the tarmac, this road was dirt top, passable for
only half the year that is dry season in the Amazon, a sea of
mud for the other half. Before it became a road, it was a wagon
track, a forty-five-yard-wide beaten path running under a telegraph line, strung in the second decade of this century by the
army colonel Cândido Rondon. Rondon, who came to be one
of the twentieth century's greatest explorers, eventually had
his name emblazoned upon this frontier territory that he trekked,
surveyed, and mapped during two decades. And Rondônia,
which gained statehood in 1986, eventually became emblazoned upon the world's imagination as the scenario of the Great
Amazonian debacle, of forests in flame, Indians besieged, and
ecosystems destroyed.

It was the next year, in November 1985, when I and a few
colleagues decided to travel the length of BR-364. The Rondônia highway gleamed with its new jacket of gray asphalt. A
blackening sky announced the imminent rains. Sunlight played
through the rents in the storm clouds, which brooded and swelled
from the steam rising off the perspiring forest. This wetness
began a thousand miles to the west, in the web of mountain
streams that stirred as the winter snows melted off of the Andes,
their trickle turning to a torrent as the waters tumbled down,
seventeen thousand feet, and spilled east into the churning
tributaries of the world's largest river basin, the Amazon.

Just thirty years ago this journey was a desolate one, often a battle with floods, mudholes, malaria, and on occasion contrary Indians. The army construction battalion that built the dirt road in the 1960s lost forty men to accidents and a host of tropical diseases. Signs posted along the way advised motorists not to dally along stretches known for hostile Amazon tribesmen. Now the road signs warned of pedestrians, stoplights, and speed bumps. Back behind the asphalt was a less predictable world, a dark, dense wall of rain forest 150 feet tall. But for now, from the safety of the solid contours of the highway, the Amazonian frontier looked like an inviting, sundappled place, shining with newness and possibility—the way, it seemed, frontiers were supposed to look.

Speeding along at sixty-five miles per hour in a rented Volkswagen Rabbit, we passed lot after lot of tidy ranch houses and lush farmers' fields. Then, just outside Ariquemes, the second-largest town in Rondônia, we slowed down as we approached a small crowd gathered in the front yard before a homestead on the roadside. The gateway was of thick logs, dressed still in their coat of bark and fitted together in a skillful fashion to make a solid, rustic fence. A crowd of about thirty was gathered on the green grass of the side yard. The spreading boughs of a mango tree provided shelter from the sun and the one-hundred-degree heat. We wondered at the time if we had stumbled upon a wedding. The idea fired our imaginations (the bride in a tiara of wild flowers, the groom in pressed overalls), and as we approached, curiosity conquered embarrassment and soon fueled the shameless reporter's habit of invasion.

There on the spreading lawn under the waxy-leafed *mangueira,* a priest in elegant vestments, draped in medallions, and clutching a beaten leather-bound Bible, was delivering a solemn mass. The house belonged to Vitório Pchek, the son of a Ukrainian immigrant who had come to southern Brazil half a century before. In the 1970s Vitório, in turn, had taken his family to Rondônia, Brazil's newest frontier, to make life over again in the Amazon Basin. The Pcheks were surprisingly gracious before this intrusion—four reporters, with cameras, notebooks, and a barrage of questions. They hesitated only at the beginning, until they were assured that none of us was "from Moscow." We stayed briefly, through the morning prayers and long enough to record a few depositions from this frontier family.

As I recall that event, I think now that what fascinated us on that sultry Sunday morning was not simply the novelty of finding living souls in this unlikely landscape or seeing the jungle toppled and the land transformed into a new farm and home. The remarkable thing was that, here, on the New World's newest frontier, something ancient was taking place. The gathering, as it turned out, was not a wedding but a simple prayer service—but not just any prayer service. The priest wore the squarish, tasseled cap of Christian Orthodoxy and, despite the heat, a bulky purple felt robe. He might have walked straight out of some stone church of Byzantium. He intoned a millennial mass, while the family said prayers and repeated the required rituals—the same rituals I imagined that the Pcheks had observed for generations, perhaps for centuries.

This Amazonian idyll was the sort of scene I supposed that had been re-created for countless years, an energetic tradition, born equally of genius, obstinance, and terrible violence that is humankind's contest with the elements in ever new settings. It had been going on ever since we were evicted from Eden and remanded to Wilderness. The contest with wilderness took many forms: journeys back to promised lands; crusades, empire; the conquest of national frontiers. Over the centuries such ventures have been ennobled, wrapped up like the Rondônia priest in a lush vestment of ideology: Providence, Manifest Destiny, the Covenant of the Calvinist Boers, and, in Brazil, Order and Progress and the March to the West.

It has been almost a hundred years since Frederick Jackson Turner announced the end of the American frontier, in 1893. It was not, of course. The American Leviathan, as Richard Van Alstyne called it, simply kept going—west beyond California to Hawaii and on to the Philippines, south of Texas into Central America, and east of Florida into the Caribbean. Empire and frontier, scholars might protest, are distinct experiences, born of distinct motives. Frontiers, after all, are mostly a continental business, the quest of a vast and sparsely populated nation to know, then to take, and finally to settle its untended regions. Empire we think of as a more brutal, club-footed affair, one nation forcing its will upon another, generally across the oceans. Those distinctions have melted away along with the invincibility of the mountains, deserts, seas, and forests that once hemmed peoples in. The technological marvels that have moved people across the globe since the Age of Discovery— the lateen-rigged sailing ship, the steamer, the automobile, and the airplane—have seen to that.

Indeed, America, before it was called that, was nothing more than "Europe's West," says Canadian historian Brian W. Dippie. Turner himself made no such neat distinctions. "The first idea of the pioneer was that of conquest," he wrote. It was not for nothing that Brazil's fiery populist and sometimes dictator Getúlio Vargas, who knew what language to invoke to whip up public sentiment, called his campaign to settle the interior both a "March to the West" and a mission of "internal imperialism." Frontiers are empires by another name.

Not all frontier episodes were glorious adventures, told by Turners and Vargases, of course. Now that we have a half millennium's distance on it, Europe's discovery of the Americas has been retold lately with far less luster. In fact, stripped of the schoolbook mythos, the Old World's thrust into the Caribbean and North and South America looks like nothing so much as a grand romp of procurement. "It was nevertheless my wish not to pass any island without taking possession of it, although when one had been annexed, all might be said to have been," wrote Columbus in his log, off the coast of San Salvador, in the Caribbean, on October 15, 1492.[1] Yet for every Kipling who sang the praises of the western empire, there was a Conrad, reeling from "the horror." For every Buffalo Bill Cody, dispatching red men and bison, there was a John Muir, railing at herdsmen and profit-possessed developers. The frontier mentality produced its own antithesis, which had eloquent and passionate spokespeople.

But on both sides of the barricades there seemed to be agreement over a fundamental point. As the literary scholar Martin Green notes, a chasm of values and sensibility separates *Roughing It,* the hard-bitten chronicles of the adventurer president Theodore Roosevelt from anthropologist Claude Lévi-Strauss's *Tristes Tropiques,* about the disappearing world of the Brazilian Indians. Yet something binds the two narrators on a single skein. "What was the most important event in modern history?" Green asks. Rough rider and anthropologist "would both answer, Europe's conquest of the rest of the world."[2] The contemporary polemics over the true legacy of Columbus only reinforce the point. To some it was a glorious discovery; to others an armed invasion. To both camps the world has never been the same since.

Nevertheless, for the conquerors, at least, frontier quests became tales that served as rough allegories of nations in the making—the stories "that England told itself as it went to sleep at night," says Green, of the literature of British colonialism. "They charged England with the will and energy to go out and explore, conquer, and rule."[3] Again and again the deeds of conquest were distilled into popular culture, literature, and legend. Europe's imperial frontiers produced Crusoe and Ivanhoe. As the U.S. society marched inexorably west, into its own New World, literature bloomed with its Deerslayers, Boones, and Natty Bumppos.

The colonization of south and central Brazil, the old frontier, also produced a brand of romantic adventure. José de Alencar and Antônio Gonçalves Dias wrote immensely popular tales of the encounter and clash of Indian and immigrant cultures. "The forest felled, now the [land's] aspect changes: on each river bank, a good shaded place to build [a home], a cow pen, a sawmill and sugar mill. In a short span of years, it has turned into a remarkable place, of progress and plenty," writes the novelist Mário Palmério in *Chapadão do Bugre* (Indian prairie), of the settlers' encounter with Indians and the rugged forests and tablelands of Goiás and Minas Gerais. The Amazon frontier has not so far spun so rich a genre of popular adventure tales. In fact, from Alberto Rangel's *Inferno Verde (Green Hell)* to Márcio Souza's *Mad Maria,* the mood in contemporary Amazonian fiction has been more the apocalyptic, antifrontier variety and often unsparingly critical of the bullish expansionist ideology.

But the story of the modern Brazilian Amazon frontier is at bottom a story of conquest. Viewed through the cool glass of history, this is only the most familiar sort of human ritual, the occupation of one more of the world's "waste spaces" and the coming to terms with the commandments of a new climate and ecology. Though such a contest has often meant pioneer creativity in the face of adversity, it has never been a clement affair. "The conquest of the earth, which mostly means the taking it away from those who have a different complexion or slightly flatter noses than ourselves, is not a pretty thing when you look into it much," muses Marlow, Conrad's pensive narrator, as he steams up the Congo to darkness.[4] Well, in the Amazon frontier everyone is looking into much, and the ugliness has become news for the world and Brazil's shame.

Since biblical times the terms of this rogue mandate have been brutally clear. "Divide and multiply and subdue the earth," Genesis instructs a people contemplating an exuberant, terrifying wilderness. "I shall make thee as a new thrashing wain, with teeth like a saw. Thou shalt thrash the mountains and break them into pieces; thou shalt make the hills as chaff," thunders the Lord in Isaiah (41:16, Douay version).

René Dubos, the thoughtful bacteriologist and philosopher, has argued in his provocative book *The Wooing of Earth* that such revisionist readings of the Bible are skewed. He notes that there are just as many passages of the Old and New Testaments schooling ecological consciousness as there are those calling for domination. For every appeal to felling there is another for sowing. Just three verses later (41:19) Isaiah reads: "I will plant in the wilderness the cedar, the shittah tree, and the myrtle, and the oil tree; I will set in the desert the fir tree, and the pine, and the box tree together."

The planting of fir, box, and myrtle is agriculture, not devastation, but everywhere it, too, has required the hand, sometimes the heavy hand, of man upon a wilderness. Sometimes there were human obstacles to these endeavors, and the results were predictably devastating to the lands' original tenants. The Boers overran the Zulu, pushing them out of the veld. The Russians trampled the Samoyed, Tungus, and Yakut as they swept through the Siberian steppe. Cherokee, Sioux, and Cheyenne were the Old West's victims. The Brazilians assaulted the Paiaguá, Tupi-Guarani, and Kayapó. Some of these peoples offered valiant resistance. But in most of the New World's frontiers, resistance of aboriginals, even fierce resistance, died quickly before the formidable array of invading weapons: from fevers to firearms. Even the very customs of invaders proved devastating. "We can see that the cultivation of the land will be fatal in many ways to savages, for they cannot, or will not, change their habits," writes Darwin.[5]

Many have written eloquently about the terrible human toll of such conquests. The Bulgarian scholar Tzvetan Todorov, in his masterful *The Conquest of America*, retrieves the critical spirit of Bartolomé de Las Casas, the Spanish priest who first and most passionately defended the Indians of the New World against his marauding countrymen. John Hemming, in his two exhaustive volumes *Red Gold: The Conquest of the Brazilian Indians, 1500–1760* and *Amazon Frontier: The Defeat of the Brazilian Indians*, deals scathingly with the protagonists of this conquest. "First the soldiers fall on their knees, and then they fall upon the Indians," wrote Alexander von Humboldt about the Catholic conquistadors. As one tribe—the whites and mestizos of the Brazilian littoral—moved relentlessly inland, with guns, rum, God, and asphalt, the myriad tribes of Brazilian

Indians were gradually pushed back, into ever-deeper recesses of the forest. Even the deepest of those recesses have been invaded now, with roads, settlements, and mines. Some communities, like the Tucano of the upper Rio Negro and the Kayapó of the Xingu, have been able to organize and mobilize eloquent defenses, before congresses, the press, and society at large. Most others, such as the Stone Age Yanomami, whose lands have been overrun by gold diggers, have grim prospects for survival, much less success.

Fernand Braudel, the *annales* school historian, put it bluntly. In the Americas, he says, "The real issue was not the conquest of men (they were annihilated) but of space."[6] The story of the Amazon is really about the conquest of space, about the quest of dominant society—first the Portuguese colonists, then the Brazilian settlers—to work its will over a new land and any who might come in the way. Each frontier where this story has played out required epic struggles with the challenges of unfamiliar terrain. In the frozen wastes of Siberia it was the cold and a truncated growing season; in Australia, the Canadian West and the United States beyond the Mississippi the challenge was aridity.

To dominant society, in Amazonia, more than men, space, and the conditions of that space were the real challenges. Once again a society on the move has faithfully followed the biblical double mandate, to devastate and then to rebuild, to take down in order to reinvent the environment. But there have been added challenges in this late frontier episode. It is a story that has meant the transformation of the world's greatest tropical rain forest.

This was not the first time a society of strangers had moved into a new, little-known, and hostile region. But most of the world's frontiers, though biotically different, were quite similar to the pioneers' home countries in terms of climate. They were neo-Europes, in the words of Alfred W. Crosby, places where Old World crops such as wheat, barley, oats, and rye took well and spread easily.[7] Like most pioneer peoples, the *colonos* of the Brazilian south, the Pcheks and their like, were also sons of a temperate zone. The northeastern-born rubber tappers and starvelings hailed from the arid tropics. Their destination, the Amazon, by contrast, was the humid tropics, the world's greatest tropical frontier and maybe its meanest.

At least since ancient Greece, the tropics have earned a bad name. This was the torrid zone, those lethal latitudes where, according to Aristotle, man and his husbanded beasts and plants had no business being and no hope of surviving. It took the polymaths of the Enlightenment to debunk the *Meteorologica*. And eventually explorers and conquistadors learned that the earth was in fact a ball, not an egg, as the sage had surmised, and did not sit at the center of the universe.[8] Even centuries after the discoverers happened upon human societies thriving at the equator, the vision of the deadly tropics took shape and potency.

"When civilized nations come in to contact with the barbarians the struggle is short," commented Charles Darwin, in 1871—"except," he amended, "where a deadly climate gives its aid to the native race."[9] So it was that the colonies of Europe penetrated only superficially in the edges of equatorial Africa and America, like barnacles clinging to the shore with an ocean of jungle beating at their backs. "This jungle," gasps a gringo in Peter Matthiessen's novel *At Play in the Fields of the Lord*. "How can you stand it?—you depraved or what? I mean, this is where God farted."

The steamy latitudes had their eternal allure, of course. Spices, gold, dyewoods, and timber beckoned comers from across the globe. But, writes the historian Alfred W. Crosby, "Until the beginning of the century, colonies of outsiders in Tropical Africa tended to sizzle and die."[10]

Countervailing these calumnies was a whole other school of thought. The tropical apologists emerged with the Age of Discovery, when European navigators crossed the oceans and pushed the boundaries of empire into another hemisphere. This was the time when navigation and investigation were the order of the day, and the whole "undiscovered" world lay before Europe like an opportunity. Columbus was hoping to reach Calicut, of course, but fell instead for the enchantments of the balmy Antilles. "Your Highness may believe," he wrote in his diary, "that this is the best and most fertile and temperate and level and good land that there is in the world."[11]

The Genoan was abetted by the English maritime chronicler and geographer Richard Hakluyt. A century after Columbus's first voyage, he wrote, "it is nowe thought that no where else but under the Equinoctiall, or not farre from thence is the Earthly Paradise." Hakluyt was thinking about Africa's Guinea Coast, but he had allies across the Atlantic.[12] Vicente do Salvador, a Franciscan priest and Brazil's first historian, met Aristotle head-on. "Experience has shown," he proclaimed early in the seventeenth century, "that the torrid zone is habitable, and that in some parts of it men live in better health than those in all the temperate zones—especially in Brazil. . . ."[13]

Often such heady claims for the tropics were pure fantasy, replete with tales of Cyclopes, anthropophagi, and a hundred versions of El Dorado. For half a millennium, however, visitors to the lower latitudes caromed back and forth between visions of Paradise and Ruin, trying to make up their minds. Over the years such visions purpled the prose of countless chronicles and misted over their *mappi mundi* in a perilous fog of illusion.

In the early part of this century the designs on the tropics were hastened by the cult of science and industry. Though the British historian James Bryce doubted that any white race could do it, "It seems certain," he ventured cautiously in 1912, after a trip to Amazonia, "that coming generations will endeavour to turn to the service of man the largest unused piece of productive soil that remains anywhere on the earth's surface."[14]

Caution was not Theodore Roosevelt's strong suit. In 1913, on a poetic pause down an unknown river in the Amazon, the former president—echoing Humboldt—waxed ebullient. "Surely such a rich and fertile land cannot be permitted to remain idle, to be a tenantless wilderness, while there are so many teeming swarms of human beings in the overcrowded, overpeopled countries of the Old World."

The dollar-a-word fee *Scribner's* magazine promised for Roosevelt's eight-part Amazon adventure series might have tinted in rose the former president's eyeglasses. But the punishing journey seemed to spoil Teddy's idyll. He battled mosquito and no-see-um, while armies of ants devoured his socks and termites ate a hole through his helmet. Later Roosevelt gashed his leg while fording a stream and fell into a raging fever, begging at one point to be left to die. That injury was to nag him until his death. "The very pathetic myth of 'beneficent nature' could not deceive even the least wise being if he once saw for himself the iron cruelty of life in the tropics," the champion of the strenuous life concluded soberly.[15]

In fact, for years the naysayers seemed to have the upper hand in these geographical debates. From Henry Ford's blighted rubber plantation to Daniel Ludwig's megalamoniacal Amazon rice and tree farm, the arrogance of the twentieth century would be brought to its knees over and over in Amazonia. In the 1970s the Brazilian military, basking in its own notion of destiny, scattered thousands of peasants along a highway that tore due west through the jungle for twenty-eight hundred miles. At first Antônio Delfim Netto, the hardheaded and wily planning minister, balked at supporting the Transamazônica as a white elephant. Yet often in authoritarian Brazil, saying was believing. And with democracy on ice and the press fairly muzzled, the generals and their technocrats spent twenty-one years listening to themselves.

In short order, Netto, too, succumbed to the reigning vision. 'The Transamazônica cannot be seen merely as an economic undertaking," the so-called economy czar now argued in August 1970.[16] After all, if Pedro Cabral, the navigator who claimed Brazil for Portugal, "had waited for an economic viability study, Brazil would still today be undiscovered." Besides,

Netto worked his fantasy, "There exists in Amazonia a strain of [fertile] red earth comparable to any state in the center-south."

The Transamazônica was built, finally, at a cost of hundreds of millions of dollars and untold suffering for peasants and indigenous peoples. It was never paved, and thousands of miles still wash out every rainy season. The rich red soils turned out to be mostly wan and weak. Though some towns along its length, like Altamira, prosper today, that has more to do with the tenaciousness of the pioneers than the wisdom of the planners who sent them there.

Of course, the years would eventually show that Brazil, most of which lies north of the Tropic of Capricorn, was indeed habitable. But as settlers and discoverers worked their way north, toward the equator, the doubts remained and even grew. The parts of the globe deemed unfit—at least for Euro-Caucasian stock—shrank but never disappeared. So it was that well into our century the humid tropics, these niggardly portions of the New World, remained as final bits of Eden. Everything from mosquitoes to microbes conspired to spare these lands from what Lévi-Strauss called "the agitations of history."[17] It would take more than shining ambitions to meet the challenge of the torrid frontier.

Science and technology may one day allow us to occupy the poles and the deserts, but the humid tropics are now apparently the last habitable spaces left on earth. What is more, population is increasing fastest in the tropical nations. So much so, in fact, that many ecologists have appealed for a new world nomenclature. Instead of the globe's being divided into hemispheres, the rich and developed North against the poor and underdeveloped South, the real division, they say, is tropical versus temperate. The temperate countries are the world's farm belts, while the tropics are far less able to produce excess food and harbor growing populations. Just how habitable is the Amazon frontier? That is a riddle that echoes throughout the

Amazon, one that settlers, scientists, environmentalists, and politicians are daily trying to thrash out—even as settlement advances.

The ecological challenge of the Amazon is the humidity, not the aridity. A delicate and complex ecosystem, with soils weaker than in almost any other frontier and more species in a single acre than in entire counties in the temperate zones, awaited the Amazonian settlers. As Dubos says, lately Europe has been bent on removing less fertile soils from agricultural production, while Brazilians are expanding, aggressively in recent years, into marginal lands in the scrub of the center west and in the forested Amazonian north.[18]

Economically there is also a riddle. The settlers, drifters, rubber tappers, and adventurers who moved into these regions for the last two centuries, and fairly poured in during the last three decades, have been the standard-bearers of official Brazilian dreams—shoring up vulnerable borders, expanding internal markets, occupying the empty spaces, giving actual bulk and body to the nation. Many of these dreams crumbled. The migrants who rushed into the region for a boom cycle rushed out again when things went bust. Until very recently this frontier was a hollow one. But over time, more and more of the settlers remained, albeit at the cost of immense suffering. Perhaps the most daunting challenge is to give them a fair deal in the frontiers they whittled out of the tropical wilderness. Even with the miracles of science, the question hovers: Is this frontier viable, profitable, sustainable?

Yet there is no turning back the clock on the Amazon to some imagined time of gentler, sylvan innocence. The Pcheks and their like are not liable to return to the south. There is less and less room there for their kind. Those were old frontiers. These people are not so much the legendary pioneers in homespun, living independently off the forest's game and the fruits of their own fieldwork. Like the settlers of the Canadian prairies, they have been brought up in an age of industry and consumer goods, automobiles and farm credit, and they expect to participate in the benefits of that society.

Vitório Pchek came to Rondônia when the highway was still an unpaved, mud-scarred track. Now there was asphalt and traffic twenty-four hours a day. Scrubbed and barbered for Sunday, Vitório might have walked out of some James Michener epic. He wore spotless denim and boots polished to shining. "This land is like a mother's heart," said Pchek. "There's always room for one more."

Six years later, in November 1990, I decided to drive once again along BR-364. The frontier had changed immensely in that short span. So much forest was gone, in fact, that locals even said the weather had changed, delaying the rains and magnifying the heat. The sweltering air and the brooding rain clouds seemed to me little different from the way I remembered six Novembers before, but the landscape had changed dramatically. The forests that hugged the highway were relegated to a distance now. The road itself was pocked and cratered, from years of poor maintenance and the relentless traffic of trucks and passenger cars. It cut an undulating line through a flattened terrain of pastures, farms, and one homestead after another. Way off in the distance a fringe of trees penciled a vague line on the horizon.

Approaching Ariquemes, I began to search the highway for the Pcheks' farm. I hadn't noted the address at the time but somehow felt sure now that I would recognize the tidy lawn, the roundlog gate, and the mango tree. Instead, around the spot where I had sworn the Pcheks' house to be, there was now a great shallow lake. It was the reservoir of the hydroelectric dam Samuel, which had been completed in 1988. The dam flooded tens of thousands of acres, forcing hundreds of settlers to move. The mother's heart had fluttered in Rondônia, and the Pcheks, I now imagined, like so much of the frontier flotsam of the Amazon, had been swept way—maybe to the teeming cities, possibly back to the old south, but probably on to some final corner of this last new world.

CHAPTER

CRABS ON THE SEA LINE

The "frontier," the open spaces to be conquered
by human settlement, was forever on the horizon
of American history, whether in Eastern Peru or
Southern Chile, whether looking across the Venezuelan llanos or the wastes of Canada, in the Far
West of the U.S. or the rolling plains of Argentina
in the 19th century or even in the Brazilian interior northwest of São Paulo in the 20th century.

—Fernand Braudel,
The Perspective of the World

At a traffic circle near the Ibirapuera Park, not far from
downtown São Paulo, a column of gray granite figures strains forward, as though marching toward the
distant horizon. They are heaving at a rope attached to a canoe,
dragging the boat overland as though over a difficult ford. At
the lead are two horsemen and a pair of colossal mounts. Some
of the men wear flowing beards; their arms are muscular and
outsize, more pistons than limbs. There are Indians, blacks,
and whites in the ranks. The rude clothing bespeaks a humble
social station; the bent shapes tell of an arduous trek. Their
faces are friezed in a mixture of determination and glory.

The sculpture, the *Monument of the Bandeiras,* conceived
in the 1920s and completed in 1936, is one of the proudest
emblems of Brazilian modernism. Begun in 1922, this was a

feverish, confusing time when sculptors, painters, poets, and musicians brashly strove to break the shackles of classical aesthetics borrowed from Europe. Symbolism and French formalist literature were tossed out; in came dada and futurism. In one sense, these Brazilian intellectuals were merely swapping one European sensibility for another. But the modernists added to this heady potion of imported ideas a twist of nationalism and set about to recast this New World republic in its own image. The "Brazilianization of Brazil," one modernist proclaimed their mission.

One of the first items on the modernists' agenda was, paradoxically, to look into the past. Sculpted by Victor Brecheret, the son of an Italian immigrant, the *Monument of the Bandeiras* was a paean to the *bandeirantes,* those sixteenth- and seventeenth-century pioneers who scaled the sheer three-thousand-foot Atlantic escarpment, groping hand over hand at times, to the tabletop plateau of São Paulo and then broke a trail west through the forbidding Brazilian hinterlands.

The marchers' mantle is a dingy gray now, spun of smog and grit from a wilderness of factory smokestacks and fifty years of megalopolitan rush hours. For millions of Paulista commuters, it is just another urban signpost, the halfway mark between the downtown office towers and the comfortable residences of Ibirapuera and Santo Amaro. Today the difficult trek is to get home by sundown without your radiator boiling over. The struggling *bandeirantes* are mostly a blur through so many rearview windows , just one brave era's fading homage to another. They trudge now under a cobalt sky toward a sierra of skyscrapers and through a jungle of steel and reinforced concrete.

Yet the city that dwarfs their monument is a metropolis they helped sculpt. Their explorations pushed the Paulistas westward, across the rich red earth of the interior, along the rivers Tietê and Paraná, to the swamps and savannas of the far west, on still farther to the north and the thick, moist tropical rain forests of the Amazon. Where the Paulistas went, the rest of

Brazil eventually followed. These probings, in turn, dilated the Brazilian colony and sent riches, fabulous riches, back to the metropolis and Lisbon. São Paulo spread and climbed. Its skyline mirrored the vast domain the dynamic Paulista economy came to influence and still dominates today. All of São Paulo is the *bandeirantes'* monument.

The *bandeiras,* as their expeditions were called, were not exactly the wagon trains of South America. The missions were never intended principally to settle the hinterlands or extend national boundaries; rather, the men were dispatched by merchants and traders mostly to procure gold and diamonds and Indian slaves. More Vikings than Pilgrims, their assignments were closer to pillage than colonization, their legacy more of scorched earth than cultivation. In *Red Gold,* his first volume on the conquest of the Brazilian Indians, John Hemming notes that the *bandeirantes* rivaled Livingstone and Speke in their jungle treks but left virtually no records behind. The one thorough report that exists tells of Bartolomeu Bueno da Silva, *Anhanguera,* "the old devil" in the Tupi-Guarani language, who, legend has it, dominated a contrary Indian group without ever having to unsheathe his sword. Coming upon the fearsome Indians of Goiás, in central Brazil, Silva set a bowl of transparent cane rum aflame and then threatened to do the same to Goiás's lakes and rivers unless the Indians handed over their gold and surrendered their sons into slavery.[1]

The *bandeirantes* worked and tricked their way west, up the Tietê River, on through the watery labyrinth of inland Brazil, and then beat speedy retreats back to the cities, often leaving "no more trace behind than a ship does in the sea," writes Fernand Braudel.[2] In many ways these rogue explorers were heroes of a Paulista myth, and not all of Brazil, imbued with healthy territorial rivalries, was eager to bow down before it. "What was the Tietê?" asks the northeastern historian Anibal Falcão, of the *bandeirante* "highway" to the interior. ". . . Above all it was the river of slavery of Indians," Falcão writes,

THE BRAZILIAN
BANDEIRAS

São Luís

Natal

Recife

CEARA

MATO GROSSO

São Salvador

Vila
Bela

Vila de
Cuiabá

Vila Boa

Porto Seguro

MINAS

Vitoria

São Paulo

Rio de Janeiro

Santos

Cananeia

Porto Alegre

SACRAMENTO

| 0 | 500 | 1000 | 1500 km |

| 0 | 500 | 1000 miles |

hardly a Brazilian "Nile on whose banks our civilization was founded."[3]

Stained in blood though they were, the *bandeirantes*, nevertheless, were resuscitated for specific reasons. They were the ones who turned Brazilian civilization away from the cradle of the seacoast, casting the nation's destiny inland, across a great unknown backland, the *sertão*. "Europe meant nothing to them," the historian E. Bradford Burns writes. "The virgin land engulfing them meant everything."[4] They were living symbols not only of conquest but also of resistance to authority and the complacent coastal life. Sent to the woods by men of wealth to plunder for more, they often never came back. That their rough encampments turned eventually into busy entrepôts, which later grew into thriving frontier towns, was nearly accidental. Not unlike the famous dictum of the British Empire, the Brazilian frontiers were also built as much out of "absence of mind" as of purpose or policy. For more than a century the *bandeirantes'* expeditions spread from the littoral like the digits on a hand: south to the Rio de la Plata, west almost to the shadow of the Andes, and north to the lands drained by the Amazon River. Thanks to their wanderings, a rosary of cities now necklaces the interior, lacing the São Paulo plateau to Paraná, in the southern farm belt, to Mato Grosso, at the bottom lip of the Amazon Basin. In many ways, the path to the Amazon began with their plunderings.

It took three more centuries, but the *bandeirantes* were followed by adventurers, gold miners, rubber tappers, and herdsmen; then telegraph wires, railroads, and highways; and finally farmers, settlers, merchants, financiers, and the men of agribusiness. The all but impenetrable rain forest that the *bandeirantes* encountered four hundred years ago is finally being occupied, more quickly than any of the most avid colonial enthusiasts imagined, more chaotically than any government has been able to control. It is a forum of pioneer genius, and destruction, on a scale that equals, if not surpasses, that of all other frontiers. No wonder Brecheret's *bandeirantes* strain at their rope.

Destiny

Frontier quests are never, of course, merely a march off toward a red sunset and some Elysium on earth. Less spiritual matters generally beckon. Furs, gold, silver, spices, and timber all were part of the traditional frontier allure. To the Russian czars, having and holding Siberia, that rich and sparsely settled territory to the east, were vital to fortifying the larder of empire. The great eastward migration begun in the late eighteenth century was wholeheartedly encouraged by Catherine the Great, who saw in Siberia a veritable "realm," prospering with sable, mink, fish, black soils, and other treasures. In *The Great Siberian Migration,* Donald W. Treadgold captures well Catherine's frontier vision. "Siberia," she insisted, "would not be a 'Canada' to Russia's 'England,' but rather an 'India,' a colony capable of supporting itself and the empire, too."[5]

But the frontier impulse is usually done up in nobler cloth. Exploration, conquest, and occupation of frontiers have long been vital parts of the script in which the drama of national identity is played out. From South Africa to Siberia, from the Australian outback to North America beyond the Rockies, the forays into new territories have been central not only to expanding the nation but also in defining its soul. Frederick Jackson Turner, who made the frontier into a religion, wrote in 1921 that to understand American history, one had to understand the American West. The U.S. literary scholar Richard Slotkin writes:

> In American mythogenesis the founding fathers were not those eighteenth country gentlemen who composed a nation in Phil-

adelphia. Rather they were those who . . . tore violently a nation
from the implacable and opulent wilderness—the rogues,
adventurers, and land-boomers; the Indian fighters, traders,
missionaries, explorers, and hunters who killed and were killed
until they had mastered the wilderness; the settlers who came
after, suffering hardship and Indian warfare for the sake of a
sacred mission or a simple desire for land; and the Indians
themselves, both as they were and as they appeared to the settlers, for whom they were the special demonic personifications
of the American wilderness.[6]

Once Siberia was in hand, its conquest was retold in loftier
rhetoric. The land east of the Urals not only attracted but compelled. One of Alexander III's officials spoke of "the historic
direction of colonization followed by the great-Russian race,
bound to move from west to east" (my italics). More potent
still, Russia's frontier also raised the hope of forming an egalitarian society, where Caucasians, Mongols, and indigenous
Siberians of all social stations were meeting and mixing. "[T]he
amalgamation of classes will consolidate and strengthen the
whole body politic," gushed one imperial official, "and should
that happy consummation ever be realised in Russia, Siberia
will have the honour of leading the way."[7]

As the Australian settlers thrust their way inland, over the
Blue Mountains, the budding colony was seen as the rebirth of
a fading Pax Britannica. "The future seat of a mighty empire
under the banner of an Anglo-Saxon race," one expansionist
proclaimed it. "When in the course of Ages, the British Lion
has waxed old, and the Sun of England's glory and power is
dimmed with age, her Australian and New Zealand colonies
. . . will carry down her language, her religion, and her might
to distant times,"[8] wrote one enthusiastic frontiersman in the
Melbourne Argus in 1849. Australia, boomed the economic
historian William Keith Hancock, had nothing less than "a
mission of civilization in the Pacific Ocean."[9]

The nineteenth-century jingoists of Canada promoted their
march toward "the last best west." "Who cannot see that Prov-

idence has entrusted us the building up of a great northern people, fit to cope with our neighbors in the U.S., and to advance, step by step with them in the march of Civilization," wrote George Brown of the *Toronto Globe* in January 1858.[10]

There is a Horace Greeley for every frontier, and in Brazil the most bombastic was Getúlio Vargas. The populist and sometime dictator, who came to power in 1930 and dominated Brazilian politics for a good part of the next quarter century, launched the famous Brazilian "March to the West." "The true direction of Brazil is westward," he declared in 1938 to an expectant crowd in Goiânia, the former cow town that was to be an early launching pad for expeditions to the wilderness and today bustles with nearly a million inhabitants. "We do not harbor ambitions towards a single palm's-breadth of soil that isn't our own," Vargas went on, amid applause, "but we have a [call to] expansionism, to grow, that is, within our own frontiers."[11] Although his "March to the West" turned out to be little more than a gale of speeches, this expansionist idea helped fuel Brazilian leaders in their drive inland, toward national destiny, for the next six decades.

His elected successor, Juscelino Kubitschek, was one of the most enthusiastic frontiersmen, and he backed his rhetoric with a lattice of highways, ports, airstrips, and railroad tracks. Kubitschek brazenly moved the nation's capital from Rio de Janeiro to the arid central plateau of Goiás, raising an entire city of sparkling glass, steel, and concrete in just five years. He called the new capital Brasília. It became the springboard to the unconquered Brazilian west, finally launching Brazil into the age of territorial expansion that nations in the Northern Hemisphere had already completed. "We are late by a century in relation to the United States," he said in the Amazon hamlet of Vilhena, where he went to inaugurate a dirt top highway in 1960. "In 1850, they had swept the country in every direction, from the Atlantic to the Pacific. . . . Brazil, a hundred years behind, begins its march now, but we will do it more rapidly than that country to the North managed."[12]

The military, which ruled from 1964 to 1985, carried the torch onward. Five military governments built highways, hydroelectric dams, mines of bauxite and iron ore, and "development poles" throughout the Amazon region. They drew settlers and businessmen to the frontier, handing out land to the landless and soft loans to entrepreneurs. "Great nations are only built in great spaces endowed with potential or real resources, capable of harboring and permitting the fecund activity of a numerous population, possessed of technology, vigor, and patriotism," said General Rodrigo Octávio Jordão Ramos, a senior member of the armed forces.[13]

The most enthusiastic of the military frontiersmen was Jordão's chief, General Emílio Garrastazu Médici, who served as president from 1969 to 1974. Prying open Amazonia was to Médici a solution for the slum-clogged cities and the landless masses, as well as an outlet for the markets of the developed centers. He launched the Transamazon highway, which tore through more than twenty-eight hundred miles of scrub and jungle. Responding, he said, to "the impositions of a Nation which has become aware of its greatness, the regime is complying faithfully with a historic mission it has assumed, of opening new horizons of our economic, social, and political universe."[14]

The Diapers of the Littoral

But the myths were to come much later. First came the deeds of conquering the interior. In fact, it took a long time for Brazilians to stir to a notion of destiny. The problem, to hear Brazilians tell it, lay to the east and Lisbon. Talk to any cabdriver, any steelmaker, any priest, any merchant in Brazil, and you hear a common lament: the Portuguese colonists. There are few woes or sins of Brazilian society—from the swollen bureaucracies to traffic jams, from the corrupt politician to the price of morning bread rolls—that are not laid at the feet of the erstwhile conquerors. The Portuguese have served contemporary and irreverent Brazil in the same way the Poles did arrogant, Protestant America—as the butt of jokes and derogatory stereotypes. Dunderheadedness, waste, and corruption are a Lusitanian ailment, planted, it is said, in 1500, with the Portuguese flag that Cabral brought, when Brazil got in the way of his passage to India. Brazil, the accidental colony, was the first joke on the Portuguese.

There is much to bolster an uncharitable view. For years, after all, Brazil was nothing more than the "milch cow" of Lisbon's empire. The Portuguese crown's greed was ignited by the dispatches of the earliest explorers. "Everything that is planted thrives!" trilled Pero Vaz de Caminha, one of the first chroniclers from Portugal. Yet listen to Father Vicente do Salvador, the seventeenth-century Franciscan friar who was not only Brazil's first serious historian but also perhaps its earliest ecologist, on why colonial Brazil, despite fabulous natural riches, simply would not develop: "Everything they want they take back to Portugal . . . not only those of them who came here, but also those of them who were born here; both use the land, not as lords but usufructuaries, purely for their benefit while leaving everything destroyed."[15]

And the Brazilian colonies were not alone in this maltreatment. The governors-general of Angola were famous for the commissions they skimmed off the top of the commerce in slaves. Nor were Portuguese clergy exactly paragons of probity. The onetime union of the "cross and the sword" that reigned during the salad days of empire mildewed in the tropics. "Greedy, lustful, rebellious and libertine," fumed one bishop in Angola of his subordinate clergy.[16]

When the united houses of the Spanish and Portuguese empires sat down at Tordesillas and drew a line from pole to pole, dividing up the world between them, most of the Amazon rain forest fell on Madrid's side of the planet. But the "Tordesillas line" was never clearly demarcated and, almost from the beginning, completely ignored, especially by Lisbon.

Myriad squabbles and doubts emerged, "so none can verely tell which hath the best reason. They be not yet agreed," commented Richard Hakluyt, the sixteenth-century British voyager. Over the next two centuries, the Brazilian *bandeiras* and the sprawling captaincies (as the first administrative districts in Brazil were called) had slopped, deliberately, way west of the Tordesillas, while the Spaniards were content to tend only to their silver lode in the extreme Andean west.

In 1750 the Tordesillas agreement was scrapped in favor of the Treaty of Madrid and the notion of uti possidetis, a pearl of New World realpolitik. It translated into something like "domain by real and present occupation." Call it squatters rights writ large. The borders would be redrawn wherever actual settlements and the dominant language determined. As a result, Brazil gradually seized and laid claim to most of the South American Amazon. These arrangements between empires spelled out well the manner in which the great powers saw the world beyond their shores. Most of the New World would be claimed long before it was even known, and coveted far more than loved.

To Father Vicente, the fall came early, after a scant few years of grace, when glint-eyed merchants rechristened the Land of the True Cross as the most mercenary Brazil, named for the dyewood so highly prized by imperial merchants. Preoccupied less with building a colony than with padding Lisbon's treasury, the rulers and elite of Brazil looked ever outward toward the voracious empire for inspiration and example and inward for quick profit. The backlands were seen less as motherland, to sow and settle, than as a mother lode, to wring dry.

For four centuries the missions to the Brazilian interior were driven by the most devastating kinds of extractive activities, the wilderness torn up for its gold and diamonds, wood and spices, rubber and cocoa. Agriculture was no less predatory. The farmers and herdsmen and sugarcane planters were agents of terrible waste. Theirs was a heritage of fire that had blazed its way across the Atlantic from Portugal. So furious were the fires set by the sugar planters of the Madeira Islands, one hapless farmer, João Gonçalves Zarco, "threw himself in the seas, with his wife and children, and other people, staying there for two days in water up to his neck without eating or drinking."[17] The account, taken from an early Italian maritime history, may be more yarn than honest reporting, but the Madeira Islands (*madeira* is "wood" in Portuguese) are today practically bare of the robust forests that gave them their name, a denuded reminder of colonial Portuguese agriculture.[18]

True, the dense subtropical forest just behind the shore, a web of unnavigable rivers, and not infrequent Indian attacks hampered the settlers' ingress, but four centuries after Brazil was discovered, the sprawling Brazilian *sertão* remained largely unknown and almost wholly ignored by comfortable society. The *bandeirantes* had done their bloody part, but civilization had not rushed in on their heels. The governors-general ruled sublimely from Bahia and the emperors from Rio de Janeiro, cities nestled between sea and mountains. History was, at most, a tussle between the port cities and the sugar plantations that folded in "along the diapers of the coast," another writer remembers.

"Of the breadth of Brazil's lands to the *sertao* I will not treat here," Father Vicente writes despairingly, "because until now no one has walked through them, out of neglect by the Portuguese, who, being great conquerors of lands, fail to take advantage of them, but instead content themselves to go about, scratching along the sea line like crabs."[19] Father Vicente was writing in 1627. It took three more centuries for Brazilians to awaken to the friar's challenge.

Intellectuals were also urban and sedentary. Responding indignantly to João Capistrano de Abreu, the historian who lionized the *bandeirantes* but branded the northeasterners a lazy lot, Anibal Falcão lashed back. The Pernambucanos, it was true, neglected the interior, but, he shrugged, only because "they had more important things to do." Great writers like Afonso Henriques de Lima Barreto, a mulatto and redoubtable creature of the city, saw the country's future as defined by the growing, bustling coastal cities and the dynamic metropolitan mix of blacks and Caucasians. Rio de Janeiro and Bahia were "the epitome of Brazil," Barreto declared. "Cannibals and brutes" was how he classified the Brazilian Indians.[20] "I, too, have been to Petrópolis," sniffed Joaquim Maria Machado de Assis, perhaps Brazil's greatest novelist, remarking on the mountain town a mere sixty miles inland from Rio.

In Brazil, though independence came early, society remained anchored by an outdated plantation system run by slave labor. There was a wide feeling that under the monarchy Brazil had largely missed the nineteenth century, with its wondrous machines, churning mills, and smokestacks belching promise. Sparked by the Enlightenment, which put a premium on philosophy, geography, and the investigative sciences, Europeans of the eighteenth and especially the nineteenth centuries had already gone to the ends of empire to peruse their annexed Edens. William H. Goetzmann has called this "the second great Age of Discovery." Goetzmann writes that "one of the hallmarks of a great and emergent nation was that it, too, developed a culture adventuresome enough and sophisticated enough to join in the exploration of the globe and universe."[21] The Amazon had a long list of famous explorers, but most of them had names like La Condamine, Spruce, Bates, Wallace, Humboldt, Spix, von Steinen, and Martius.

There were some eminent exceptions. One of the most noted of the eighteenth-century naturalists, the Bahian-born Alexandre Rodrigues Ferreira, spent a decade exploring Amazonia. "The land," he wrote to Lisbon, "is a Paradise; it produces so much that I do not know which way to turn." A century later, in 1863, came Couto de Magalhães, who began systematically to catalog ethnic groups. But through much of the last century the Amazon remained mostly a paradise for European scientists.

Scratching Inward

Though Father Vicente might bitterly complain about the sedentary Brazilians, the world's great powers were not so very far ahead in consolidating their frontiers, both overland and overseas. Russians had swept through Siberia by early in the seventeenth century. But at the beginning of the nineteenth century Siberia's population still numbered only about a million. That population expanded sixfold in the next hundred years, with the freeing of the serfs and a vigorous official migration policy. But it took the opening of the first leg of the Siberian Railway, in 1896, to flood the East with migrants. In the next twenty-five years Siberia's population nearly doubled, to more than eleven million.[22]

Similarly, it was not until the late 1800s, and the maturing of formal colonialism, that Europe began to look in earnest to the overseas empire for markets and opportunities. In the late 1800s, in fact, most Old World capital was still invested within Europe or the United States. Only in 1841 did the first European settlers reach California, and even well after that date most pioneers leaving the East still preferred Texas to the Pacific Coast.[23] In 1910 only half a million souls were spread thinly over the Canadian prairies, despite the quarter century of rail service that connected them to Montreal.

But by the dawn of the new century all that was changing. At World War I Britain had twenty billion dollars, a quarter of its wealth, invested abroad, and both France and Germany put a fifth of their respective annual gross product into their colonies. This was the era of science and investigation, when the quest for "modern civilization" became a "kind of substitute religion."[24] The tumultuous politics of Europe during the previous century had already set in motion events that nudged Brazil forward to an early independence. After Napoleon's army rolled over Portugal in 1807, the Portuguese royal family fled to Rio, becoming the first European monarchs to run an empire from the colonies. In 1821 the king, Dom João VI, returned to rule in Lisbon, leaving Brazil in the hands of his son, Prince Pedro. The prince, a bon vivant, liked life in tropical Rio, and rather than obey a call by the Portuguese parliament to return to Lisbon, he declared Brazil independent in 1822. The emperor's son, Pedro II, a poet and philosopher, took over the fledgling monarchy in 1840. He enjoyed a long and popular reign, but by the end of the nineteenth century, in a time when republicanism and the miracles of the industrial age were taking hold worldwide, a monarchy seemed musty and out of place.

Much of the energy to conquer and settle the Brazilian interior also came on the boisterous eve of the new century, set in motion with the fall of the Emperor Dom Pedro II of Brazil.

The end of the Brazilian monarchy was sealed on a warm November day in 1889. The royal family threw its last party on a small island in Rio de Janeiro's limpid Guanabara Bay. Invitations were embossed in gold. The empress, Tereza Cristina Maria Bourbon, wore Chantilly lace. The guests—forty-five hundred in all—were regaled with caviar and pâté de foie gras. The menu went on for twelve pages, and the merriment nearly until dawn. Ladies' garters were found the next day bobbing about the bay.

The Fiscal Island ball was held in honor of a visiting admiral from Chile, but it was also the sort of affair meant to flatter the vainglory of the aristocracy and awe the *povão,* the teeming masses. But while blue bloods danced and commoners ogled, army officers gathered onshore in Rio's Clube Militar, a gathering place for officers and a hothouse of republicanism. The Brazilian Army had become increasingly restive since the war with Paraguay. The Brazilian victory, in 1870, had catapulted the military to national prominence. But ever since, it had never again enjoyed the prestige or the important role the soldiers desired. Inexorably they turned against the monarchy. General Benjamin Constant Botelho de Magalhães, the chief republican conspirator, exhorted his young volunteers to rise against the regime that was "carving the ruin of our country." Six days later the monarchy fell at gunpoint. The coup was nearly bloodless (the navy minister pulled a revolver and was shot in the buttocks), the first of many such short circuits of democracy to follow.

It was not a popular uprising; the *povão* was genuinely fond of Pedro and his royal family. For all their extravagances, they had not only freed the slaves but also ably refereed among plantation owners and merchants who argued over Brazil like medieval lords fighting over fiefs. Such a sagacious moderating force would be sorely missed during the next tumultuous century; whenever troubles surged, time and again it was the army that clumsily, often brutally, stepped into the breach, replacing presidents at will and holding sway over politics well into modern times. The direct election of Fernando Collor de Mello, in November 1989, marked the end of a thirty-year period dominated by the military, the longest bout of autocratic rule since Pedro's. Six coups d'etat rocked Brazil during the republican century.

But at the beginning, anyway, the republicans had brave ideas and set out to replace a regime run by personal fiat with a modern state, guided by the rule of law, and liberty, and reason. They sought nothing less than to reinvent Brazil. The national face-lift involved debates over the form of government, the national character, and the boundaries of the nation.

Discovering the hinterlands was part of this search. A few of the republican illuminati fretted over the fact that this continent-size nation was also sparsely populated and vulnerable. At the end of the monarchy only two of Brazil's eleven borders had been definitively demarcated. The Treaty of Madrid had remanaged the map according to the more realistic notion of actual settlement. But this was also a recipe for conflict and delicate diplomacy. As a result, eight treaties had to be hammered out between Brazil and its neighbors between 1889 and 1910. Important accords were reached with Argentina in the south. But Amazonia, the vast and—to the powers in Rio de

Janeiro—underpeopled jungle that bordered on seven countries, was particularly sensitive territory.

In the north, Bolivia, Peru, and Britain (in the Guianas)
jockeyed for parts of the Amazon. José Maria da Silva Paran-
hos, the Baron Rio Branco, who was the father of modern
Brazilian diplomacy, set about to solve the myriad disputes
and to map the untamed portions of the nation. In 1909, when
Brazil had already made significant inland advances, a con-
gressmen suggested swapping the plain green curtain that hung
behind the president's chair with a national map. "A map of
this great country should be constantly before our eyes," he
declared.[25]

The idea of Latin America's west began to take hold among
intellectuals in many South American capitals. The Argentine
Jesuit Domingo Fausto Sarmiento waxed poetic on the importance of peopling the pampas, the grassland prairies to the west
of Buenos Aires. However, unlike Abreu, who celebrated the
mestizo *bandeirantes,* Sarmiento wanted the peopling done by
vigorous and, to him, superior Europeans, not by the native
gauchos, "neither learned or powerful men." Uruguay's
acclaimed writer José Enrique Rodó wrote *Ariel,* a novel on
the power of the interior to transform the human character.[26]

In 1889, four years before Turner wrote his famous essay
heralding the role of the West in forging the budding U.S.
nation, the Brazilian historian João Capistrano de Abreu had
already laid out his own frontier thesis. He wrote a series of
articles, "Old Roads and the Peopling of Brazil" ("Os Caminhos Antigos e o Povoamento do Brasil"), for the important
Rio daily *Journal do Comércio,* which elevated the *bandeirantes* to the role of national heroes. Rough men born of the
subtropical climate of the New World, the *bandeirantes* were
sons of a land where all the races mingled and collided—
mamelucos, mulattoes, and caboclos as the varying permuta-
tions of Portuguese adventurers' liaisons with slaves and Indians and river dwellers became known. The *bandeirantes* were,
by breeding and deed, the true pioneers, Abreu's articles argued,

and their expeditions conquered the interior, opening the way for settler society and consolidating the Brazilian nation.

Though their monument is tarnished and their legacy neglected today, the resurrection of the *bandeirantes* served as important impetus for a country on a journey, both geographical and spiritual; the journey inland was also a quest of a nation in search of itself. The Brazilian modernists, who rose to prominence during the historic Modern Arts Week in São Paulo in 1922 and continued to mark the national intellectual scene through the 1940s, were perhaps the most illustrious of the seekers. Not only did they retrieve *bandeirante* history and, like Brecheret, cast it in bronze and granite, but they went further, exploring the special amalgam of races and regions from which this nation was forged. Greece and medieval Europe were no longer the beacons. They shunned symbolism and Parnassian poetry, the aesthetics that sectors of the Brazilian elite had enthusiastically swallowed whole and only half digested. ("We have no need of a machine to make verses," wrote Oswald de Andrade. "We have the Parnassians."[27]

The modernist manifesto made an iconoclastic toast to the brutal *bandeirantes*. "We want to write with blood, what humanity is all about," said Graça Aranha, one of the preeminent authors of the day, in a thundering speech delivered at the Modern Arts Week in 1922, ". . . with electricity, that is movement, the dynamic expansion of the century; with violence, that is the *bandeirante* energy." These artists were looking for authenticity, and some of them went far and wide to find it. "Let us forget the marble of the Acropolis and the towers of the Gothic cathedral. We are the sons of the hills and the forests," Ronald de Carvalho, a leading modernist, declared. "Stop thinking of Europe. Think of America."[28] Suddenly traits that had long been dismissed as Latin maladies—miscegenation, a mystical bent, the spurning of a Protestant work ethic— were recast as virtues.

Amazonia, especially, with its wealth of Indian cultures and myths, was fuel for dozens of creative works. Novels with

indigenous legends or fantastical characters—*Cobra Norato,*
Macunaima, and *Amazônia Misteriosa* (mysterious Amazon)—abounded. Heitor Villa-Lobos, the renowned Brazilian
composer, found inspiration for his most famous symphony,
A Floresta Amazônica, in the Amazonian north. The writer
Mário de Andrade scoured the countryside for the grammar
and customs of Brazilian society. "Sleep, *seringueiro*/ In enormous friend's love . . . Brazilian sleep," he wrote, in a lullaby
to the rough class of rubber tappers whose sweat and blood
created vast wealth in the late nineteenth century from the
Amazon's wild rubber groves. It was his way not only of repa-
triating this alienated and suffering class but also of recharging
the rest of Brazil with its energy and spirit. "God, so far from
me/ . . . This man is a Brazilian just like me."[29]

These efforts would help kindle a new appreciation of the
backlands and, though the modernist artists hardly intended it,
help fuel official pronouncements and programs of a number
of Brazilian leaders who aimed to drive settler society deep
into the interior and succeeded. Slowly, deliberately Brazilians were beginning to turn their backs to the sea and scratch
inland.

ORDER AND PROGRESS

This scientific exploration, a commonplace thing
in all the countries, is the first obligation of our
progress.

—Euclydes da Cunha,
A Márgem da História

A thousand miles due west of São Paulo begin the red-earth tablelands of Mato Grosso. Here, at the lower lip of the Legal Amazon region, where the great marshlands of the Pantanal meet the scrub and squat jungle of the region Brazilians call the *cerrado,* is the starting point for many modern overland journeys north into the forests of Amazonia. Mato Grosso harbors the geographical center of South America, where two of the world's greatest river basins meet: to the north, the Amazon, on its four-thousand-mile eastward path from the Andes, draining the lands above and below the great river; to the south, the Rio de la Plata, fed by streams and tributaries from Bolivia to Argentina. In the wet season these watery empires swell and their waters nearly mingle. "Whoever drinks by morning the waters bound for the mid-Atlantic in the afternoon can quench his thirst in those destined for the equator," mused Edgar Roquette-Pinto, a historian of the Brazilian backlands.[1]

This is the Brazilian far west, a land of azure skies and

endless ranges, where migration is intense, farms are giant, and a family with a bit of money and fool courage can still find a plot of land and carve out a new life. This is also the southern gateway to the Amazon frontier. Many men have passed through the Mato Grosso. The *bandeirantes,* driven by word of gold and diamonds, tore through the landscape but left little behind except a few raggedy towns and a plenteous issue of mixed-blood mamelucos. Early in the last century Georg Heinrich von Langsdorff, the Russian consul in Rio de Janeiro, plunged into the bush for nearly two years with a band of explorers, packers, and artists. It was a disastrous expedition, marked by bickering, illness, and death, and Langsdorff returned stone mad, in "a lamentable condition," according to one diplomat. In 1913 Theodore Roosevelt set off to the Mato Grosso for a bit of adventurous hunting and nearly died on the way down an uncharted and treacherous water course, the River of Doubt.

Until well after the turn of this century, Mato Grosso (Big Bush) meant dread and difficulty for anyone who dared pass through it. But all that changed in the twentieth century. In three decades this land at the bottom of Amazonia was thoroughly walked and mapped, and its sprawling scrub and bushlands were modestly peopled. Traders, adventurers, and drifters led the way. But the real architects of this Brazilian west were a pair of explorers whose lives were devoted to discovering and opening the Brazilian hinterlands.

For all the dreams and delusions it has generated, the Amazon frontier has a fairly thin rostrum of heroes. But two of the earliest, Cândido Mariano da Silva Rondon and Euclydes da Cunha, were also key figures in the emerging Brazilian republic. They were classmates at the military academy in Rio de Janeiro, where the overthrow of the monarchy was hatched. And both were positivists, disciples of the philosopher Auguste Comte, who made science into a burning faith and whose faith Brazilians made into a powerful national movement. They spent most of their lives buried in the barely traveled backlands and shared the bold idea of bringing "order," that most cherished of positivist maxims, to the "chaos of the Brazilian jungles." But in many ways the story of Cunha and Rondon begins not in the wilds of the Big Bush or the rain forests of the Amazon, but back east, in the sun-dappled and sea-lapped city of Rio de Janeiro.

The Brazilian Positivist Church in Rio de Janeiro has faded some since its glory days at the end of the Brazilian monarchy, but it still retains touches of its turn-of-the-century majesty. The imposing stone and brick edifice faces the delivery door of a giant hospital on a street named, fittingly, Benjamin Constant. To enter, a visitor must slalom a blockade of parked cars, which have invaded the cracked cement of what is still euphemistically called in Rio a sidewalk. Yet once inside the churchyard a visitor feels an uncanny quiet. The huge Parthenon-like facade of the church rises behind a green metal fence and is crowned with the odd and intriguing slogan: "The living are always and ever more governed necessarily by the dead."

From the great portico sprouts a forest of pillars supporting the lofty roof. A steady breeze whispers through the garden with its sweet-smelling flowers, called manaca and dois-amigos, a slim *cordon vert* between the temple and the rush of downtown traffic. Here nature has won back a little space from the city. Moss has worked its way through the fissures of the entryway, and water stains darken the pilasters. Overhead, above the square archway, a frieze of a woman clutching an infant is done in blue, yellow, and mauve mosaic. She wears a blue shawl, her skin is brown, her hair golden. Her infant is a miniature swaddled likeness.

Inside, a veil of dust settles over the deeply stained hardwood pews. The church is hung with portraits of the curious pantheon of the faith: Copernicus, Dante, Toussaint L'Ouverture, Lord Cromwell, Galileo, and Shakespeare—the fathers of empire, revolution, art, and science. The altar supports a

bust of Comte, and behind him, in the place where Christ on
the cross would be in a Catholic church, hangs a painting of
the woman and infant seen at the entry. The edifice looks less
like a church than a courthouse or a government building and
has a feel that is somehow both hallowed and secular.

I visited the church on a hot summer day in 1991. Alfredo
de Moraes, then eighty-four, a retired navy admiral and the
church's keeper (there are no presidents or directors in the positivist order), opened the doors to the cool basement that was
his office and library. On one wall, in a glass and wood armoire,
was a collection of leather-bound texts on philosophy, mathematics, and chemistry. Here again the world's great scientists
and artists stared solemnly from dark portraits hung on every
wall. Most prominent, resting on a large easel, was an oil of
Texeira Mendes, an early Brazilian convert to Comte's philosophy, who, together with Miguel Lemos, spread the word back
in Rio de Janeiro.

It was this word that soon leached through to the restive
citizens of the late Brazilian monarchy and so sealed its end.
Engineers, doctors, geologists, mathematicians, and soldiers—especially soldiers—found inspiration in Comte's
teachings. Propelled by this cult of science, this professional
class not only changed Brazil's political regime but went to
the ends of vast countryside to explore and investigate and to
make the country anew.

The Heroic Geographer

There was perhaps no more earnest a frontier ideologue than
Euclydes da Cunha. He was an engineer and a geographer by
vocation and an early follower of the philosophy of positivism.
He was also a fervent republican. The republican movement
was marbled with positivists. At the time Cunha attended the
military academy, Comte's ideas dominated the officers' acad-
emies and the technical schools. Though the positivists never

managed to gain power, their ideas seeped into all levels of
the republican government and society. Comte's faithful helped
write the first constitution and fashion the Brazilian flag, a
green and yellow standard with a star-spangled circle representing the heavens in the center, bordered by the Comtean
motto "Order and Progress."

The positivists called for an enlightened dictatorship. A tal-
ented and trained elite would guide society according to the
inexorable plan of humanity as revealed by modern science.
They believed in social harmony and progress, without the
impedimenta of democracy; voting, party politics, and political liberties, like freedom of speech, they argued, would only
confuse and anguish the masses. In a time when Europe heaved
and boiled with social conflict, the positivists talked instead of
a firm hand guiding society from above to a slow but sure
evolution to enlightenment and prosperity. "Liberty consists in
subordinating oneself to laws," Cunha said.[2]

Their inspiration came from France, but more than any other
of Comte's apostles, the Brazilian positivists refashioned his
vision into a national utopia. They dreamed of nothing less
than overhauling society, though their ideology was a heady
and confusing potion of imported and homespun thought. Positivism called for a quiet revolution and found its most ardent
advocates in the army, which believed in "a consortium of
thought with the sword." This posed a problem for the soldiers. Comte, after all, was biliously antimilitary and insisted
on the peaceful evolution of society. So the Brazilian follow-
ers in uniform had to do some ideological acrobatics. How
were they to maintain allegiance to their caste—instrumental
in toppling the monarchy and bringing on the republican century—and at the same time respect the distance from civilian
politics their religious calling imposed?

They settled on the notion of the "soldier-citizen," according to the historian José Murilo de Carvalho, recasting themselves as a "society with arms." In that way they appropriated
for themselves an array of civil rights and a leadership role

within society. They were not aristocrats. In fact, they hailed from the strata of society that depended less on pedigree than diplomas. They were technically trained professionals, the "Bolsheviks of the middle class," in Carvalho's words. They sought to provide a dignified wage for the proletariat, improve the living conditions of the humblest citizens, and respect all the races.[3]

To paste together this national ideal, the positivists and other republicans had to break the allure of the coast. Their mirror was no longer the sea but the vast interior, with its dense forests, imposing sierras, and web of rivers. Immigrants were a driving force, but the imperative was to break away from this "loaned culture," as Cunha called it, and create something wholly Brazilian.

Cunha was not only one of the most brilliant voices of positivism but also an acclaimed journalist, explorer, and naturalist. He was never an orthodox, churchgoing positivist but was in thrall to Comte's cult of science. The Brazilian scholar Nicolau Sevcenko, who tracked his career, writes that Cunha, who wrote at the dawn of the twentieth century, really straddled two eras. He drank from the curious elixir of romanticism mixed with the new era's reverence for exact science and historical determinism. He had Rousseau and Victor Hugo at one elbow, Spencer and Darwin at the other. He began as a fervent believer in the nascent republic and set out to plumb its innards and so to find the soul of the nation. By the end of his career he was deeply disillusioned with the republicans and sought in the countryside a refuge, an antidote to that dilapidated urban regime.

A man of the rough interior, he never failed to invoke the value of those motley beginnings. He described himself, variously, as "the son of the farm," the "son and lover of the land," and a "hillbilly." He wrote:

Let others adore the vast capitals
where brilliantly

> *voices are raised in magical respect*
> *for the triumph of Industry and Science.*
> *Not me, I much prefer*
> *the desolate quests of the desert*
> *full of shade, silence and peace. . . .*
> *And I seek at this hour*
> *the cities that majestically*
> *hide themselves*
> *in the solemn sadness of the* sertão.[4]

His amblings deep into the core of Brazil bolstered his faith in the virtues of the countryside while at the same time confirming his bitter disillusion with the foundering republic. As one dream of utopia crumbled behind him, he burrowed after another, deep in Brazil's heart of darkness. The nation's first genuine war correspondent, he covered the campaign of the Brazilian Army's campaign against a messianic and antirepublican uprising in Canudos, the dusty, parched backlands of the northeast.

He was shocked by the brutal republican assault against a people armed with little more than the muskets they captured from their foes and a burning faith. The ragtag Canudos army, which sympathized with the deposed monarch, rallied behind a charismatic leader, Antônio Conselheiro, humiliated the Bahia state militia and twice turned back federal troops before being slaughtered in a final battle. (Even so, the Bahia state and republican armies lost a total of one thousand and forty-four men.) Cunha saw in that war a national "crime" against a people "abandoned for three centuries." At the same time he marveled at the capacity of these *sertanejos* to cope and prevail in that desert.

Amazonia held a special place in his romantic geography. At the time, in fact, the northern region of Brazil was nearly an independent country. In 1839 Charles Goodyear invented vulcanization, a chemical process that made rubber resistant to heat, cold, oils, and solvents. He patented his invention five years later, and suddenly the whole world demanded the Amazon's gold that grew on trees. The rubber boom of the nineteenth century created tremendous wealth and a local elite, whose prosperity and culture owed nothing to Rio or Bahia. It also laid the ground for exploitation.

Thousands of northeasterners, fleeing drought and pursuing hopes of land and wealth, migrated to the Amazonian rubber groves. They were the miserable underbelly to so much wealth. Cunha was shocked at the condition of the rubber tapper, "a fellah bending all his efforts to the most abject and proletarian servitude . . . much less than a man and little more than a machine." But it was in this underclass that the genuine national heroes were to be found. There, in the jungles of Amazonia, as in the parched *sertão,* were the sturdy souls who represented "the vigorous core of our nation," the "living bedrock of our race."

More and more he came to dismiss the city and its glittery imported culture and tastes as products of decadence and mediocrity—and injustice. Despite the republican ideals of progress and modernity, a chasm yawned between Brazilians.

Inflation and monetary speculation ran wild. Fortunes were made and lost nearly overnight, and the poor got even poorer. The republic split in two, wrote the novelist Aluísio Azevedo. "[There are] those who lost everything and those who won everything. The first cry out in hunger while the second tremble in fear. Some hide to mask their misery; others to flee justice."[5]

In a matter of a decade the republic had shown itself to be as infected by snobbishness and hierarchy as any monarchy. Underneath the patina of egalitarian rhetoric, the protagonists of the republic lolled on a bed of privileges. The lettered men, in the fashion of the French Jacobins, flaunted the word "citizen" but that, too, was amended for more refined sensibilities. "It was 'doctor citzen' here, 'general citizen' there," writes José Murilo de Carvalho about these haughty republicans. The worst offender, he noted, was also one of the most famous, the renowned jurist Rui Barbosa. "He was 'general doctor citizen,' " Carvalho writes.[6]

The *sertão,* by contrast, was seen not only as a frontier of opportunity but also as the wellspring of purity and authenticity. For Cunha, then, Brazil's noble savage was not the aborigine but the mixed-blood *sertanejo.* (Later, during the modernist period, the celebration of miscegenation blossomed into a fullblown theory of "racial democracy," put forth by the sociologist Gilberto Freyre, a potent myth that survives till this day. Brazil was no such thing, of course, and racial barriers were often as implacable as they were dissimulated. But the easy mingling of the races in contemporary Brazil is still confounding and refreshing for many North Americans, used to the gaping divide that separates the colors and cultures in the United States. the brave *sertanejo* was "the only hope" to rid Brazil "of the cosmopolitan stigma . . . and a borrowed culture."

A wiry man with a gaunt aspect and a mustache waxed into points at each end, Cunha was an anguished soul. He wrote long, poetic, but tortuous tracts, devoting hundreds of pages to landscapes and geological minutiae. He was enamored of the stouthearted *sertanejo* but harbored nagging doubts as well. For all their stoicism and virtue, *sertanejos,* too, were rude, incomplete souls. "We are condemned to civilization," he wrote. "There we shall progress or we shall perish." He had a tragic homelife, losing his wife to a lover while he sallied forth, for months at a time, in the outback. He lost his life not in an adventurous "duel with the desert," as he had imagined, but to a bullet from the gun of his wife's lover in a jealous domestic brawl.

Cunha has been held up in recent writing on the Amazon as an early ecologist. His text rings with powerful denunciations of the manhandling of the Brazilian environment. "We have been a disastrous geological agent, an antagonistic and terribly barbarous element against the very nature that surrounds us," he wrote. He decried the wanton practitioners of plantation agriculture, who promoted "the impoverishment and the sterilization of the earth. They fill up the land by emptying it out."

But this was no Muir to Brazil's untamed west. Nature, to him, was not some object of sublime reverence but instead a force to be dominated and harnessed for social ends. If the people of Amazonia were exploited and abandoned, then the accoutrements of civilization—roads, telegraph wires, food, and justice—must be brought to their wilderness.

He lost himself in the Amazon, a place for which he felt a mixture of both wonderment and fear. This realm of nature was "portentous, but incomplete"—there, he said, to be not only revered but improved upon. "It is a stupendous construction that lacks all interior decoration. Amazonia is perhaps the newest land on earth. It has everything and it lacks everything."

What Amazonia lacked was human design—that of white humans, in any case. "Our engineering has no nobler calling than the rational conquest of our earth," he said. So Cunha called for railways and roads to stitch the vast interior. Environmentalists today finger the Brazilian military and the ruthless capitalist developers in Japan for their crusade to build a route to the Pacific, a highway that they say would pillage the tropical timber and destroy the delicate ecosystem. But Cunha was perhaps this route's earliest advocate. Enamored of the stupendous Panama Canal, which burrowed a way between the seas, in 1905 he was already calling for a Brazilian route to the Pacific, "the Transacreana."

Imperialism was also an enemy. He made his journeys when Peru and Bolivia, and U.S. capitalists, were jockeying for parts of the Brazilian Amazon. In a proviso that has echoed over and over again during this century, Cunha called out for the settling of the Brazilian interior, in order to "integrate" Amazonia with the rest of nation. "The imperialist expansion of the great powers is a growing fact," he warned. "The most natural spilling over of an excess of lives and the surplus of riches and the conquest of peoples, it is a simple variant of the conquest of markets."

Taking hold of Amazonia, then, was imperative. And Amazonia could not be had unless it was also known. He had come of age reading the treatises of the world's great discoverers—Humboldt, Bates, Wallace, and Darwin. Investigation was one of the noblest badges of progress. "The exact definition and complete dominion of the great physical base of our nationality—there is the true mission," Cunha trumpeted. "Because just as we do not have a complete science of the physical foundations of our nation, neither do we have a history."

The adventurers and woodsmen who stubbornly carved out their homes in various corners of this country were promoted as the foot soldiers of this campaign. These "admirable caboclos of the north," he said, "are the ones who can impose our tongue, our habits, and eventually, our destiny . . ." on the backlands, thus "establishing . . . the dominant component of our nationality." So here, three centuries later, was the link between the *bandeiras* from São Paulo and the Amazon. The forest, underpeopled and vulnerable, was "the inevitable destiny of the Paulistas and the *sertanejo*."

Cunha played an important part in casting Brazil's destiny inland. His design for Amazonia, a utopia of science wedded to the purer vigor of the backlanders, was fashioned from the disillusionment of a decadent republic. But it took the efforts of a colleague, General Cândido Rondon, to turn the call into a deed of the expanding Brazilian empire.

"Moses in Reverse"

Mimoso—"affectionate" in Portuguese—is a sleepy village in the southwestern corner of Mato Grosso. A dirt road and irregular bus service connect it to Cuiabá, the state capital. It is a hamlet of squat houses on dirt streets, caressed by the meandering Cuiabá River. Bats roost in the cool darkness of the Catholic church by day and wing through the streets for prey by night. Life is governed by the heat, the rain, and the sluggish rhythms of fishing, farming, and herding. Mimoso is also the home of Cândido Mariano da Silva Rondon. A small plaque marks the modest house where he was born. Despite these modest beginnings, Rondon became this country's, and one of the world's, most accomplished explorers. He trumped John the Baptist, spending forty *years* in the Brazilian wilderness, mapping the backlands, stringing telegraph wires, and making contact with Indian tribes. No one—not Stanley or Livingstone nor even Humboldt or Wallace—spent more time exploring the tropics. He navigated through nearly as much of the jungles behind Rio and São Paulo as Columbus did the seas.

He systematically charted twenty-four thousand square miles of territory and strung thirty-six hundred miles of telegraph lines that, end to end, would stretch from Lisbon to Warsaw.[7] Just one of them traversed twelve hundred miles of scrub and jungle virtually unknown to white society, between Cuiabá and Rio Branco, in the extreme northwest Amazon. Shortly after his failed attempt at reelection with the Bull Moose (Progressive) party, Theodore Roosevelt spent six months with Rondon, traveling an unknown river in the Amazon. He called Rondon's Strategic Telegraph Line, connecting Mato Grosso to Acre, one of two "cyclopean accomplishments" in the Americas. (The other, of course, was Roosevelt's own, the Panama Canal.)

A remarkable part of Rondon's legacy, one that distances him from most of the world's wilderness explorers, was his zealous dedication to the cause of defending Indians. He was the founder of Brazil's Indian Protection Service, in 1910, and paved the way for policies that would protect "our brothers of the jungle" from the crush of an expanding civilization. Trained in the natural sciences as well as in engineering, Rondon contacted and coaxed into complacency dozens of tribes. His work allowed the first scientific census of the nation's Indian population, and he personally recorded dozens of Indian languages, which he also mastered.

Brazil's official hero is Tiradentes, a dentist who led the Inconfidence movement against the Portuguese crown. The movement failed, and Tiradentes was executed for his plotting, but his death is remembered in a national holiday. Rondon never received such formal acclaim. No one remembers his birthday, and no statues of the intrepid woodsman adorn city parks or plazas. (A discreet bust of Rondon is tucked away in Rio's Laranjeiras neighborhood.) Finally, in 1990, the government minted a new currency note, of a thousand cruzeiros, stamped with his image, but in inflation-battered Brazil, where old heroes depreciate every day, that is a dubious honor. If he did not make it into the national pantheon, Rondon did become at the very least a crucial pillar in the construction of the Brazilian frontier.

For his efforts, a state the size of Wyoming, Rondônia, was named after him. Brazil's domestic Peace Corps, in which young professionals served in poor country communities, was called, fittingly, Project Rondon. (The service was discontinued after heavy budget cuts in 1990.) Amazonia's maps are speckled with towns like Rondonópolis, Vila Rondon, and Marcos Rondon, as well as those named for half a dozen other positivist eminences. A major highway that traced part of the path of his telegraph wire is named for him. There are butcher shops, hardware stores, bus stations, and bars that bear his name. Even the occasional baby is still named after him.

Yet these homages to the great Indianist are the emblems of a settler society; they crowd a landscape once occupied by the tribes he set out to protect. The devout positivist who cherished all the races and worked his whole life for the protection of Indians ironically played a fundamental role in making Mato Grosso safe for "civilization."

Rondon was born in 1865, a few months after Paraguay's megalomaniacal dictator Francisco Solano López, *El Supremo,* invaded Brazil, sparking one of the continent's bloodiest conflicts. The War of the Triple Alliance pitted Brazil, Argentina, and Uruguay against tiny Paraguay and cost that landlocked nation perhaps a fifth of the entire population. It had taken forty-seven days for a messenger to get through to Rio de Janeiro with word of the Paraguayan invasion, and the delay dramatically exposed Brazil's weak western flank. Rondon, whose family was caught in the caldron of that conflict, was to dedicate his life to remedying that dangerous situation.

Rondon never knew his father, who died of smallpox a few months before he was born. His mother gathered the infant up shortly after birth and fled with thousands of western Brazilians before the marauding Paraguayans. She, too, died two years later of smallpox, which had swept through the teeming camps of war refugees in Cuiabá. Rondon was brought up by a grandfather of distant Indian descent and grew up speaking both Portuguese and Bororo, the language of a large Mato Grosso tribe.

Rondon was sent off to Rio to the military academy, where he studied engineering, mathematics, and the natural sciences. A short, frail, timid young man, he was awed by the ways of the big, rude city. Donald O'Reilly, who scoured Rondon's life for a Ph.D. dissertation, describes his arrival: "In December, 1884, wearing a celluloid collar and no undershirt, Rondon arrived in Rio de Janeiro; determined to make a bold front, he listened to a waiter read the entire menu in a restaurant. He ordered bread, rice and beans, the cheapest items listed."[8]

Abstemious, often severe in his self-discipline, Rondon rose regularly at 4:00 A.M. to swim in the Atlantic and routinely began his studies before sunlight. He lost a year of school to a nagging illness that left him a wraith. An orphan from the humblest of backland origins. Rondon was a world apart from his wealthier, more urbane classmates. An accomplished athlete, he spent his weekends scaling the thousand-foot Sugar Loaf Mountain and swimming in the ocean. Painfully awkward in social settings, he was branded "the hairy brute" by his classmates.[9]

But Rondon made up for his lack of social skills by his ardor. He became an avid student of Benjamin Constant Botelho de Magalhães, who was a lecturer in mathematics, a burning positivist, and a leading republican, despite his close association with Emperor Dom Pedro II. (Constant even tutored the emperor's grandchildren, but Pedro apparently never saw coming the coup d'etat that Constant sparked.)

Constant soon inducted the young Rondon into the burgeoning positivist fold. To Euclydes da Cunha, positivism's appeal was the reverence for science and philosophy; Rondon was swayed by the dogma of this "Religion of Humanity." He became a leading member of the Brazil's Positivist Church, one of the largest in the world, and one of the faith's most dedicated apostles. In fact, he saw his whole life in the Brazilian backlands as an extended positivist mission.

The cool, quiet basement of the Positivist Church was a tonic from Rio's steamy and busy streets. I asked about Rondon, and Alfredo de Moraes lit up. He had known the general quite well and recalled how they often sat for hours debating philosophy in the church basement. "He used to sit, not like you and me," said Moraes, slouching in the wooden chair for effect. "But like this." He sat bolt upright, his spine straighter than the chair back. "Discipline. That was Rondon." Moraes apologized for not having a portrait of Rondon on display. It was not a slight to the renowned explorer, he said, just a question of space. To prove the point, he took me to another room, where every inch of the walls was again covered up with the framed idols of the faith, from Aristotle to George Washington. He picked up a dusty frame showing the unmistakable visage of a steel-eyed, bearded, mustacheless man. "There isn't even room for Lincoln!" The icons of the "Humanitarian Religion" apparently were always being renovated.

Then Moraes scurried into another closet and dug out an old poster of Rondon as a young lieutenant colonel. It was a sepia portrait, showing a small man with sharp, blemishless features that owed more to Europe than to the neotropics. Bookworms had eaten holes through the margins of the poster, and the humidity had left dark stains. But the image was clear, and the face commanding, less a portrait than an adulation. It showed an elegant officer in a crisp officer's dress uniform—with a choke collar buttoned high up his thin throat and a stiff-billed cap—as if in sartorial defiance of the tropical heat. The shoulders were set at a slight angle, and his head turned another few degrees from that axis, the eyes veering slightly off to the right. The expression was placid, almost beatific, the gaze lifted toward some destination in the mezzo distance.

The positivist patriarch Auguste Comte had two phases, the first scientific and secular and the second more spiritual and mystical. His liaison with a platonic lover, Clotilde de Vaux, is credited with the transition. The image of Clotilde, usually portrayed, as on the church's facade, hugging an infant in her arms, is the most prominent symbol of the positivist's faith. And it was after meeting Clotilde that he elaborated the views on race and family. Positivism was a secular religion, a faith "without fear of hell and without the reward of heaven," said Moraes.

The positivists' Trinity was the extended family, the *pátria* or nation, and humanity—ever-larger families, in a sense. Positivists opposed slavery and favored the separation of church and state. Catholicism was not bad; it was just not enough, at best a way station between atheism and positivism. To Comte, the belief in an almighty God was a useless abstraction. He called monotheism the inkling of reason's struggle with the imagination. In Catholicism faith superseded scientific observation; believing was seeing. The positivists stood that on its head. Seeing was believing. God was but a mystification, whose proppings would come undone before the revelations of the observable sciences.[10]

The positivists also chafed under the heavy hand of Catholic authorities in political life. Indians were to be protected and ministered to—not by religious missionaries but by agents of the state. Rondon, too, became ever more disdainful of the collapsing republic and its failure to make real the ideals it espoused. Such broodings sent Cunha off to the backlands to find a purer reality. Rondon, likewise, buried himself in the *sertão*, but he never failed to answer the call of the nation's leaders.

From the time Cabral stumbled ashore at Porto Seguro, in 1500, until nearly the beginning of the last century, there were still many more Indians than whites in Brazil. However, the colonials were persistent, expansive, and often truculent. You could say the Indians had a settler problem. In Rondon's lifetime the balance swung brutally in the other direction. White society was expanding west now, finally resuming the trails of the *bandeirantes*. There were open spaces, lands to be colonized, from Cuiabá to the upper Rio Negro, and society was now on the move.

What to do with the Indians? The debate was intricate, and it was heated. The positivists played a key role in defining the Indian question. They had put forth some extravagant and mystical ideas about racial union. In the positivist republic a special role was reserved for the darker races. An ornate statue adorning an arbored courtyard in downtown Rio is a thick column topped by a leading positivist hero, Floriano Peixoto. On a square pedestal at its base are a white Portuguese colonial, an Indian, and a black. Also sharing the pedestal are a priest and a woman, holding a rose. This elaborate, if cluttered, iconography represents the positivists' notion of the Brazilian "race."[11]

To the positivists the blacks were the embodiment of affection and emotion. The white race was dynamic, the agent of change, movement, and industry. The "yellow race," which included Amerindians, was the repository of intelligence. The Indians, though primitive in technology, were "fetishists" and therefore purer—unencumbered, that is, by the mystifying cant of monotheism, which the positivists believed only retarded social evolution to scientific enlightenment. The Indians had an order, but not yet progress. That put the Indian race closer to the pinnacle than the dominant whites.[12]

All these elaborate ideas and icons were part of a deliberate effort to forge a national identity, and the positivists were not alone in the foundry. Brazil is a country, after all, which has tried harder than most to create an ideology of racial unity. The modernists contributed their part, most notably Gilberto Freyre, with his theory of Lusotropicalism, the idea of a great racial symphony, where all shades of humanity lived in a special, tender harmony. Many of these advocates were trained social scientists and professional artists. Yet their works read more like poetry than objective contemplation. After all, they were working on nothing less than a Brazilian myth of origin.

The Brazilian claim to a special racial dynamic is based partly on solid fact. Everywhere in the Portuguese colonies, where colonial women were latecomers and the men hardly puritans, miscegenation was winked at or actively encouraged. The marquês de Pombal, the all-powerful overseas minister of Dom José I of Portugal, who virtually ran Lisbon's empire from 1750 to 1777, actively advocated miscegenation in Brazil, particularly in the Amazon region.

"The colonial clerks of the merchants sit at the same table as their employers without embarrassment," said an enthusiastic Livingstone, of a visit to Angola. "Nowhere in Africa is there so much good will between Europeans and natives as here."[13] Yet the notion of a rainbow colony was also a deliberate flight of fantasy. Often there was a more concrete agenda at work. Pombal's racial "tolerance" was meant, at least in part, to breed away the "Indian" problem and also to wrest the Brazilian Indians and their vast lands from the hands of Jesuit missionaries, who presided over villages in key regions, from Argentina to Amazonas.

Some of the early Brazilian novelists, notably José de Alencar, and the poet Gonçalves Dias, looked to the Indian as the repository of Rousseauist values. Although African slaves had been drafted early to replace Indians, the romantics ignored the blacks. (It took another half century and the emergence of Lusotropicalism to add blacks to the Brazilian racial blend.)

But they were passionate about Indians. Alencar wrote *O Guaraní,* about a doggedly loyal Indian who forsook his people's faith to protect his master, a Portuguese colonist.[14]

These were not so much realistic portrayals of Indians as they were literary domestications. Stripped of their original surroundings and culture, which were real and or imagined threats to the expanding Brazilian settlers, these fanciful remakes were less terrifying, even appealing. In *O Guaraní,* Alencar's Indian hero, Peri, is so blindly devoted to his master he abandons his wife and tribe, forsakes his religion, conspires with the settlers to defeat another tribe, and finally even sacrifices himself to save the colonist's daughter: "This girl, this blond angel, with blue eyes, represented divinity on earth." Peri is not an Indian at all, of course, but a medieval knight done up in loincloth.

Contemporary critics have dismissed these writers as second-run romantics, whose style and vision were but pale copies of the novelists of North America and Europe. Yet they were also portrait artists of a frontier drama, and their tales only exaggerated versions of the real sagas of settlers, bad hats, adventurers, and Indians. Their stories sold wildly, especially back in Rio and São Paulo. These fictions served something of the same imaginative role as the tales of noble savages and whites in buckskins who people the fiction of James Fenimore Cooper and the works of Francis Parkman (both of whom inspired Alencar). The telling of clashes between white savages and red and of the opening of the way for good homespun settler types was, to paraphrase Martin Green's words on English colonial literature, part of "the energizing myth" of the frontier.

In both Americas this was fiction of conquest. When Alencar wrote, Brazilians were still scratching at the coastline, and other than the *bandeirantes,* only a few intrepid Paulistas had pressed very far west. Indians were formidable obstacles—until they were defeated. Then they became the objects of curiosity, pity, and finally stony indifference. "They were 'former

savages,' " writes Lévi-Strauss; "as soon as they were no longer
a 'danger to Society,' civilization took no further interest in
them."[15] This literary domestication mirrored the historical one
happening swiftly, brutally in the countryside, even as Alencar
spun off more of his adventures.

Rondon's self-made career and backland origins seemed
perfect material for mythmaking. The official descriptions of
Rondon generally extol his "Indianness" and his woodsman's
ways, often with colorful hyperbole. Even in his portraits he
seemed to grow more Indian as time went by. The younger
Rondon is generally painted as almost fair-skinned and fine-
featured. Later portraits color his skin cinnamon, pull the almond
eyes back slightly at the corners, and raise the cheekbones.
His biographers often described him as "half Indian" or of direct
Indian descent. "A full-blooded Indian," reveled Theodore
Roosevelt. In fact, anthropologist Antônio Carlos de Souza
Lima discovered a far less exotic lineage. In a carefully recon-
structed family tree, Souza Lima demonstrated that Rondon's
"Indianness" was practically restricted to two mestizo relatives
four generations removed and to Maria Rosa Rondon, his
paternal grandmother, who had "a few drops of Guaná Indian
blood."[16]

Nevertheless, such claims to indigenous heritage were not
mere idle picture making. Rondon held a key position in
smoothing the way to the Brazilian frontier. The Indian-like
Indianist, lifelong humanitarian, and ardent positivist finally
helped make Alencar's stories of conquest into history.

The Indian Protection Service

Brazil's Indian problem began when the first Portuguese put
to shore early in the sixteenth century. The Indian policy problem started four centuries later, at the International Congress
of Americanists, in Vienna in 1908. At first there was little to
rattle nerves. This was, after all, an academic affair, where

eminent scholars debated the arcana of primitive peoples. Reports of violence against Indians were troubling, to be sure, but atrocities against aboriginals were taken more as a loss for science than as a crime against humanity. The trouble started in the afternoon session, when a twenty-seven-year-old Czech ethnographer, Vojtěch Albert Frič, brazenly accused Brazil of genocide. He pointed a finger at the settlers of European descent, particularly the Germans, who were carving out a frontier in southern Brazil. Frič spoke passionately of whites engaging in the wanton killing, maiming, rape, and enslavement of tribes-people, as well as the deliberate spreading of disease. He called the Indian hunters of the day, the *bugreiros,* "human hyenas." Frič's contract as a naturalist working in Brazil for the Berlin and Hamburg museums was summarily canceled, and he was nearly expelled from the Vienna conference. But Frič's denunciations provoked a fury of debate within Brazil and without. It was this debate, plus the efforts of the Brazilian positivists, that led eventually, in 1910, to the establishment of the Brazilian Indian Protection Service.[17]

David Stauffer, in a doctoral thesis on Rondon, points out that behind these diplomatic and scientific frays was an unprecedented expansion into the Brazilian interior, from the pampas of Rio Grande do Sul to the Amazon Basin. In the far south the cultivation of maté herb tea turned into a booming industry, attracting thousands of former slaves to the maté plantations that were opening up in the interior. In the center south, two railroads, one connecting Rio Grande do Sul and São Paulo, the other traversing west, through Paraná, advanced into the backcountry, where dozens of Indian tribes dwelt.

In 1877 an epic drought in the northeast drove thousands of starving peasants from the dusty backlands. Many went to Amazonia, having been recruited by merchants who bought and sold rubber latex, cacao, quinine, and sarsaparilla—the so-called drugs of the *sertão*. In the first of what were several waves of migration to the Amazon from the northeast, these desperate *sertanejos* soon came into bloody conflict with the

Indians. Word of ambushes and massacres, on both sides of the barricades, drifted downriver to Manaus and Belém and on to Rio and São Paulo.

Central Brazil also felt the crush of migration. The invention of cold storage in Argentina revolutionized the beef industry and, inadvertently, sparked a land rush. The frozen beef dealers paid top prices for high-quality meat, driving up land values and eventually pushing the less competitive "rough stock" cattlemen (who served Brazil's meat extract and jerked beef industries) north into the unoccupied and cheap savannas of central Brazil. As the land market boomed, squatters were no longer tolerated, and they, too, streamed north to the plains of Mato Grosso and Goiás. In 1906 one southern Brazilian rancher reported some two hundred squatters and their mule trains passing by his ranch every month.[18]

This was also a time of intensive migration from Europe, which sent German small farmers to settle the south and Italians to work the Brazilian coffee plantations, smarting still from the loss of chattel labor. In 1909 there were nearly a hundred thousand immigrants in twenty-six colonies all over Brazil, from the gaucho grasslands to the Amazon.

The Indian question was in part a philosophical one, with positivists and lay missionaries on one side and frontiersmen and developers on the other. But the debate also broke down along geographic lines, pitting São Paulo against Rio. In Rio the Indians had already been expelled by the earliest colonists and driven beyond the mountains. To Cariocas, as Rio dwellers are called, Indians lived only in the pages of Alencar and Gonçalves Dias. São Paulo, however, was already halfway inland and the engine of the frontier. To the Paulistas, the Indians were often just over the next hill—some tribes such as the Kayapó and Paiaguá offered fierce resistance. But for the most part the Indians were judged to be less a menace than a nuisance to Paulistas pressing westward. The other side, led by the German-born entomologist Hermann von Ihering, the director of the São Paulo Museum, simply wanted the Indians out of the way. "It seems we have no alternative but to exterminate them," he concluded icily. "The life of a woodsman and colonist is certainly worth more than the life of a savage" was Ihering's infamous and often-cited pronouncement.[19]

The railways of the nineteenth century had encroached upon the Xokleng of Santa Catarina, the Kaingáng of São Paulo, the Pataxó of Espirito Santo and Bahia, and the Parintintin of Amazonas. Now the surviving Indians were a stone in the shoe of those on the move. "We are seeing a new and grandiose combat of the modern *Paulista* civilization with its three million inhabitants held hostage by some 3,000 savages," declared São Paulo rancher José de Campos Novaes.[20] The Indian, who had already surrendered the littoral, was now in the path of the Brazilian march inland.

Yet even as society rolled relentlessly westward, Rondon clung fervently to the belief that Indians not only were to be protected but had a role in society. Though he rejected outright assimilation and preached respect for Indian culture, he saw them as essentially citizens in the rough. Like the North American ethnographer Cadwallader Colden, who wrote five volumes on the Iroquois, Rondon believed that Indians were not devoid of spirit, nor did they necessarily have to be converted. Just as Colden believed that in every Indian was a "Christian waiting to blossom," Rondon argued that the native Brazilians, treated with a gentle hand and left to ponder the wonders of science, would come around (to positivism) of their own accord. They, too, would be Brazilians someday. "As a patriot, I yearn for the reconciliation of the three races that constitute the ethnic base of the Brazilian people so that, once forged, they will form a united population of this great republic," he stated.[21]

But Rondon performed another role that came inexorably into collision with these brave ideals. He was not merely the symbol of the expanding Brazilian will into the interior but for half a century the primary mover. In the first years of the republic the government set out to tend to its vulnerable western and northern flanks, those great splotches of the map marked *decconhecido* (unknown). Binding the interior with telegraph wires and rails was the way to bring it under control. This was a bold, risky time, the era of "heroic geography," according to the noted engineer Francisco Behring.[22] To the Indians, it was the first wave of what became a relentless invasion.

Rondon actually hastened the invasion into Amazonia when he took on the Olympian task of building the Strategic Telegraph Line from Cuiabá, in southern Mato Grosso, to Santo Antônio (now Porto Velho), in what is current-day Rondônia, nine hundred miles due northwest. To that time it was river travel that had defined journeys through the Amazon. Until nearly the middle of this century it was far easier and far quicker to sail to London than to trek the savanna, bush, and jungle north of Cuiabá. The telegraph lines would do for Amazonia what the railways had done in southern Brazil.

The telegraph construction brigades, called, suggestively, commissions of penetration, spread their web of lines and men and herds all over the Brazilian backlands in the span of thirty years. Often they were made up of an assortment of unsavory characters, including misfit soldiers and those serving punishment for shirking other duties. They were an unruly bunch and frequently spoiled for trouble with the native populations.

Rondon's commissions were notably different. Though he lost several men to Indian attacks, not a single Indian was killed by his crews. A stern disciplinarian, he frequently resorted to the lash to control his men, a practice that once had him hauled before a military tribunal to answer for the death of one of his soldiers. Yet Rondon would be the first one systematically to break the jungle barrier. Not only did he string a discreet, one-inch-thick copper wire, but he also opened a monumental wagon trail beneath it, 150 feet wide in parts, tearing straight through the jungle. Maintenance stations were built, and small outposts sprang up. Corrals for cattle were constructed.

In this task, and in many others, Rondon belonged undoubtedly to the conquering race. He once said:

> The problem of the west depends today on one factor, population. But the question of peopling [the west] cannot be resolved without . . . a railway. We should do in this field what the North Americans did: tear railway lines through our interior, and go planting nuclei of population along the tracks. This is the efficient solution to the problem to which I have dedicated myself all my life. The more I meditate on it . . . the more I am convinced that this question can only be resolved with the intelligent and systematic intervention of man.[23]

In two scant decades the land was dotted with corrals and encampments, roads and rails; the land of the Mato Grosso Indians had become occupied territory.

Rondon had a curious, sometimes uneasy relationship with the republic. The governments he served had long harbored plans to move society inland, and his task was largely to see that it was carried out with the minimum of fuss and unseemly violence. True to his positivist precepts, he declined repeated attempts to draft him into politics. He even defied an executive or two. Yet he ended up serving every ambitious Caesar nonetheless. The man who had taken up arms against the emperor answered the call from President Artur Bernardes twenty years later to suppress a military rebellion. He chased the young rebel leader Captain Luiz Carlos Prestes throughout the southern backlands, to preserve the government.

He stood up, briefly, to Getúlio Vargas, who had him arrested shortly after the coup d'etat and removed from government service. Vargas then systematically gutted the Indian service Rondon had founded, making it an appendage of the Labor Ministry, shutting down many outposts, and slashing the budget. Yet later Vargas astutely grasped the value of Rondon's pioneering work. Nothing like the services of a "soldier-saint" to buffer the iron heel. He coaxed him back into the Indian service, and soon Rondon was doing the dictator's bidding, too. (Vargas had also relented some, restoring the Indian service to the more supportive Ministry of Agriculture.) Rondon accepted the directorship, working without pay.

Soon Rondon was praising the demagogue as nothing less than a "positivist dictator." He hailed Vargas's policies as those of "a responsible government, alien to rhetoric, theological and philosophical fictions' and, most important, opposed to "the absurd majority process." To Rondon, after all, the republic, with its cant of popular democracy, was nothing but a "bourgeois orgy." Vargas's coup had squelched the "irrational and immoral" call for universal suffrage, which was nothing but an invitation to "disorder."[24]

More and more, as the telegraph lines and railways stretched forward into forests, the Indians reacted. The northwest railway claimed many lives on both sides. One report told of a train returning from the backlands to a station with five bodies aboard, each missing its head. Lévi-Strauss recounted the story, told again and again on the Strategic Telegraph Line, of a telegraph worker "buried up to his waist, with his chest riddled with arrows and his automatic sender perched onto his head."

Rondon was the human buffer to these escalating conflicts. He was elevated to a role as laudable as it was impossible: the mediator of two societies on collision course. To the Indians he was hailed as "a friend" and even a "great chief." To the white man he was the "last *bandeirante*." Juscelino Kubitschek, who drew and quartered the nation with roads and power lines, called him "Moses in Reverse," leading his people *into* the wilderness.

Everyone, even the most ardent of Indian advocates, has treated Rondon with unbridled reverence. Rondon's intentions were, undisputably, humane. His often quoted slogan, "Die if necessary. Kill, never," reflected not some abstract ideal but a praxis. Often he physically punished his charges for shooting at Indians, and he repeatedly retreated from areas contested by hostile tribes. He was personally inured to punishment and extreme danger. He lost a toe to a piranha. His dog took a Nambikwara arrow meant for him.

But Rondon was a curiously tragic figure. Personally a humanist, he was single-handedly responsible for prying open the impenetrable Brazilian *sertão,* from Cuiabá to Rio Branco in the extreme west, from the river port of Manaus on the Amazonas to Boa Vista, not far from the Venezuelan border. All the time that he was protecting and defending Indians—from ruthless farmers and ranchers, from rubber tappers and adventurers—he was preparing a secure and permanent way through their lands and so sealing their demise.

In fact, as much as protection, the Indian agency he founded was really the state's attempt to define a crucial question: Once they were defeated, what was to be the proper role for the Brazilian Indians? As anthropologist Souza Lima has noted, the official Indian agency was officially called the Service for the Protection of Indians and Localization of National Workers. Many tribes knew Rondon as the "white chief," and he, for his part, frequently called on friendly Parecis and Bororo Indians to serve as guides and laborers along the telegraph stations. Once he even went so far as to persuade one tribe to move its village to the opposite side of a heavily traveled river. It was the agenda of dominant society, much more than indigenous rights, that defined the terms of the Indian question.

Under Rondon, Indians were protected but not empowered. Today, eighty years later, the Indian service has changed names, but the same agenda reigns: how to mediate the role of Indians within dominant society. More than ever the requirements of the latter still dictate the fate of the former—despite all the outcry against the slaughter of the Indians and the invasion of their lands.

Alfredo de Moraes shook his head sadly when asked what happened to Rondon's bright utopia for racial reconciliation. "Ruined," he said. It was, he said, the Catholic Church and its leftist mission work, combined with a more strident posture by the military, that buried Rondon's humanitarian goals. They wouldn't respect his example. Moraes wagged his head again. Indeed, the military governments have often been accused of betraying Rondon's humanitarian legacy. Yet that would be a half-truth. They did so only in style, not in content. In 1987 the military launched Calha North, the Northern Headwaters project, establishing a series of barracks along Brazil's northern perimeter. The idea was to shore up the vulnerable borderlands with soldiers, settlers, and towns—nodes of development in the empty jungle, it was called. It was a supremely Rondonian idea.

The modern military saw its mission in Amazonia as a peculiar mixture of conquest through caretaking. It built health clinics, schools, and housing. Indians and caboclos, or the half Indian peoples of the Amazon, were recruited as soldiers. These peoples of the Amazon were to be "repatriated," turned into the modern sentinels of the fortified borders. In this way, the military was tending to the needs of poor Amazonian communities as a way to influence more directly the question of control and "proper" use of land, including Indian land.

Everyone—left-leaning missionaries, environmentalists, ranchers, and soldiers—had a say on the Indian question. Everyone but the Indians. Their fate hinged on a heated debate by the different strata of the master society. Less than a corruption of Rondon's ideals, the military was really only carrying them out to their final, agonizing contradictions.[25]

Rondon gave his last interview to the *Jornal do Brasil* in May 1957, nine months before his death. Reporter Edilberto Coutinho described the ninety-one-year-old, dressed in a white shirt, buttoned at the throat, and gray trousers, thin and wrinkled, blind in one eye. It was a brief interview because Rondon was weary and under strict medical care. But Coutinho found him lucid, if slightly disengaged. He was laconic about current events but effusive on the deeds of the past. He also wore an Indian pendant, which had been hung on him earlier that day by an Indian chief.

The chief had come to try to urge him to return to the jungle to die in dignity with his darker brothers. If he remained in Rio, the white man's capital, he would only be forgotten, the chief warned. Rondon stayed in Rio, where he died in February the next year. Everyone, including President Juscelino Kubitschek, attended the funeral. The body lay in state for twelve hours at the Clube Militar, the exact place sixty-nine years before where Rondon and his fellow cadets listened to Benjamin Constant rail against the emperor and then decided to take history into their own hands.

Though he was not totally forgotten, in a way Rondon's life and work were expropriated at death. Rondon, the lifelong orthodox positivist, mysteriously called for a Catholic priest on his deathbed, as though to repent for something. His grandson, an ordained priest, administered extreme unction, and Rondon's last words were, strangely, "Long live the republic!" the institution he helped make and then watched in disdain as it lapsed into decadence. Likewise, the funeral was a Catholic affair, complete with mass and a wake. Though he never accepted or sought an political office, he was buried with ministerial honors. His coffin was wrapped in the Brazilian flag, the standard of Order and Progress, the positivist slogan the republic adopted. This backcountry peacemaker was lowered into the ground to the din of a twenty-one-gun salute.

It seems fitting, though, that Rondon's funeral was presided over by Juscelino Kubitschek. Getúlio Vargas was the noisiest booster of the west. But it took Kubitschek, invoking the spirit of this "reverse Moses," to pry open the Brazilian wilderness. After Kubitschek, the Amazon was rent, much the way Rondon had imagined, only with asphalt and not railways. But as Kubitschek conquered the backlands, Rondon watched this utopia fall apart.

"The transformation of the savage is slow by their very

nature," Rondon once wrote, hopefully. ". . . It requires a moral and social atmosphere capable of affecting the soul of the Indian with moderation, without profound shocks. . . ."

The shock, when it came, was profound and the means anything but moderate. The numbers alone tell part of the story. When he graduated from the military academy in 1889, there were an estimated million Indians in Brazil, two-thirds of them in Amazonia. When he died, in 1958, at the age of ninety-two, there were fewer than two hundred thousand. The survivors would just about have fitted, Coutinho reported, in Rio's Maracanã football stadium.[26]

At the height of his career Rondon's work had already crumbled around him. The telegraph line fell out of use almost as soon as it had been completed in 1915, when radiotelegraphy came to Brazil. Its maintenance trail became first a road and then BR-364, a superhighway, traveled by thousands of whites, who tore through Indian lands. The reservations he argued for are now repeatedly invaded by miners, loggers, small farmers, and ranchers. The Indian Protection Service he began is routinely denounced as ineffectual, discredited among professional anthropologists and indigenous communities and rattled by not infrequent exposés of cronyism and corruption.

In the end he was something like Kipling's Kim grown up and out of place, bent on the harmony of two tragically opposed nations. Or maybe he was more a kindly Gunga Din, pliantly leading the way as the empire's legions overran the darker races. The "less protected brothers," whom Rondon championed, were by Kubitschek's day already reduced to a few tens of thousands. It was not what Rondon wanted, but it was what he had made possible. History had taken care of the rest.

FRONTIER OUT OF SEASON

> But the wilderness had found him out early, and had taken on him a terrible vengeance for the fantastic invasion.
>
> —Joseph Conrad, *Heart of Darkness*

> This was not the hour or the day for white men. . . .
>
> —Graham Greene, *The Heart of the Matter*

The man from the power company was talking about kilowatts. A knot of journalists gathered around him dutifully scratched down the details. On a grassy bluff he gestured toward the Xingu River, swollen and roiled with silt from the pounding winter rains. There, on the mightiest affluent of the Amazon, the mightiest river in the Western Hemisphere, a great hydroelectric dam would be built. With a sweep of his arm he traced an imaginary concrete arc across a bend in the river. The muddy Xingu would do the work; in wet season, thirty-seven thousand cubic meters of water would plunge over the parapet of the dam to drive twenty turbines that in turn would send eleven thousand megawatts coursing through hundreds of miles of transmission lines to light up living rooms as far away as São Paulo and Rio de Janeiro. The man from the power company dressed as precisely as he spoke; a fine gold necklace danced against a deeply tanned neck, a cotton shirt striped broadly like a soccer goalkeeper's jersey hung loosely over pressed indigo jeans.

Off to the side, Chief Kupato was taking a break. While the power company man lectured, the chieftain had held separate court, compliantly drawing and redrawing a tall wooden bow, scowling convincingly for the television crews and motor-driven Nikons. His people, the Kayapó, are mostly beyond the age of long bows and favor instead hardwood cudgels for brawls or pump-action Winchesters for hunting. But bows and arrows make for better theater, and when the world is watching, theater is what the world gets. And the world was watching that day.

At ease a few minutes later, and free of the paparazzi, Chief Kupato began to speak. Like the power company man, he gestured at the broad Xingu. In a mixture of Portuguese and his native tongue, he told a quiet little tale of disaster. "See that tree with Brazil nuts," he said. "We eat those. See the river, we eat the fish. This used to be a living forest. Now there are dead things all over. We Indians used to live all over this land, as far as Rio and São Paulo. Now we are few." He gestured again, this time at the imaginary dam. "We don't hate the white man. We're not going to attack Rio and São Paulo. We just don't want them coming here and interfering with our land. It is like they hate us. It is like a sickness." The chief wore a loincloth, rubber sandals, and streaks of red urucú and black genipap war paint that converged in a point when he frowned.

Had Beckett gone to Brazil, he might have staged the encounter. Side by side, universes apart, the two men recited their separate scripts, the power company man going on about energy and asphalt and the totems of progress, the chieftain about survival and heritage and other poetic notions. Perfect foils, they held forth on the banks of the Xingu, protagonists in the battle of wills and words that was shaping the fate of the Amazon forest.

This was February 1989, the middle of the wet season, though this year the rains had only just begun to fall in this eastern corner of the Amazon. The landscape was tinged in fecund greens and sorrel. Cicadas thundered as the sun rose fat and white, burning off the gauze of morning mist. The town was Altamira, a sleepy river port of about forty thousand inhabitants. Altamira was for years just another stop on the way upriver. Then came the Transamazon highway, that muddy incision that sliced the jungle from east to west, and this river entrepôt, like so many other addresses in the Amazon, turned into a frontier town and grew too big too fast. Surrounded by fertile purple soils, Altamira was like early Texas, a ranchers' haven, a land of cowboy hats and gleaming silos and smoky barbecue joints. But that week in February the cast of characters and the scenery abruptly changed.

The potholed streets and lone star hotels were the stage for an unprecedented meeting of Indians, ecologists, bureaucrats, and politicians, rounded up from across three oceans and a handful of continents. For five days delegates from some dozen conservation groups and Indians from all over Brazil took over this tiny hamlet on the Xingu, where a remarkable event is a cattle fair or getting your cousin elected to city hall. The muddy streets filled with hordes of foreigners and echoed with a babel of German, Japanese, English, Italian, and French. Hard currency flowed like the Xingu that February.

The First Encounter of the Peoples of the Xingu River had a many-tiered agenda. It brought together, and then into collision, some basic notions about politics and development and human rights—and about the chaotic way that all these things have been arranged on the planet in recent times. More immediately it also signaled a new era, a time of soaring awareness and angry confrontation, and the tardy awakening on this part of the map to a theme that had already gripped the rest of the globe: ecology.

Suddenly, it seemed, all the world had gone green, from the World Bank board to Prime Minister Thatcher. The worry,

worldwide, had become repairing the ozone hole, reversing
the greenhouse effect, and curbing the smoke-belching factories that mar our skylines. It was also high season for Amazonia. The cause of saving the rain forest, and those who lived
within it, seemed to be sprouting everywhere then, silk-screened
onto Peter Max T-shirts ("Save the Rain Forest" "Kiss a Tree"),
bellowing from apocalyptic brochures that crowd our mailboxes, pondered in whither-the-ozone conferences, and aflame
in fierce debate in the world's halls of government. The discussion had reached around the globe and come back now to
the Amazon Basin itself.

The issue at hand was the government's proposal to dam the
Xingu. The Brazilian government came to peddle a pricey piece
of merchandise, the $5.8 billion Kararaó hydroelectric station,
meant to power this energy-hungry South American nation.
Only the twelve-gigawatt Itaipú Dam on the Rio Paraná in
southern Brazil, was larger. Summoned by the charismatic Chief
Paulinho Paiakan, a leader of the Kayapó nation, 480 square
miles of whose land was to be flooded by the dam, the Indians
weren't buying. It was a heady week.

It was not that the Kayapó, whose technological parapher-
nalia includes Sony minicameras and chrome-paneled ghetto
blasters, opposed electricity. Indeed, the Kayapó own five airplanes as well as tractors, pickups, and bulldozers, and their
chiefs live in houses of aluminum and brick. They command
a gold mine, where twelve hundred white prospectors pay them
royalties for the ore. They regularly drive to Tucumã or Belém
to move money in current accounts and money market funds.
Nor did there seem to be any doubt in Altamira that the project
would bring some benefits: commerce, jobs, and a bit of pavement for the cratered streets.

Though many giant public works projects in Brazil have
been tremendous wastes of money, there was also agreement
that dollar for kilowatt, Kararaó seemed a well-designed, economical plant. A high run-of-river dam, it would flood an area
about a third the size of Rhode Island—a relatively modest

area for Brazilian dam reservoirs—to produce a formidable eleven million kilowatts, making Kararaó the largest dam anywhere in the tropics. However, the companion dam, Babaquara, said to be necessary to regulate the flow and so to maximize the output from Kararaó, would pose a far graver threat, flooding 2,240 square miles. That reservoir would put all of Delaware underwater.

The real catch, it seemed, was something unforeseen, the sort of factor that had rarely figured into the Brazilian government planner's charts. Kararaó was but one in a network of Amazon dams, called Plan 2010, that at one time projected 136 dams during the next two decades. The plan included some 80 dams in the Amazon region, which would flood an estimated forty thousand square miles of forest, according to the noted biologist and Amazon specialist Philip Fearnside.

This plan had been drawn up in an earlier, less complicated time. Until just a few decades ago the policy bosses in Brasília saw the vast river-entwined Amazon Basin as a perfect venue—both economically and politically. Unlike the fertile south, Amazonia had notoriously weak soils, and flooding them was considered no loss to agriculture. In the south, dam projects had also come under fire from unions representing peasants whose family lands had been drowned in the reservoirs. Planners call such factors externalities, pebbles in the paths of the earth-moving machinery. By contrast, the Amazon was judged to be "empty"—except, of course, for Indians and humble river dwellers, who were hardly expected to make a fuss. But by the time of the Altamira gathering things were changing.

For the tribes of the Amazon Basin, like the Kayapó, such landmarks of progress have generally come with the whiff of cordite and the color of blood. Grand construction projects, like dams and mines, not only displaced Indians and farmers but almost always loosed an inevitable flood of the poor and landless when word of work and opportunity spread. Ecological—and human—disaster have followed. It happened along BR-364, the World Bank-financed highway through Rondônia, which sent tides of settlers spilling headlong onto park-lands and Indian reservations. It happened at Tucuruí, the Amazon's first megadam, where a lavishly expensive new town was jerry-built in the jungle, crowding out an entire forest tribe and turning the old city into a near Bantustan of workers' shan-ties, bars, and brothels. Though Tucuruí did not provoke the ecological disaster that alarmists had prophesied (in which sea-water would back up into the Tocantins River, devastating fish and plant life and corroding the turbines), it did create a human inferno. Scores of residents on the reservoir have been plagued for the last five years by swarms of mosquitoes that breed in the trees left to rot in the shallows of the reservoir. Well before he became a Kayapó chieftain, Paulinho Paiakan got a glimpse of the designs of the white world in Amazonia in the 1970s, when he worked as a translator for work crews on the Trans-amazon highway, which ripped straight through traditional Kayapó lands.

Though the Northern Hemisphere had long been in the eco-logical belfry, the clarion was a new sound for Brazil. Only a couple of decades ago, when big was still beautiful and foreign finance flush, grand public works projects crowded the draft-ing boards of government planners. For a century, at least, Brazil had trained an ambitious eye on its vast interior. After all, this continent-size nation had its own west to win. The technology and finance of the late twentieth century were going to bring about these nineteenth-century ambitions.

Roads, dams, bridges, and boomtowns followed. They were not mere symbols of development but progress incarnate, and for years on end progress had been a mantra for the third world (especially in Brazil, where it was a religion). But the lan-guage and times were changing. In country after country, revolt at the ruin wrought in the name of progress was welling. It boiled over with the burnings that engulfed the Amazon forest every dry season, when farmers, ranchers, and squatters slashed and burned their way ever deeper into the forest. Where there was smoke, there was also blood. In December 1988, just two months before the Altamira gathering, and shortly after he had won the United Nations Global 500 conservation prize, Francisco Alves ("Chico") Mendes Filho, a union organizer and Brazil's best-known ecologist, was slain by a gunman as he stepped out his back door in the western state of Acre. Late in 1990 an Acre rancher was convicted of ordering his son to pull the trigger, a small stroke of justice in a jungle of impunity.

Scientists also sounded the alarm. Poring over satellite images, Brazilian and American climatologists found that twenty million acres of virgin rain forest—an area slightly smaller than Maine—had gone up in smoke the previous year. Protests were staged in foreign capitals, on behalf of Indians and rubber tappers, the pawns of past policies now cruelly driven out of their homes. Survival International, the London human rights center, staged vigils every Thursday for the Yanomami, the Stone Age Indians threatened by an invasion of gold prospectors. Time and again the ecology lobby had blown the whistle on such wanton destruction and kept honest the banks that had financed ecologically dubious projects. But now the ante was up, and just about any scheme of development for the rain forest could provoke tidal waves of international indignation.

Some of the demonstrations were sincere; others, merely showy and exaggerated. At a tourist fair in Milan the Brazilian stand was swarmed by a militants from the Italian Green party. They threw sand all over the booth and through bullhorns denounced the startled travel agents as "murderers." The Friends of the Earth (FOE) took the drama overseas by building a fifteen-foot-high replica of the Xingu dam before the Brazilian Embassy in London. FOE also took out an ad campaign in major British newspapers charging that the Xingu dam threatened to displace "70,000 people and [would] probably kill the proud warriors and their families who have vowed to stay put." That number represented fully one-third of all the Indians in Brazil. (The official estimates identified 344 people whose lands would be flooded by Kararaó.) But there was always room for hyperbole in the jungle theater of ecology. Why all the fuss

over a distant jungle? Because "the Amazon is ours, too!" U.S.
Senator Robert Kasten, the Republicans' greenest legislator,
unabashedly declared to a congregation that included the Brazilian ambassador.

The backlash came just as swiftly. The waves of indignation
caught Brazil just as the generals were losing their grip. In
1985 power had passed from the military-backed Democratic
Social party to a civilian coalition, composed of opponents to
the military and disenchanted defectors. José Sarney assumed
power when the president-elect fell ill and died, and he had
his hands full with Brazil's unruly inflation rate, which soared
from 200 percent to 2,000 in his five years. As he fought one
losing battle, the ecological war flared. He waffled and fumed
and finally lashed out clumsily at ecological militants. The
military dismissed the demands from the Northern Hemisphere
to curb development schemes as just a greener version of
imperialism, and Sarney decried the attempts to turn Amazonia into "a green Persian gulf."

Playing underneath the indignation from Brasília were some
confusing but potent notions about sovereignty and development and the limits of national freedom in an environmentally
imperiled world. The protests struck a chord that resounded
deeply in Brazil's past. Historically the topic of Amazonia has
provoked paroxysms of xenophobia among Brazilian rulers,
especially sectors of the military, which saw an expansionist
foreigner behind every palm. Only in 1867 did the Brazilian
monarch open the Amazon River to international navigation.
Noted scientists, from Bates to Lévi-Strauss, practically had
to go on bended knees to secure permission to travel the Brazilian jungles. Part of the nationalist mythology of the Amazon, told as gospel even today, is that the decline of the rubber
boom was an imperialist conspiracy, by which a wily British
naturalist "smuggled" Amazon rubber seeds out to Asia. The
truth was far more prosaic. The naturalist Henry Wickham did
not steal away with the seeds at all but exported them in a
perfectly legal transaction. In fact, the decline of the rubber

boom owed much more to the failure of the Brazilian government to implement a serious plan to plant rubber trees.[1]

The angst over Amazonia, Sarney imagined nonetheless, masked nothing more than timeless "international greed" for the jungle's riches, real or imagined. As late as June 1991, in fact, the Brazilian Congress had launched an inquest into a supposed plot to "planetize" the Amazon, in the suggestive words of the justice minister Jarbas Passarinho. (The next month the government launched an investigation into American Protestant missionary groups, accusing them of meddling in sovereign affairs, and threatened to close down several missions in the north of Brazil.) But even common Brazilians who had no truck with the generals, paranoiacs, and the fumblers who called the shots in Brasília resented the pronouncements from the upper hemisphere, which had long ago dispensed with its forests and aborigines in the name of development. François Mitterrand did not help ecological diplomacy much by his statements in a press conference that on matters of ecology, nations would have to accept "limitations to their sovereignty." How, Sarney bellowed, could the industrial world, with its monstrous fleets of motorcars, acid rain smokestacks, and ozone-tearing gases, point a finger at Brazil for environmental misbehavior?

But the boundaries seemed to be definitively crossed at Altamira. The Amazon was burning then, much as it always had. But now its blaze had caught the attention of the world— first through the weather satellites, next through the eyes of ecological organizations in the North, then in the halls of the U.S. Congress and European parliaments, and finally down below the equator. Something was out of step, in Brazil and on the globe.

Suddenly some potent ideas were smacking one against the other. The first was that of the ever-expanding domain, the spatial frontier. This was as old as empire and lingered through the 1970s, fueled by the conquests of the green revolution. Only very recently has science helped change this concept.

The spatial frontier has been replaced by the less tangible one of biotechnology, genetics, and agronomy. The gene revolution retired the green one. It is information and invention, not geography, that mold and move societies today. Yet Brazilians, like Americans, have long eyed a vast territory, largely unoccupied by white society, and felt impelled to take possession of and tend to it. "Filling" such territory was, for decades, less a mission than a compulsion, like a social law of gravity. All brands of government—military, populist, and democratic—abided by that law. What is more, Brazilian people were picking up and moving on their own. Ever since the first Portuguese landed, Brazil had been a remarkably restless society, a "country on the move," as John Dos Passos once marveled.

But this idea bumped up rudely against another, driven by a sea change in world sensibilities. Brutality and ecological devastation are the ugly subtext to all these frontier stories, from Oregon to Rondônia, from the Australian outback to the South African highveld. Brazil is conquering the Amazon just as the age of the environment conquers hearts and minds. And environmentalism has recast the vocabulary. Frontiers now are viewed no longer as badges of vigor and opportunity but as synonyms of violence, aggression, and the squandering of resources. There may be nothing especially new about the violence of this episode of territorial conquest. Yet never before has a frontier nation had an international audience to scrutinize its every move and misstep. The Amazon is a frontier in an antifrontier age, a frontier out of season.

On both sides of the equator the argument was now being forcefully made that the destruction of a rich forestland was too high a wage to pay for "progress." The American Congress, pushed by environmental groups, sent delegations to the jungles, and elementary schools in wealthy Connecticut suburbs held school socials and raffles to buy up acres of rain forest, from Belize to Brazil. "Save a piece of Paradise," hawked a full-page ad in *Cosmopolitan*. "They can't burn it if you own it." Militant ecological movements even called for boycotts of tropical wood and other Amazon products extracted by predatory or, in the argot of environmentalism, "nonsustainable" means. Our sins do not justify yours, these first world groups were saying. Now ecological concerns must figure shoulder to shoulder with those of justice, poverty, and development, the banners of an earlier era.

The new government of Fernando Collor de Mello, ever attuned to the anxieties of the first world countries he so admired, abruptly changed its tone. His weekend jog in Brasília featured T-shirts emblazoned with slogans to save the whales and the forests. He made lavish preparations for the United Nations Conference on Environment and Development, scheduled for Rio de Janeiro in June 1992. He named the renowned ecologist José Lutzenberger to the post of environmental secretary. "The age of mutual recrimination is over," Lutzenberger said, over and over. We have to save the planet, he intoned. Real changes in policy would be slower in coming under Collor, and occasional spasms of retronationalism, such as Passarinho's, still seized the capital. But even if this ecological fervor was mere gesturing, Collor was keenly aware that the environmental lobby was on to things in Amazonia. The world had soured on conquest of late and, like Marlow, was "looking into it much."

Though the initial fracas was over the Xingu dam, the Altamira encounter broke new ground for Brazil. For in Brazil ecological organizations had had a late start and little public clout. All of sudden they were meeting one another face-to-face and feeling their oats. Likewise, most of the tribespeople from twenty-four Indian groups, from distant corners of Brazil, had never laid eyes on one another. Indians from North America crossed the equator to lend a hand, another first. Some of the Brazilian Indians had come from so far away, in fact, they were caught short of funds; one Xavante man had to take up a collection just to get back home.

In a hundred ways, in gesture and in deed, the message was repeated at Altamira. As the two sides squared off, there was plenty of room for debate and eloquent oratory, angry confrontation, and comic relief. When business got under way in Altamira, there was a familiar sort of order to things. The Indians, some six hundred of them, came in splendid feathered headdresses and body paint. The ecologists were the ones in blue jeans or cutoffs, baggy T-shirts, and knapsacks full of leaflets. The journalists toted cameras, tape recorders, and laptops. The bureaucrats came with briefcases and sheaves of documents. Almost everyone was peaceable, in fine spirits, and, for a time, reasonably well behaved.

Every day brawny Kayapó warriors, wielding their cudgels and wearing splendid headdresses, sat cross-legged on mats of buriti palm fronds before a speakers' dais and under television klieg lights. Like Tom Wolfe's Samoan mau-mauers, they hoisted their hardwood clubs simultaneously into the air to show their approval on any particularly debating point. A bare-breasted Kayapó woman rushed the dais to spook the appropriate white man—the power company official—slapping the flat of her machete blade against the engineer's cheeks. The woman warrior later appeared a bit chagrined by her behavior. She had had a bit too much to drink, it seemed, and did not mean to hurt the man from Eletronorte. The ritual attack was just so that the government man "would not forget" about the Kayapó—though, to judge from the power man's pallor, there seemed little danger of that.

Gradually the scenario changed. White people began to appear with their faces and limbs streaked in glorious red and black genipap. Layers of clothes began to peel off. Soon gringos in skimpy bathing gear were appointed with brilliant macaw plumes, feathered bracelets, and alligator bead charms. As the Kayapó relaxed, some of them left the floor of palm fronds for proper folding chairs and grandstands.

A small scandal emerged when British Labour Member of Parliament Tam Dalyell told the ecologists he was all for saving the rain forests—and then called for the expansion of nuclear power plants as the answer to the third world energy deficit.

"Did he really say that?" asked an incredulous Fernando Gabeira, president of Brazil's Green party. Simon Counsell, of the staunchly antinuclear Friends of the Earth, who had invited Dalyell to the conference in the first place, looked stunned.

Then there was the recently converted Amazonophile Sting, who dropped into Altamira like a raja, sweeping into the Indian encampment behind a cordon of Kayapó bodyguards and with his man Friday, Belgian cineast Jean Pierre Dutilleux, at his elbow. Dressed in designer camouflage and lace-up black suede boots, Sting cameoed a press conference, uttered the appropriate pieties ("If the forest dies, my country is in danger"), scribbled some autographs, and airplaned off again with his new friend medicine man Raoni, for a few days' retreat in a distant Kayapó village. (To be fair, Sting went on to log hundreds of hours in the Amazon and made an international tour to raise money for the demarcation of the Xingu Indian reservation. After widespread press reports that Dutilleux was basically along for the ride and interested mainly in promoting his own career, Sting parted company with the Belgian and removed him from the board of his environmental group, the Rainforest Foundation.)

Kayapó warriors were aghast as journalists clambered up trees, stood on one another's shoulders, and elbowed one another viciously for vantage during the Sting press conference. One inspired cameraman even took to howling. The club-wielding Kayapó looked positively pacific next to the horde of reporters and their arsenal of tripods, telephoto lenses, and giant-stemmed microphones.

Each day, as Chief Paiakan climbed the steps to the rooftop restaurant at the Palace Hotel, breezes of adulation rippled through the tribe of foreigners. The handsome young chieftain, then only thirty-five, held court like a don, answering inquiries, granting interviews, and nodding graciously at admirers. One afternoon Barbara Pyle, representing broadcaster-turned-conservationist Ted Turner, loosed a war whoop and began kissing Paiakan up and down the forearm. A California woman had her pate shaved, à la Kayapó, because, well, "I wanted to."

Curiously, for all its bellicosity, the Brazilian government was badly outgunned. Eletrobras, the central power company, had often come under heat for its ecological and economical blunders. The northern branch, Eletronorte, was accustomed to launching strident apologies; after all, its works not only involved billions of dollars, mostly in foreign credits, but also predictably drew fierce criticism. The power company thought of sending eight technicians to Altamira, but by the time they looked into it, all the flights were booked solid, as were the hotels. The ecologists, Indians, and reporters were way out in front. (Most reporters. When I arrived, I managed only to secure a room in the local short-time motel, the Kiss Me, with its round beds, chartreuse lighting, and a kissing couple silk-screened on the pillowcases. It was not the best ambience. For reporting.) Eletronorte managed to hustle up one senior executive and a few technicians, but they seemed sorely unprepared, let alone underdressed, for an audience done up so formidably in feathers and war paint.

Maybe it was only fitting for a gathering that had earned the sobriquet "Woodstock on the Amazon" long before it began. Though there were no screaming Stratocasters this time (nor were consciousness-raising drugs in evidence), the comparison was still apt. Just as all the decibels generated on Yazger's farm blared for peace and drugs and unfettered love, the merriment at Altamira heralded ecology, the utopia of a newer generation. The summit also served notice to the policy makers. Gone were the days when soldiers ran things: Brazil's new democracy—and its financiers—would have to start listening to ordinary mortals now. Even ecologists and Indians.

Altamira also signaled another theme that has marbled the narrative on Amazonia: disaster. The Amazon apocalypse is worked and reworked in the media, in protests, and in political arenas. We are warned again and again that this splendid ecosystem is going up in smoke, or down before chain saw-wielding armies, or under the vast reservoirs of hydroelectric dams like Kararaó. The message cries out from four-color glossy mailers that crowd our mailboxes and full-page ads that blanket the morning paper. There is some good sense in these warnings. The Amazon is not only a cathedral of nature but also a vital tool for human survival. It is the repository of a multitude of germ plasm, untold medicines, and unimagined foods. Squandering the forest is to annihilate a part, perhaps a crucial part, of our own survival kit.

Yet this eloquent saying of doom seems grounded in a much deeper disenchantment, one that speaks of an end to the romance with development and the wonders of progress. It was this romance, born of the nineteenth century's faith in science, industry, and technology that rekindled expansion into the world's farthest reaches. Now, in the late twentieth century, those notions have been stood on their head. Our machines and methods have brought us prosperity and wisdom, but also to an inkling of ruin. The specter is not, as some would have it, "the end of nature." Our handiwork has made countless species disappear, but nature, finally, is indifferent to the disasters we may induce. All our aggressions combined are like spitting into ocean. The planet and its maelstrom of elements will go on, with or without us. What we are suddenly faced with is our unique and deadly talent to provoke our own undoing. We can merely scratch the universe but very probably rub out the conditions we require to remain a part of it.

There was a glimpse of this, of course, during our own frontier conquest. Walt Whitman, Aldo Leopold, and John James Audubon railed against the fury of developers and nature-gobbling enterprise. Eighty years before Altamira, John Muir sponsored, almost single-handedly, his own Altamira protest at Hetch Hetchy, the dam that he warned would destroy the spectacular Yosemite National Park. Muir lost that battle and died, disconsolate, just a year later. Though it took time, his lonely crusade gathered soldiers. It was really only in this century, when our frontier was long spent, that American sensibilities began to change. A rural nostalgia tugged at Americans who chafed at the bounds of civilization and the tedium of a comfortable life. The real terrifying "jungle" was now, as Upton Sinclair told it, the city, not the wild outdoors.[2]

Today this awareness has turned to poison. We revile our own works and cast ourselves as the enemy. Amazonia takes on a special role in the disaster narrative. Its magnificent rain forests have often been compared with the Garden of Eden. They were hardly paradise, of course (as the frustrations and sufferings of countless explorers and settlers later confirmed), but served as the rough emotive equivalent. To the early explorers of the New World, after all, the earthly paradise lay "somewhere to the west." It was not so much a place on any map but a moral zone, an area of imagined innocence, even redemption. Lévi-Strauss, who meditated on the New World on a ship's voyage from the Old, wrote about the sea and the meaning of discovery in his classic *Tristes Tropiques:*

> This lugubrious frontier area, this lull before the storm in which the forces of evil alone seem to flourish, is the last barrier between what were once—quite recently—two planets so different from one another that our first explorers could not believe that they were inhabited by members of the same race. The one hardly touched by mankind lay open to men whose greed could no longer be satisfied in the other. A Second Fall was about to bring everything into question. . . . [T]he spectacle of a humanity both purer and happier than our own in reality (it was neither, of course, but a secret remorse made it so) made the European sceptical of existing notions of revelation, salvation, morality and the law.[3]

Today the "secret remorse" has gone public. The Amazon, in flames and trampled, has brought it out of the closet. The Second Fall is banner headlines. Now the klieg lights play mostly on Jeremiahs. They chant their eloquent monody of ruin and folly, and to their credit they have made a generation stand up and take notice. The meeting at the banks of the Xingu was also about them.

Heroes

Yet the story of the modern Amazon frontier is also about another kind of messenger. Nearly lost in the din of denunciations are the discreeter voices of those who have worked steadily, often thanklessly, on retrieving the Amazon from devastation and on puzzling out its mysteries. In no small way these people are the heroes of the Amazon. They are heroes in somewhat the same way that the Gudgerses, Rickettses, and Woodses were famous men to James Agee and Walker Evans. They believe that things are possible and, despite the fabulous odds, are trying to stretch human talents, and generally threadbare budgets, to meet the challenge of this new and perplexing frontier. They are pharmacologists, scouring the jungle for new drugs to cure maladies ranging from skin rashes to leukemia. They are agronomists, trying to improve and adapt crops to the tropical ecosystems.

They are also simpler people—union leaders and rubber tappers—trying to organize some of the most exploited laborers in the world and bring to the frontier the principles of law and justice and the right to prosperity. They are ranchers, struggling to make pastoralism work on this difficult terrain, plagued by erosion, pests, and plummeting fertility. They are peasants, looking to the land for a key to the prison of subsistence cropping that depletes the soils and condemns them to poverty. They are Indians, trying to come to terms with the invasion of settler society and somehow retain their traditional lands and ways.

These people, botanists and rubber tappers, Indians and engineers, know well the immensity of the puzzle that is the Amazon. This is, after all, the humid tropics, a mouthful for which countless fortune seekers and conquistadors "had the teeth but not the stomach," in the words of Alfred W. Crosby.[4] "It is the thousand years' war against the unknown," wrote Euclydes da Cunha in 1905, of the naturalists' investigations of Amazonia. "The triumph will come at the end of incalculable labors, in the remote future. . . ." Since Cunha's time, the Amazon frontier has been settled at a dizzying pace, and the people there need some answers. For them the remote future is now.

Brazil's Amazon pioneers launched headlong, often on their own volition, but just as often with government blessings, into the tropical wilderness. They were encouraged by promises, tempting and often unrealizable promises, of land, roads, markets, and a guiding hand. They were, after all, agents in myriad visions of utopia that have driven Brazilian soldiers and intellectuals and statesmen since the emperor was overthrown in 1889. They were nation makers. "We were told we were going to be the new farmers of Brazil," said Avelino Ganzer, a burly red-haired southerner, who was swept up in a government program to settle the eastern Amazon.

"In Rio Grande they put up posters showing lush vegetation and speaking of fertile soils. They even showed a photo of a plant, called the *jurubeba,* which they said was a cross between a cactus and a tomato." Ganzer laughed. Echoing Pero Vaz de Caminha, the Portuguese chronicler who sailed to Brazil with Cabral, the official propaganda declared that "everything planted thrives in the Amazon." So in 1972 Avelino, his mother, his father, and eleven of his thirteen brothers and sisters were flown to Belém, 3,000 miles from Iraí, a colony of German immigrants in Rio Grande do Sul, then bused to the middle of the jungle. They were deposited on a 250-acre lot in an *agrovilla,* a ratty government peasant colony along the dirt road that authorities called a highway.

Like thousands of other pioneers of the Transamazon, Ganzer felt at first proud to be recruited for this bold task of colonizing the Amazon. He even posed for a cover story in a glossy

Brazilian picture magazine on the taming of the Amazon. The Ganzers, like most of the Transamazon's pioneers, were soon abandoned by the pundits who had put them in the bush. Then came years of sweat and malaria and washed-out roads and stores of rice and beans rotting every dank, rainy winter.

Nevertheless, the bewildered, the poor, and the adventurers of the Amazon often endured. In many cases, though not the majority, they triumphed. Ironically Ganzer is in a way a man made by his bitter frontier experience. He left the Amazon to become the vice-president of the powerful Unified Workers Central (CUT) and a champion of the Amazon peasants the government forgot. He turned defeat into a vocation, then a mission. Another brother, Waldir, went on to become first a local union leader in the Amazonian state of Pará, then a state legislator, and in 1990 was elected to the federal Congress. In all, eight of the eleven Ganzers remained rooted in the Amazon.

The town of Altamira is also, curiously enough, a symbol of frontier endurance. True, Altamira enjoyed advantages that many Amazonian towns did not. It was blessed by fertile soils, bounteous mineral deposits, and—no matter how the opponents might protest—extraordinary hydrological resources. Once a wide place in the road, it is now a solid, prosperous settlement and a pole of growth and commerce for the entire eastern Amazon. Today ranchers depend on it for marketing their cattle, gold miners peddle their ore there, and Indians ply their wares and stock up with supplies for their distant villages.

Yet like the Ganzers, the people of Altamira were left mostly on their own. They survived first the hostile tropical environment, then the lack of credit and aid, and finally the treachery of a policy that changed with every windy pronouncement gusting north from the capital. The gathering at Altamira was also, in an oblique way perhaps, about these people and the town they built. Over and over Amazon pioneers have had to piece together their lives out of the junkyards of official utopias.

At Altamira the acrid debate over ecology and development also was taking on a new dimension. Why, many were asking now, do we need to see the two notions—development and the environment—as enemies? Ecologists and scientists have launched a search for "sustainable development." The finite inventory of resources has underscored the urgency of finding some way of development that does not undo itself, economic growth that can be maintained over decades or centuries. Though Amazonian communities may be a long way from such sustainability, there was already money to be made in the search.

Indeed, while Indians postured and white savages played, other participants sniffed about Altamira in pursuit of more concrete objectives. If the Black Panthers turned berets and bullet belts into high fashion, then the ecology movement may just go down as the font of Amazon chic. A pair of British restaurateurs scoured the riverbanks for anglers who might provide frozen Amazon river fish for export. Anita Roddick, millionaire owner of the Body Shop, a British-based beauty boutique, prowled for jungle perfumes, makeup, and vitamins. U.S. anthropologist Jason Clay collected several pounds of Xavante Indian trail mix at the behest of an American yogurt company. This was only the beginning of Clay's Amazon entrepreneurship. Thanks largely to his efforts, in two years two dozen companies in the United States and Europe would be marketing "rain forest products," from Brazil nuts to perfume.

The jury is still out on many of these activities. Potentially marketable goods must be culled, processed, packaged, and shipped. Daunting obstacles—from untrained laborers to competition from laboratory-made synthetic goods—still stand in the way of making a living from the rain forest. But part of the message at Altamira was this: Whatever the obstacles, it was time to tread lightly and learn to heed the hidden rules of this complex ecosystem. Time—to borrow René Dubos's words—to try wooing the Amazon instead of flattening it.

The Xingu encounter ended almost as it began, in a potent brew of high hopes and cross-purposes. The atmosphere clouded over only at the end, when camera crews, with the customary etiquette of their tribe, muscled into the center of the ritual Kayapó corn dance. The cameras created so much disruption that the Kayapó called the whole thing off after ten minutes, and the painted warriors retreated in frustration to their chartered bus. But like the morning mist over the Xingu, a sense of good spirit lingered over Altamira until well after the meeting was done.

In a way the whole thing was a standoff. The government said it would cancel the companion dam, Babaquara. However, the conveniently timed announcement seemed a publicity stunt more than a concession; it was finally austere finances, plus reduced energy demand brought on by the Brazilian recession, not a sudden twinge of green conscience in Brasília, that shelved that and other Amazon dam projects. On the other hand, the power company stood firm on Kararao. The one concrete gesture to the Indians was cosmetic. In the language of the Kayapó, *kararao* is a battle cry, uttered defiantly in the face of some enemy group that has been imprudent enough to stray beyond the bounds of civil conduct. By some peculiar but fitting irony, the bureaucrats in Brasília had chosen the same word to christen a huge hydroelectric dam, the mere idea of which had loosed a cry of war among these very forest Indians. The government caved in on that one. Belo Monte (beautiful mountain) they rechristened the dam project. The Indians were still not impressed. "They are going to build a dam," said Chief Kupato, eyes set deep beneath his handsome headdress. "I can tell you, Indians are not going to be dancing on it."

CHAPTER **5**

FORGING CONTROVERSY

n an August day in the Amazon, when the earth is brown and parched, you can smell the sprawling railroad town of Açailândia long before you arrive. Even as the train heaves toward the distant stop, the acrid aroma of charcoal is everywhere, invading nostrils, clinging to clothing, and even impregnating the clapboard of the shops and houses that gird the main road to town. The skyline is smudged in a permanent dusk of woodsmoke and dust, lit only by a ruby moon and the winking blue neon sign of the Santa Maria Hotel.

The scrap wood fires that glow night and day in the backlots of local sawmills are partly to blame. But mostly this ashen ambience is the work of hundreds of kilns, ten-foot-tall mounds of brick and clay that blister the gently rolling landscape like a strange pox. All about, armies of half-clad men and boys, dusted from head to foot in soot, stack the ovens with lengths of roughly sawn wood.

To the people of Açailândia, this booming frontier town on

the eastern edge of the Amazon region has always had the whiff of prosperity. These kilns turn wood from the surrounding forests into charcoal. The charcoal, in turn, fuels the area's pig iron smelters, which generate steel, revenues, and jobs.

But in recent years the charcoal ovens have also stoked a raging controversy over the destruction of the primary forests of the Brazilian Amazon. Here, according to the world environmental movement, the steelmakers were gobbling up the most magnificent of tropical woodlands to make the crudest of metals. Technology from the last century, they warned, was turning into problems for the next.

By 1990 their protests had grown shrill. Brazil's outspoken secretary of the environment, José Antônio Lutzenberger, fumed and threatened to quit if the pig iron industry advanced any farther into the Amazon region. The agency he commanded, the Institute for the Environment and Renewable Natural Resources, Ibama, handed out millions of dollars in fines against the steelworks for illegal charcoal production and unlicensed transport of timber. "These companies are technologically backward and bring very little in resources to our state," charged Violeta Loureiro, head of the Development Institute of Pará, a research and advocacy agency in the state that harbors two large smelters. Abroad the environmental lobby pressured European buyers to limit, or halt altogether, purchase of Brazilian pig iron.

The steel companies launched their own counterattack. Some charged environmentalists with trying to embargo development in the Amazon region. Crusades for preserving the rain forests, they said, were fine for the comfortable classes above the equator, whose own wilderness had long since been demolished, but a "straitjacket" for underdeveloped society. "The debate has grown hysterical," said Mauro de Almeida, a consultant to the steel industry and the former president of the forestry division of Itaminas, a major Brazilian steelmaker with a subsidiary in the Amazon. "And no one even wants to hear our side."

In the fireworks over pig iron, there has probably been a good deal more heat than light. Yet sorting out this brawl will be of vital importance. Açailândia lies in the heart of the region planners call Grande Carajás. This is ninety-eight thousand square miles, an area larger than Oregon and fully 10 percent of the Brazilian Amazon, girdling a railway that stretches from the Atlantic coast to a giant iron mine in eastern Amazonia. The forests fell first here to make way for highways, grazing lands, settlements, and mines. For years the government waved on the newcomers, lavishing many ranchers and industrialists with tax breaks and credits.

Largely because of this sponsored spoliation, the 1980s were dubbed the Amazon's "decade of destruction." But by the next decade the campaign to repair human damage and rein in the rush to the Amazon was also beginning. Scientists and planners were debating how to recover overgrazed pastures, replant leveled forests, and bring spent soils back to fecundity. These efforts were only beginning. But they promised to be crucial in working out the larger puzzle of Amazonia: how to develop this complex tropical ecosystem without devastating it.

Three decades ago the region's only inhabitants were Indians in scattered villages and river-dwelling peasants. Isolation ended rudely in 1960, when the government opened the Belém–Brasília highway, a north-south road linking the nation's new capital to Belém, near where the Amazon empties into the Atlantic. Another interstate highway, the Transamazônica, would follow in 1971, this one cutting west, from the palm forests of Maranhão to the dense, humid jungle of southern Pará. Regional routes were added during the seventies, seaming the map with dirt top and asphalt. Eventually Açailândia came to be known as "the biggest intersection in the Amazon."

But the crucial development came earlier, when iron ore turned up in the Carajás Mountains. On a clear July day in 1967 José Aguiar eased a bulky Bell helicopter down into a stubbly mountain clearing, praying that the low scrub would not foul his rear rotor and leave the craft crippled and the crew stranded in the middle of the jungle. A passenger, Breno A. dos Santos, was charged with the important duty of looking out for the rear propeller, but the young geologist was distracted. What riveted his attention was the lumpy, xanthous terrain below. Only the thud of touchdown jerked him out of his trance.

The chopper survived the abrupt landing, but the twenty-seven-year-old geologist would never be quite the same. The yellowish earth was only scantily clad in bush, grass, and low trees, a telltale sign of hematite, or iron ore. A quick survey showed that the baldish sierra was indeed shot through with iron ore. Santos and another Brazilian geologist were on contract by United States Steel to survey the hills and dense forests of Pará State for manganese, used for the manufacture of batteries. But the more they poked about, the more hematite they found. The manganese hunters had stumbled upon Carajás, now the planet's largest-known reserve of iron ore. Curiously the find that July day did not spur immediate action. Santos phoned the head of the exploration program in Rio de Janeiro, and the response was lukewarm. There was, said his boss, plenty of iron ore being mined elsewhere in the world, and plenty elsewhere in Brazil, for that matter. Santos and his team were ordered to get on with their search for manganese. Union Carbide, it seemed, was also closing in on the Carajás region, and the American steel giant wanted first claim to the manganese reserves.

But more and more hematite kept cropping up wherever the geologists turned. Finally, on September 9, a cable marked "urgent" spit out of the telex at U.S. Steel headquarters in Pittsburgh and found its mark. The coded telex told cryptically of an iron find potentially bigger than anything yet found. "Strongly recommend you or person of equivalent authority come Belém next few days," Gene Tolbert, an American geologist at U.S. Steel headquarters in Rio de Janeiro, was saying. "Estimate lid will depart in seven to ten days."

It took another month for the lid to blow off the Carajás secret, but in short order the scramble was on for the world's largest and richest deposits of iron ore. U.S. Steel, Union Carbide, and Alcan of Canada all fought for a piece of the iron lode. Militant independence movements in Africa and other former mineral-producing colonies had made the multinational mining conglomerates uneasy. Brazil, whose military had just snuffed a nationalist-minded civilian government in the 1964 coup, looked like a safe bet for investment. So they thought anyway. After two more years of haggling with U.S. Steel, the Brazilian generals, who had their own ideas about the Amazon's treasures, took over the Carajás find in 1967 and handed over the concession to the state-controlled mining conglomerate, Companhia Vale do Rio Doce (CVRD), which bought out U.S. Steel's interests for fifty-five million dollars.

It was quite a prize. Stretching over 4,240 square miles of the states of Pará and Tocantins, the province of Carajás contained an estimated eighteen billion metric tons of 66 percent pure iron ore, some of the highest-grade ore ever mined. In addition, the rolling hills of the sierra harbored millions more tons of aluminum, nickel, copper, and zinc and thousands more of gold, tin, tungsten, and chrome—as well as manganese.

CVRD officials still do not know the total bounty of Carajás, and survey work is likely to go on for several years yet. But expectations are enormous. As of late in the last decade, only about 30 percent of Carajás's potential reserves were known. "We are presently discovering only what are the easiest minerals to find," Santos said. "We are only just getting to the filet mignon, while in other parts of the world the best deposits are beginning to give out." I talked to Santos in 1984, when he was heading CVRD's prospecting company, Docegeo. Seven years later Carajás was still serving up plenty of filet. By 1990 some thirty-five million tons of iron ore were being shipped out of Carajás along the railway every year. A small part of the ore was destined to industry at home. As part of the financing deal, CVRD committed some 70 percent of the raw ore to long-term contracts with the industrialized nations, led by Japan. By the mid-1980s, thanks to Carajás, Brazil had bypassed Australia as the leading iron ore producer. In 1990 a significant new gold mine, sixty miles from the main iron ore operation, also went into operation. This was El Dorado for the machine age.

Installing Carajás was a feat of engineering acrobatics. In the early 1970s CVRD built an entire city in the jungle, which in 1990 housed eleven thousand people, and began to install the massive project. But the mining operation would not be possible without massive amounts of energy, an ingredient the Amazon has lacked for sluggish decades. The electric company, Eletronorte, built the $4.5 billion Tucuruí Dam, a 3,800-megawatt generating station to power Carajás and a portfolio of megaprojects. The dam harnessed the rushing waters from the Tocantins River, whose peak flow of 1,000 cubic meters (35,000 cubic feet) per second made it the mightiest river ever to be dammed. Enough concrete was poured to build a wall 54 miles long. The reservoir covered 972 square miles, better than twice the size of metropolitan Los Angeles.

More highways followed, and in 1985 CVRD opened the Carajás–Ponta de Madeira railway, hauling iron ore 534 miles from the jungle mine site to a deepwater Atlantic port. Sixty-one bridges had to be erected over the streams and rivers along the route. With the Carajás railway, the "problem of the west," as Rondon had envisioned it, was a long way toward a solution. The problem of the environment had only just begun. For now the land was torn with rails and roads and pocked with boomtowns. The kilns at Açailândia would soon be smoldering away with what Rondon might have called the "intelligent and systematic intervention of man."

There is a bitter irony to the current controversy over Carajás. While many third world governments took fat foreign loans to build bridges to nowhere or opulent shrines to national vanity, the $3.1 billion mine, funded by the World Bank, Japan, and the European Community, was hailed as a model project. The mine was completed under budget and before deadline.

Rarer still, it combined sound finance with sound ecology. A battalion of botanists, ecologists, and anthropologists was deployed to plant forests razed by excavation crews, protect watersheds from industrial waste, and insulate indigenous peoples from outright collision with this invading culture of machines and megawatts.

Beyond the company gates is another story, however. Once company officials boldly courted investors by touting the development opportunities along the railway. A company brochure sang the praises of the region: jobs, reliable transport, and the "establishment of townsites in a sparsely inhabited region." Now CVRD takes pains to distance itself from the mess without. Even before the railway the roadways had made this region a magnet for problems. But since the opening of the rail, the peasants, prospectors, and ranchers have seared their way through this backlands at a dizzying pace.

Many of the travelers and drifters end up in Açailândia, halfway between the sea and the mine. Census takers, in the roughest of estimates, put Açailândia's population at 70,000 in 1985. But frontier statistics are no sooner recorded than out of date. Visitors are proudly informed that in ten years the population there swelled from about 15,000 to 280,000. This would make Açailândia one of the fastest-growing cities on the planet. The other towns in the orbit of the Carajás project have expanded accordingly. Officially Marabá, the next stop west on the railroad, grew from 14,200 in 1960 to 178,614 in 1990. Paragominas, further up the Belém–Brasília highway, expanded almost tenfold, from a mere 5,400 people in 1960 to 56,000 in 1990. And in the same thirty years Altamira's population dilated from 9,400 to 156,000.[2]

As a social gesture, CVRD added a passenger train, charging only a token fare. In a terrain where most roads are dirt top and virtually impassable during much of the six months of rainy season, the all-weather railway became a vital transportation link. Soon the passenger train was operating six times a week—three trips west, three back east—with the tattered seats and aisles jammed for the entire eighteen-hour journey. In just five years the handful of maintenance stops had turned into eighteen stations, each with a town burgeoning behind it. They were raggedy, haphazard villages, built of hope and accident, and had exotic names like Presa de Porco (Pig's Prey) and Santa Inez and Dufilândia. The trip west to Açailândia was once a passage through an unsullied landscape, from the unbroken palm prairie of Maranhão to the dense rain forests of central Pará. In half a decade the train was running a gauntlet of scruffy small farms, withered pastures, and overgrown villages.

Some 280 miles west on the railroad the train shuddered to a halt at Dufilândia, the newest stop. A dozen passengers waited to board; a dozen others lined up to get off. The "station" was four posts stuck into the ground holding up a roof of banana leaves. The waiting passengers squatted on their heels under the paltry patch of shade. Here, and at the dozen stops along the way, the passengers clambered aboard, filling each of the rickety cars to brimming. The CVRD officials tried once to restrict the passenger load, at least to within safety limits. But that effort was soon scrapped altogether. One too many desperate peasants, having walked twenty miles to get to a station and slept all night under a plastic sheet, had pulled a gun on the terrified station men. Now the boarding whistle loosed a mad scramble for the cars.

Yet the passengers seemed surprisingly cheerful and somehow resigned to the impossible conditions of their journey. They were bathed and barbered, many of them in pressed Sunday clothes, and their faces were lit with the dull glow of quiet expectation. They spilled over from the seats into the aisles, grasping any grip they could find. Some dangled chickens by their feet; others held straw baskets full of papaya and banana. There were ladies in high heels and shiny bijouterie, humble but elegant figures tossed about in the undulating, grimy coaches. Some were on their way to visit relatives they had left behind in the interior; others were returning to an Amazon gold dig.

Every day hardship and hope jostled over these iron wheels toward a dozen destinations.

Rolling on roads and rails, the settler tide on the Grande Carajás corridor laid low more than 25 million acres of forests in under ten years. So extensive was the ruin that Brazilian President Fernando Collor de Mello in late 1990 announced initiatives to replant 2.5 million acres. Brasília would again offer incentives, but this time to businesses that agreed to replant the deforested areas.

A thornier problem was the arrival of steelworks in the Amazon. By mid-1991 five were in place and three more were being installed along the railway. They produced roughly five hundred thousand tons of pig iron, simple steel used for engine blocks, stoves, and refrigerators or as an ingredient for finer steels and alloys. Nearly 80 percent of the pig iron was exported to Europe, the United States, and Asia. Though they were late-comers to the Amazon, the steel mills suddenly became a lightning rod for Grande Carajás.

Despite the polemics, the government and steel executives still defended the program to industrialize the Carajás corridor. One of the aspects that distances Brazil from the club of less developed nations is its portfolio of manufactured products. This continent-size country, once known for coffee, sugar, and rubber, now includes battle tanks, airplanes, and software on its export list. Critics on both the left and the right agree that exporting primary materials is, in fact, the scarlet letter of underdevelopment. Yet so far the vast majority of Carajás's treasure was still being sold as raw ore, at a meager profit of two to three dollars per ton, to the rich countries overseas. "Is this country so badly in need of jobs and industry that we are going to give ourselves the luxury of continuing to export only raw iron ore?" asked Mauro de Almeida. Almeida, who designed a forestry plan for Cosipar, the largest steelmaker in the Cara-jás corridor and who later joined an energy consulting firm,

Del Rey Serviços de Engenharia, answered his own question: "As a Brazilian citizen, I don't think so."

However, in the wake of environmental protests and lawsuits, the grandiose Grande Carajás program, drawn up behind closed doors by a handful of technocrats and military men, was scaled back drastically. The early plans spoke of nearly thirty factories of pig iron, iron alloy, metallic silica, and cement, powered mostly by charcoal. But in September 1990 Brasília canceled incentives that had been earmarked for twenty-one industries, including five steelworks.

"Many of these companies were out of compliance," said João Urbano Cagnin, of Brazil's Office for Regional Development. Urbano said some companies even turned the official subsidies into a kind of commodity, "selling their incentives to third parties." Urbano, astutely, chose a high-profile seminar on Amazon rain forest ecology to announce this decision. His audience included respected biologists, botanists, tropical foresters, and environmental activists—hardly a crowd to be wowed merely by flush trade statistics and official propaganda on the importance of the Amazon's industrial potential. No more perks and credits would be offered to Carajás industries, Urbano now insisted, unless they planted their own forests for charcoal at least five years before installation. "We won't approve any industries that can't present serious reforestation plans."

This was new talk from Brasília, the futuristic "Capital of Hope," raised thirty years ago on a dusty central plateau. Built by President Juscelino Kubitschek, Brasília was the engine that he believed would move this country "50 years in five" and serve as a hub for expansion to the hinterlands. In recent tracts on the vanishing Amazon, most of the thunder is directed at the Brazilian military, which ruled from 1964 until 1985. The generals did have their own visions of superpowerdom, and taming the Amazon was part of the design.

In fact, the military tackled the Amazon frontier with a sense of urgency. The generals sank billions of dollars into dams, roads, communications, agriculture, and pioneer settlements. Bertha Becker, a geographer who has long studied Amazonian development, notes that in one five-year span the military built 7,200 miles of improved roads in the Amazon region and in just three years planted 3,066 miles of microwave telecommunications towers.[3] Much earlier Getúlio Vargas, the booster of the Brazilian west, had proudly created the Superintendency for the Economic Valorization of Amazonia (Spvea). But Spvea was largely bogged down in financing the antiquated system of collecting latex from the feudal rubber groves of the Amazon. The military gave the agency a face-lift, renaming it the Superintendency for Amazonian Development (Sudam), with a fat budget and an aggressive new agenda. In a decade Sudam created fifteen development "poles," declaring that 60 miles of land bordering federal highways belonged to the state and would be used to settle small farmers.

But for all its muscle the military's approach to the Amazon was hardly an innovation. Instead, the generals' Amazon policies were but a loud and exorbitant extension of a time-honored Brazilian political tradition. Since Vargas's days frontier development had been a matter of crony statesmanship, marked by grand, expensive construction projects and generous subsidies that kept contractors content with new cash flows and local politicians busy at ribbon cuttings. The military did add its own twist to things, projecting the Amazon frontier not only as the space for creating new opportunities but also as a solution for nagging social pressures. "Difficult social problems—such as the misery in which at least a third of Brazil lived—would be solved not by nationalizing or redistributing the wealth or income of anyone else," writes Thomas Skidmore, a longtime scholar of Brazilian politics, "but by finding new resources."[4]

But the real innovator was the civilian Kubitschek, who in the late fifties drew and quartered the nation with roads, rails, airstrips, and electricity lines. Between 1955 and 1961 Kubitschek added 10,800 miles of roads, mostly in the Brazilian interior, and 3,480 miles of asphalt, tripling the total of paved highways. The most ambitious of Kubitschek's oeuvre was the Belém–Brasília, the "Highway of the Jaguar," tearing 1,080 miles through the backlands. In 1961 Kubitschek matched it with the Brasília–Acre, a 2,300-mile road cutting northwest through the *cerrado* to the Amazon. (In the 1980s part of this route became Highway BR-364.) He even mounted a bulldozer and personally toppled a 150-foot tree, the last obstacle of nature that "blocked the way of man," he declared. Later, dressed in a dark suit despite the heat and standing next to his daughter, Kubitschek bared his frontier vision to an adoring crowd in the tiny Amazonian village of Vilhena. "We had to realize in this nation works that represented a bit of dream, a bit of poetry, because only poetry has the power to create great things," he said. Both the Brasília–Acre and the Belém–Brasília roads were later paved and became roaring expressways to Amazonia.

Back then ecology was still mostly a pastime in the Northern Hemisphere, and scoffed at down south. In the sixties, after all, Brazil had its own destiny to manifest, and Amazonia was to be the next great pioneer zone, a twentieth-century reprise of the conquest of California. "We cannot remain as crabs on the beaches of our coastline," boomed Kubitschek, recalling the lament of Father Vicente do Salvador. "Brasília," he intoned, "is a city whose only purpose is this: to force national integration. . . . These highways will constitute the powerful seeds that will bear tomorrow the admirable fruits for which this nation has waited for 400 years."

The world eventually tired of that bully pulpit talk. But through the 1970s and well into the eighties, in fact, this classical frontier vision, of conquest as creative energy and space as opportunity, was to reign in Brasília. Rondon blazed the way to the Amazon frontier, Kubitschek made it into an aggressive national policy, and the military turned it into a crusade. In thirty years the results were bustling in the streets of countless boomtowns and cooking away in the charcoal kilns and blast furnaces of Grande Carajás.

In a way the Carajás pig iron industry is not so much a symbol of a frontier as a relic of the bygone days of metallurgy. China gave up smelting steel from charcoal a thousand years ago. The tradition lingered in Europe as long as there was plenty of timber to fuel the blast furnaces. "Civilizations before the eighteenth century were civilizations of wood and charcoal, as those of the nineteenth were civilizations of coal," writes the historian Braudel.[5] By 1810 there were no more charcoal furnaces left in Britain. All had been replaced by coke and coal.

But in the United States it was a different story. This growing New World territory had plenty of timber to gobble up and toss into its roaring iron smelters. Michael Williams, in his encyclopedic study *Americans and Their Forests: A Historical Geography,* reports that in the United States iron was made almost exclusively from charcoal fuel until well into the nineteenth century. The first coal-fired plant arrived in America only in 1835. The last charcoal smelter was shut down only in 1945.[6] Largely because of the vast forest reserves and the furious cutting on the American frontier, Frederick Jackson Turner proudly reported that in 1907 the United States had overtaken Germany, Great Britain, and France in production of pig iron.[7]

Russia, Sweden, and Norway, all endowed with bountiful forests, still burn charcoal to make some pig iron. But Brazil has turned making steel from charcoal into a national industry. In 1990 almost 35 percent of Brazil's yearly output of twenty-five million tons of pig iron, and 18 percent of its total crude steel, were still smelted in charcoal furnaces. Everywhere else coal has long since replaced charcoal.

Despite their ill fame, the Amazon smelters are not so much predators as scavengers, living off the excesses of a society that is still relentlessly on the move. Forests, after all, were seen not only as one more resource in a land of abundance but principally as an obstacle to settlement, sowing, and the work-aday business of civilizing the wilderness. It was the detritus from this settler invasion—logging, ranching, and scorched-earth agriculture—that fed the Amazon's blast furnaces. And even then the steelworks could consume only a fraction of the surplus wood; the rest was burned in the backlots of Açailândia as scrap.

But charcoal-burning steelworks have never been exactly models of conservation. Braudel writes that the raging demand for charcoal posed the obvious dilemma of how smelters could better utilize this dwindling resource. "But it would appear that no attempt was made to economize on fuel in either glass- or ironwork," he notes of the eighteenth-century Europeans. "The response was to move the factory." It was not environmental consciousness but a new, abundant resource—coal—that eventually saved what forests remained.[8]

The Amazonian steelworks hardly have a stainless record, either. In 1989 Ibama (the Institute for the Environment and Renewable Natural Resources) fined one industry thirty-five times. Another, Simara, closed down its blast furnace in 1990, mostly because of management problems, but also because of the $670,000 it paid for environmental violations. In 1991 Ibama fined Cosipar five times. "We have even found Brazil nut trees in the kilns," said Norberto Neves, a regional Ibama inspector, referring to the stately nut-bearing tree that is "protected" by the forestry code. In fact, as early as 1965 the forestry development agency required steel industries to plant their own forests or pay a reforestation tax.

This was one of the more scandalous episodes in the larger scandal that was Brasília's program of fiscal incentives for frontier development. Sawmills, lumber companies, and steel-makers were taxed for their wood consumption, and the tax in turn went into a pool of funds for reforestation. Each industry could either plant its own forests to replace the ones it cut or buy shares in reforestation projects, undertaken by independent companies. These shares were called CPRs (Certificates of Participation in Reforestation). The CPRs soon became hot commodities, bought and sold like stocks. Reforestation never really took root, however. The flush replantation fund was like flypaper in a candy store; dozens of companies suddenly were swarming for a piece of the action. Few of them had had any hands-on experience in reforestation, and many probably never had any intention to do so. But in the bureaucratic wilderness violations were either unseen or winked at by officials on the take. Fortunes were paid for forests that never sprouted.[9]

In the state of Minas Gerais for example, the volume of CPRs sold represented an area of 6.25 million acres—large enough to sustain eucalyptus and tropical pine plantations for the entire charcoal needs of that state's steel industry, according to industry officials. However, the forestry was so poor that these plantations supplied only 30 percent of the Minas Gerais steel industry's charcoal needs.

By the end of 1989, however, Ibama had started cracking down on the outlaws. Clandestine lumbermen and sawmills and fraudulent reforesters all were under fire. Helicopters, airplanes, and ground teams now scoured the Amazon for predators and clapped industry with stiff fines for illegal cutting and transport of timber. As of June 1991, 201 reforestation companies faced charges of misuse of public funds. Ibama estimated that perhaps as much as half the $1.5 billion earmarked for replanting projects between 1966 and 1988 was squandered through mismanagement or simply stolen. The crackdown also meant a major shakeout was pending for the pig iron sector. Under Ibama's new rules, by 1995, manufacturers would have to supply all their own charcoal, either by replanting large areas of the Amazon or by learning to log an area without degrading the native forests.

Those who operated shy of the law were still angling for loopholes. In these days of environmental impact statements and forest management inventories, the imprimatur of government inspectors was key. Overnight, environmental consultancy was booming in Brazil, and while many of the consultants were professionals, many others cranked out pretty environmental blueprints meant, in the colorful Brazilian expression left over from the days when British engineers held sway here, *para inglês ver,* to fool the English. Luís Carlos Cardoso Vale, a forestry consultant for the Vale do Pindaré steelworks, turned down two handsomely paying offers from "backyard" steel companies that wanted him to produce "instant" environmental impact statements.

Jean Dubois, a Belgian forester who has worked for four decades in the tropics, said many industries were still "dreaming of impunity"—gambling, that is, on getting away with illegal forest cutting. "After all, they've lived that way for a long time."

Yet even before Ibama's blitzes, most of the industries had already become acutely aware of the high stakes. It was not fines but the exigencies of the market that hemmed them in now. In southern Brazil steel mills were increasingly squeezed between falling pig iron prices and soaring charcoal costs. Pig iron prices have gone up and down over the years, but more recently they sank to a low point of about $108 per ton. Only a relatively cheap energy source can make pig iron smelting profitable. Most of the Amazon smelters are subsidiaries of larger firms from Minas Gerais, in central Brazil, where their charcoal costs have soared as the result of the tremendous distances they must go to secure it. Many smelters there now have to travel up to a thousand miles to secure their wood from the scrublands of Mato Grosso, where deforestation is still intense. "We are at the end of a cycle of expansion of ranching and extensive agriculture. Those industries who do not plan for this are going to be in trouble," said Almeida.

Some companies accepted the challenge. In Açailândia, in mid-1990, the Vale do Pindaré steel mill was harvesting wood from fifty-five thousand acres of a previously logged forest. A small cleared area of fifteen hundred acres had been reserved for planting "exotic" species, such as eucalyptus. But most of their efforts were devoted to forest management, or the selective logging of successive strips of forest. Cutting crews felled medium-size trees, leaving a variety of healthy ones for natural regeneration. The cut wood was then hauled out by mules instead of soil-crushing tractors or bulldozers.

In Marabá, the next stop west after Açailândia on the Carajás railway, Cosipar, the subsidiary of Itaminas, also drew up a detailed forest management plan. But the company looked as well to another novel source of charcoal. Until recently the 210 million cubic feet of timber drowned in the reservoir of the Tucuruí Dam, a lake nearly the size of Luxembourg, were chalked up as a loss. But a fifty-eight-year-old mechanic, Juarez Crispino de Jesus Gomes, built an "underwater chain saw" and invented the art of submarine logging. Now "lumbermen" in scuba gear "fell" the larger trees. The heavy ones are hauled up to the surface by ropes, while the floating timber is allowed to shoot to the surface, like a Polaris missile. This form of logging has proved far cheaper than cutting timber in standing, dry forests in the Amazon.

Sawmills will exploit the valuable hardwoods. Cosipar is counting on Tucuruí's waste wood to supply half its charcoal needs over the next decade. Ibama officials were chary of the plans to exploit Tucuruí's reserves; the agency's natural resources division doubted there was enough wood in the bottom of Tucuruí's lake and enough goodwill on the part of the industry. But Crispino's aquatic chain saw created an alternative that at least gave the smelters—and the forests—a fighting chance.

Far from the smoke and dust of Açailândia, behind the tinted glass of a fifteenth-floor office tower suite, overlooking Rio de Janeiro's sun-gilt Guanabara Bay, Ulysses de Freitas, secretary of development for the Companhia Vale do Rio Doce, gently coaxed the conversation away from pig iron. "Let's philosophize," said Freitas. What we need, he said, is an agenda for an ecologically bruised, but still resource-starved, planet.

"What is the entire world worried about?" He waited half a beat, then answered his own question. "The greenhouse effect, right?"

In the future, Freitas predicted, Carajás would be known not as a corridor of destruction but as a garden that pumped life's breath back into a carbon-sopped atmosphere. There millions of eucalyptus and tropical pine trees would reclothe the denuded Amazon. These fast-growing species, which soar to maturity in just seven years, would not only produce oxygen but also be the fuel for an enormous industry of paper and pulp. Brazil, he reminded me, had already pioneered the use of short-fibered eucalyptus for producing fine paper products on plantations in the south.

Many ecologists bristle at the idea of planting eucalyptus, a latecomer from temperate Australia, in a region where the magnificent Brazil nut, rosewood, and mahogany once reigned. The objections are not merely aesthetic but turn on fears that a monocrop of eucalyptus would disturb the intricate Amazonian ecoystem. Studies by the cellulose manufacturers in southern Brazil, where eucalyptus has been planted for years, show that in properly managed plantations the feared problems—high soil acidity, desiccation, the impoverishment of soils—have not proved significant. There is less certainty about the long-term effects on the weaker Amazonian soils. Yet bringing back the native forest species of the Amazon would take years, perhaps centuries, virtually ruling out any viable commercial activity. "The Amazon is never going to be reforested if there is no project which offers economic returns," Freitas warned.

Of course, planting twenty-five million acres, on 10 percent of the Brazilian Amazon, only with eucalyptus presents its own problems—chiefly a glut of wood that no pulp mill or steel plant could possibly consume. So not all of the deforested Amazon could be replanted with a view to profits. Hence Freitas's idea of a greenhouse tax. A suffocating world, he said, will have to face facts and dig into its pockets to bankroll such reforestation projects in a vital exchange for the air we all breathe.

Still, turning green tropical biomass into industrial gray steel had put Carajás's smelters to a severe reality test. The American billionaire Daniel K. Ludwig nearly went broke trying to plant trees in the Amazon for pulp and paper. But his Jari project survived him, and twenty-three years later, despite setbacks and nagging debts, the 250,000-acre plantation of eucalyptus, gmelina, and tropical pine was producing respectable yields (of up to 20 cubic meters, or 700 cubic feet, per hectare, according to one Jari forestry official). A search for alternative fuels and methods that spare the forests was also under way. The coconut hull from the babassu palm, the feather duster-like tree that is bountiful along the eastern railway, makes a high-quality charcoal. The coconuts could be piled onto the empty cars of the iron ore train on its return trip from the sea. The problem would be to collect the scattered nuts efficiently and without generating conflict; much of the babassu prairie falls within the bounds of private ranches, whose owners are ever on the alert for trespassers and squatters. Carajás steelmakers are also studying use of modern blast furnaces that consume 30 to 40 percent less charcoal, so reducing the demand for raw wood.

Some conservationists have called for coal to substitute for charcoal. Increasing use of coal would, of course, reduce the demand for wood. But the rest of the world has curbed its coal appetite in recent years. In the last decade most industrial nations have cut back on crude steel production, largely as the result of decreased domestic consumption and plant modernization but also because of environmental concerns. Charcoal burning does produce its own cocktail of pollutants, chiefly methane and tar, but they are more easily, and far more cheaply, controlled than the emissions from the monstrous sulfur-belching coal plants. Firing smelters with coal would spare the Amazon forests in the short run, but there is no telling what havoc acid rain and clouds of particulate matter would eventually wreak on the tropical rain forest. (It would also be simply one more demand on a nonrenewable resource and transfer the devastation to the strip-mined landscapes of the coal countries.)

Yet one São Paulo steel company, Prometal, has made plans to install a coke-fired plant for specialty steels along the Carajás railway. The company's president, Eduardo Seabra, argued that coal would be not only possible but preferable. Initially the company would have to invest heavily in pollution controls to clean up the coal-burning smelters. But Seabra calculated that these increased costs would be more than offset by savings from recovery and recycling of sulfur and other coal by-products and from the greater economy of scale afforded by the larger coal smelters. Seabra firmly believed that this would mean a double gain—a cleaner plant that would also spare the standing forests.

But by far the sorest of controversies has been over the plans to harvest wood for charcoal from native forests. There has been little experience in prolonged forest management, as this is called, in the tropics and no guarantees that it can be done without depleting the polysplendored Amazonian ecosystem. Some observers were not waiting for the final verdict. "There is no way these forest management schemes are sustainable," stated ecologist Anthony Anderson, who prepared a lengthy report on Grande Carajás for the World Bank. Anderson suspected the pig iron makers were cynically betting on ample supplies of cheap charcoal from bootleg forest cutters and on inspectors looking the other way.

The steelmakers readily admitted the risks. "We don't know how much wood we can produce or how much it will cost. We don't know how long the regeneration cycle will be," said Luís Carlos Cardoso Vale. "We will be learning as we go along." Ecologists might well shudder at the prospect of using the Amazon forest as a laboratory. Yet many in the steel industry believe this is precisely Brazil's unique opportunity. "In a country with vast open areas, plenty of sun, and a hospitable climate, we ought to discuss the possibility of using a renewable natural resource," said Rudolf Bühler, director of the Brazilian Steel Institute. Bühler's optimism may be appropriate for eucalyptus plantations on already deforested land, but the jury is still out on management of native forests, and so far it is mostly wood from native forests that has fueled the pig iron industry.

But in 1990, when Ibama was on the prowl and environmentalism on the rise, discussion bogged down. Ibama had yet to come up with a clear master policy on forest management. The state environmental agencies, which must sign off on such plans, had vastly differing opinions, but not the technical staff to make solid evaluations. As a result, the state of Maranhão approved the forestry plans for the Vale do Pindaré steelworks, in Açailândia, while down the railway in Marabá, just across state borders, Cosipar's forestry plan had not been approved. A year and a half after the plan was filed, it was still sitting on the shelf in Belém, at the Pará state environmental agency. "Environmentalists are talking to environmentalists, and industry is talking to industry," said Almeida. "Everybody is listening to his own echo."

The storm over Carajás will likely get worse before it abates. The pig iron controversy has forged deeper awareness, but also painful problems. The steelmakers are a step, though maybe a primitive step, toward planting industry and jobs in a region where people have long been chained to the grueling rhythms of agriculture. Yet barreling ahead unchecked, with smokestacks and assembly lines, into the tropical woodlands could leave marks that may prove to be indelible. Wood, harvested either from native forests or from man-made plantations, could represent not only a vital resource but also a replaceable one for the fledgling industries of the frontier. How to use this resource without impairing the environment that nurtures it? Like the smoke veil over Açailândia, that question looms now all along the Grande Carajás corridor.

FROM FORESTS TO TIMBER

What will the axemen do when they have cut their way from sea to sea?

—James Fenimore Cooper

A skidder is a bulky machine, jointed in the middle like the body of an insect. Unlike a bulldozer, it may writhe and twist its way through a dense stand of trees. Great rubber wheels, taller than a grown man, roll individually over rocks and stumps. Each of these tires costs about two thousand dollars and is filled not with air but with water to keep them cool as they bully through the bruising jungle terrain. In back of the snout, just over the thorax, the driver sits behind a steering wheel and gearbox, in a compact wire mesh cockpit, immune from lashing branches and flying debris. Its tail is armed with a giant winch and one hundred yards of industrial-strength cable to strap and haul the fallen timber.

My first skidder ride was on an old Caterpillar, Model 526. It belonged to Ovídio Gasparetto, a lumberman with a large logging reserve in the high forests of the central Amazon, a leading wood export business, and a special sense of humor. At the end of a winding dirt road, deep in the forest behind the

Tapajós River, his crewmen in overalls and hard hats were revving the Caterpillar, preparing to fetch a load of fallen timber. Gasparetto stayed put in a wide forest clearing but told his crewmen to give me a ride on the back. Just to see what it was like, he said.

This one was yellow and aging, its armor blemished from sixteen years of punishing labor. Its motor rumbled, a sotto voce baritone, as diesel exhaust issued black and pungent from a corroded tailpipe. When the driver opened up the throttle, we leaped into the woods, the motor bellowing now, in search of our prey: a hundred-foot ipê, with a reddish blond core, felled moments before by two men with chain saws. I crouched over the abdomen, head low, feet straddling the middle joint, fingers locked on to the wire mesh of the driver's cage, holding on for my life. For though we went no more than ten miles per hour, the skidder bucked and shuddered, careening at seemingly impossible angles as the wheels bounded over stumps, craters, and fallen boughs. The workmen lashed the cable around the ipê, and the driver worked the winch deftly, spinning and rolling the great tree into position. After an agile about-face, the driver steered back to the logging clearing, the lashed ipê tree ripping a path as wide as a dump truck through the forest.

Gasparetto's logging project lay in a pristine stretch of dense rain forest, sixty miles upriver from Santarém, where the Tapajós was still half a mile wide and boiling thick and brown with the silt disgorged by a hundred streams. To get there, we had flown in a single-engine Cessna, a twenty-minute flight over nothing but the churning river and an ocean of jungle spreading out from each bank.

We piled into the cabin of a ten-ton truck and drove onto a logging road that penetrated straight back from the riverbank, toward the center of the forest. The treetops met ten stories overhead, nearly closing in over the dirt track. Dappled light played through the boughs and leaves, dancing delicately on the ground. Butterflies with blue wings flashed like new chrome, now dark, now blinding, in and out of the woods. Lianas as thick as a man's leg dangled, seemingly out of midair. The road wove around giant trees with musical names that the woodsman sang out as we passed them: massaranduba, samaúma, tatajuba, and jatobá. There were ipê and cedro and muiracatiara. Some, which I couldn't record in time, had roots that flanged like the most outrageous of bell-bottoms. Some had bark as smooth as oilskin, while that of others was knobbly and rough as gravel.

Gasparetto was the owner of this majestic tract of woods and also a self-proclaimed lover of nature. He studied the passing ranks of trees and also recited a bit of silviculture. João, the woodsman, gently intervened to correct him now and again. Gasparetto made a fuss now of chasing a bee off the windshield, coaxing it onto his forefinger, and safely delivering it out the window to freedom. "My grandfather taught me to save all the bees I found," he said. "I grew up in the woods," Gasparetto announced. Wind whipped his silvered hair.

Such earnest environmental consciousness seemed a touch rehearsed, especially for an Amazon logger. Perhaps it was a penance of sorts for the spotty record accumulated over the centuries by the practitioners of his indelicate vocation. Or maybe it was an homage to his ancient namesake, the Roman poet who wrote that, before the coming of civilization, "not yet had the pine tree been felled on its mountainside."[1]

John Perlin, in his book *A Forest Journey,* notes that it took the Age of Iron and of Empire to lay low the Roman pines. From then on, of course, forests fell like dominoes, straight around the world, from Athens to the Adirondacks. The trees are falling in the Southern Hemisphere now, and Gasparetto, a distant descendant, by way of his grandfather, of Ovid's land, is in the business of felling. At sixty-two, he was in formidable shape, with a barrel chest and square, sturdy shoulders; he would have looked right wrapped in flannel and hefting a poleax. Yet along with logging implements, he had learned how to wield the sharply honed vocabulary of environmentalism. His trade, after all, has become the target of shrill protest worldwide, condemning studies, and even consumer boycotts, driven by a movement that accuses loggers of being on the front line in the destruction of the world's dwindling tropical woods.

Gasparetto seemed not only keenly aware of this movement and its seething passions but also anxious to show how, despite his trade's illfame, logging and conservation are not doomed to be enemies. "The wood industry depends solely . . . on the forest as its source of raw materials. Once it is eliminated, this industry will follow suit," he told a gathering of the International Hardwood Products Association, in a speech in Orlando, Florida, in 1990. He spoke of a "new mentality" among loggers, one that guaranteed "there will be no danger of depletion of our Amazon Forests."

There was a great deal at stake, of course, in his apology. His company, Amazonex, is a major tropical hardwood dealer, and his sawmill in Belém receives one million dollars a year from Europe and the United States for finely crafted products, from cheese boards to kitchen paneling. He also is a leading voice in the Amazon timber exporters' association. His class, the lumbermen, millers, and wood craftsmen, have a multi-million-dollar business. They sell to a world hungry for handsome tropical hardwoods but suddenly thrown into remorse over such extravagant tastes.

So far, however, it is not the doubts that have prevailed. World trade in tropical roundwood, or unsawed logs, represents a fabulous eight-billion-dollar business.[2] Japan is the leading consumer; Indonesia and Malaysia are the leading producers. And until recent times the only issues that moved the two sides, both customers and producers, were the tandem questions of a fair price and a reliable timber supply. The environmental agenda has been placed square in the middle of the hardwood negotiating table, however. Now, wherever the forty-two-member countries of the Tokyo-based International Tropical Timber Organization (ITTO) meet, they are shadowed by a like number of NGOs (nongovernmental organizations), which fret over the disappearance of these spectacular forests.

For all its wealth of wood, Brazil is not yet a big player on the ITTO roster. Less than 5 percent of the world's tropical hardwood comes from Brazil, and the number is increasing only slowly. By contrast, Indonesia, which is only one and a half times the size of the Amazon logging state of Pará, produces nearly half the world's supply of tropical timber. However, the potential from the 875 million acres of the forested Amazon—the largest tract of tropical forest left in the world— is tremendous. Amazon hardwood is already a big business within Brazil, whose own voracious demand for building materials and other wood products consumes the lion's share of tropical timber.

The south of Brazil with its deciduous forests was traditionally the major source of woods, hard and soft. More and more, the business has migrated north. In the 1850s the naturalist Alfred Russel Wallace marveled at how the traders of the Amazon, though surrounded by "virgin forests" and "inexhaustible quantities" of fine tropical hardwoods, imported pine packing crates from Europe. "For centuries the woodsman's axe has been the pioneer of civilisation in the gloomy forests of Canada, while the treasures of this great and fertile country are still unknown," he wrote.[3] One hundred and forty years after Wallace, the situation is radically changed.

Many of those old-growth forests are depleted now, and the logging industry has moved north, into the timber-rich Amazon Basin. In Amazonia only a relatively small area is being forested, but the increase in lumbering has been dramatic. In 1976 Brazil's bureau of census and statistics reported that 14 percent of Brazil's sawn wood came from Amazonia. That number leaped to 44 percent just ten years later.[4] Christopher Uhl, a biologist who has long studied logging and the timber trade in Brazil, has estimated that if all its timber were harvested, the Amazon would yield six hundred billion dollars in marketable roundwood and two trillion dollars if it were all cut and sawed.[5]

In fact, green gesturing aside, Gasparetto's logging project was an attempt to do something rare in Brazil and nearly unheard of in Amazonia: to put back some of the bountiful timber loggers have removed. On his hundred-thousand-acre property in central Amazonia, he had undertaken a bold, expensive, but uncertain experiment in reforestation. Not even Gasparetto ventured a guess about how it was going to turn out. And no wonder.

For close to two decades reforestation has been carried out in the south of Brazil for pulp and paper. But there it is a precision affair, more like agriculture than logging, where eucalyptus after eucalyptus stands in immaculate rows, stretching from horizon to horizon. Jari, the megaplantation started (and then abandoned) by the quixotic billionaire Daniel Keith Ludwig, is a 250,000-acre reforestation project in northeastern Amazonia. But again, Jari's forests are of "exotic" species, such as eucalyptus, gmelina, and Caribbean pine.

The real challenge for loggers is how to log profitably an area of the primary Amazon forest, with as many as four hundred species spread over a single hectare, without degrading the native forest—how, in other words, to cut trees and at the same time preserve the biodiversity of the forest. It is this biodiversity, after all, that is the genetic savings bank of human life. Once a species is eliminated, no laboratory can conjure it back again. And as tropical forests contain so much of the gene stuff that is vital for our own lives—curare for anesthesia, the rose periwinkle for leukemia or Hodgkin's disease, quinine for malaria, and a dozen analgesics, not to mention the possible keys to pest and disease controls for agriculture—depleting the species pool is lighting the long fuse of a time bomb for humanity.

Logging has long been one of those venerated and paradoxical occupations that have built great societies in every continent even as they tear down the natural bounty that sustains them. "The rifle and the ax," Frederick Jackson Turner once proclaimed, "are the symbols of the backwoods pioneers." The ax, especially, has had a key role on all the world's frontiers.

The able use of timber has gone hand in hand with the development and conquest. From Mesopotamia to Minnesota, timber and its myriad by-products were vital tools, often more vital than any other. "The forest," writes Braudel, "enabled man not only to warm and house himself but to build his furniture, tools, carriages and boats." For centuries, having wood also meant having power. Venice even demanded that the Holy League put Turkish seamen to death in the sixteenth century "because the Turks, having ample forests, could only be stopped by stanching another resource, human beings."[6]

Though Rome is remembered for its statesmen and their politics, its power lay in no small way in the pine forests that inspired Ovid's verses, and wood was probably Rome's most valuable product of exchange for the products of more developed nations.[7] Wooden ships propelled Europeans all over the globe. Before coal, wood fueled the ovens that made Europe's steel, baked its bread, and warmed its hearths. So much wood was cut for fuel, in fact, that in Medina del Campo, Spain, it grew scarce, and "heating the kettle was just as expensive as filling it." Likewise, the decline of forests has presaged the decline of civilizations based on wood. Europe's eventual triumph over Islam was decided in no small part by its bountiful forests. "Against it, Islam was in the long run undermined by the poverty of its wood resources and their gradual exhaustion."[8]

There is much fury unleashed today against the nations, such as Brazil, that waste these pristine tropical woodlands. Indeed, the 1980s were a devastating time for the Amazon. Between 1978 and 1990 some 105,320 square miles of forests, or more than twice the area of Greece, were cut in the Brazilian Amazon, according to satellite data collected by Brazil's Institute for Space Research. But we had our own decade of destruction in the United States—the 1850s, when eastern forests were sacrificed by a nation on its way to becoming a great industrial power. In these ten years, and well before the days of chain saws and bulldozers, the ferocious frontier expansion leveled nearly 39,705,000 acres (62,039 square miles) of virgin forest, according to Michael Williams. That represented fully one-third of all forest clearing that had been carried out in the two previous centuries.

In Great Britain it happened much earlier and over a longer period. The Irish geographer Gerard Boate reported that between 1603 and 1641, thanks to the barrel makers, charcoal burners, and farmers, Ireland became "so bare of woods that in many parts the inhabitants do not only want wood for firing, but even for building." So much forest was felled that Ireland's map had to be redrawn at mid-century to register the newly denuded areas.[9]

In Brazil today there is precious little of the dyewood left that gave this country its name. Rosewood and jacarandá, two other prized timbers of the colonial days, went the same way as brazilwood. The Atlantic forest that stretched nearly unbroken from Maranhão in the extreme northeast to São Paulo in the south has been cut and largely cleared, and no more than an estimated 8 percent of the original forest remains. Dye making has been left to chemical companies, while the forests, what remains of them, are relegated to the agenda of the environmental movement. The axmen, all the while, have hacked their way deeper and deeper into the Brazilian interior.

Though logging has been going on in the Amazon since the days of the Portuguese captaincies, until very recent times it was a low-tech affair that turned mostly on brawn and perseverance. Native Amazonians, or caboclos, as the mixed-blood peasants and riberine folk are called, were the lumbermen, and their tools were not much more sophisticated than steel axes, handsaws, machetes, and canoes. Their logging roads were the rivers, and the weather, as much as the forces of supply and demand, controlled their trade. Biologist Uhl, of the Institute of Man in the Amazon, concluded in a recent study that the impact of such logging practices on the surrounding forest has traditionally been negligible. More a craft than an industry, the finding and felling and collecting of a single virola tree, a blond wood species used for plywoods and basic construction board, could take more than seven hours. The footpaths created to get to the targeted timber were fashioned by peons with machetes, and the logs were dragged over the ground to the river by groups of men or mules. The roundlogs were then lashed together and canoemen floated them downriver to the nearest sawmill.[10]

The modern timber trade is not so benign, nor are its methods so precise. Bulldozers and chain saws have replaced mules and machetes. Upland forests that were all but untouchable in times of river travel have been lacerated by the highways and feeder roads. Many trees are toppled to get at the prized few, and even the most selective of modern logging leaves a trail of destruction. The tree crashes down, creating a sizable clearing, often seriously damaging dozens of other younger trees around it. Hauling the log through the forest tears away still more of the fragile understory. The use of skidders, which can weave deftly through a treescape instead of barreling straight ahead like bulldozers, reduces the damage somewhat. Gasparetto reported that total damage from his logging operation claimed no more than 15 to 17 percent of the forest. However, Uhl found a higher casualty rate: Fully 26 percent of the total forest was damaged in a typical logging operation in the area of Paragominas.[11]

Often the result has been thinned-out and picked-over patches of woods, less forests than tall stands of weeds. A typically logged forest too often is not only stripped of its natural diversity but also left with commercially useless species. Worse, logged-over forests are generally loaded with dry slash, or fallen stumps and boughs, that in dry season are dangerously fire-prone, particularly when adjacent to clearings, such as cattle pastures, where burning is frequent.

In defense of his class, Gasparetto claimed that it is not the axmen who are to blame for deforestation. In fact, historically it has been society's demand for fuel wood, building materials, barrel slats, and ship hulls that sent lumbermen ever deeper into the woods. They stopped, in the past, only when the trees finally gave out or when some alternative energy source, such as coal, was found. The small peasants who generally follow the logger's trails have been every bit as destructive, penetrating along the logging roads and cutting their gardens and pastures farther into the woods. Cattlemen are also culprits. Rather than be bothered with harvesting marketable timber, cattlemen have often felled and then burned as waste millions of dollars of valuable timber. (Uhl found that between 1966 and 1983 some 193 million cubic meters of marketable roundwood—or 48 million trees—went up in smoke. That represented four times the amount of wood actually marketed in the first five years of the 1980s.)

Yet lumbermen, if they are not the principal culprits, have rarely been preoccupied with the repercussions of their trade, much less with replanting the timber they harvest. Societies have paid dearly for that lack of foresight. Pará State, in Amazonia's "old frontier," with three thousand sawmills, is the center of the timber and sawmilling industry. There, and in many other Amazonian communities, the forests are balding, and suddenly the lumber industry is stumbling on a crisis it helped precipitate together. The call is shrill now for sparing the surviving wilderness, especially the primary forests, from the terrible genius of the axman. Loggers won't be able to enjoy the hit-and-run practices that have kept them moving, like locusts, across the woodlands for millennia.

The drive into Pimenta Bueno, midway up the state of Rondônia, along the asphalt highway BR-364 took me through a corridor flanked by hulking sawmills. Roundlogs, some wider than trucks, were stacked in the muddy mill lots, awaiting cutting. Black fingers of smoke reached up from dozens of smokestacks and dissipated into the dirty clouds above. The whine of band saws and the thunder of diesel generators announced that a furious enterprise was under way.

At the backlot of one mill called Sulmap, where a low warehouse and huddle of office buildings perched on a deforested knoll, Írio de Bortoli gazed over three-story stacks of the noblest of woods of the Amazon—mahogany, tropical cedar, ipê, and cherrywood. But standing before all this treasured timber, de Bortoli could talk only about his frustration. Sulmap, he explained, was a subsidiary of a big timber dealer in Santa Catarina, which ventured north to Pimenta Bueno in 1979, drawn by the bountiful Amazonian timber and the equally coveted tax breaks offered by Sudam, the Amazon development superintendency. Business was good at first, and by the mid-eighties fifty sawmills had sprung up along the newly paved BR-364. But by late 1990 the scenario had changed drastically.

The first problem Sulmap faced was a national recession, provoked by the government's draconian monetary policy in 1990, which tightened money supply, sending demand plummeting and wood prices tumbling right behind. De Bortoli could see the way out of that woods; navigating through the frequent government economic "packages" had become a national sport among businessmen by then. However, another far more serious crisis was pressing in. The most precious hardwoods had almost disappeared. This crisis was the lumbermen's own doing. Worse, in the short term, there was little they or anyone else could do about it.

Now, the best wood was gone, and loggers had to go up 150 miles away to find and fetch it, driving up the production costs even as prices fell. Belatedly Sulmap had begun to draw up a plan for reforestation. This was new ground for lumbermen. After all, they had become experts in removing, not sowing, the wood wealth of Amazonia. "It's for the future, I guess," said Luiz Appi, de Bortoli's manager. Appi dug at the sawmill lot with the toe of his boot as he spoke, as though to find an answer in the sand. "But it's already late. Everyone saw this great abundance of wood all around, and no one thought about reforesting. We all thought it would never end. Anyway, reforestation was Ibama's business."

Abundance, the blessing of nations with vast spaces to fill, is also a curse that has plagued Brazil since it became a colony. Natural bounty, where resources spread over endless forests and plains, is a pioneer's dream and a conservationist's nightmare. John Norden, the seventeenth-century cartographer and surveyor of England's woods of the crown, lamented the "universal inclination to hurl down" and the fury of those seeking merely the "profit present" In Rondônia they called it building a frontier.[12]

One of the state's most avid frontiersmen was the air force colonel Jorge Texeira, who had served as appointed governor of Rondônia when it was still a federal territory. He was the keyman on the ground in the outgoing military government's land giveaway, which drew tens of thousands of displaced southern farmers north to the newly paved highway. All up and down Highway BR 364 he would summon thousands of peasants to gather on town greens. There he would don his paratrooper's cap and climb onto a town gazebo to make triumphant speeches. His compliant audiences were generally the *colonos,* or settlers, he had had bused in from their temporary lots. After a windy speech he would personally hand them permanent land titles. The greatest land reform of all times, General Figueiredo, the fifth and dourest general to command in Brasília, called this policy.

The military government was replaced by a civilian one in 1985. Rondônia became a state, and Colonel Texeira died. But the *colonos* he waved into Rondônia kept coming. So did the cattlemen, the gold prospectors, and the lumbermen. Together, in twenty years, they removed an area of forest one and a half times the size of Massachusetts in a state the size of Wyoming. But back in Texeira's time, a state had to be built. The colonel would lose no sleep over such trifles as trees. People, not woods, was his business. The more of them the better.

Some Rondonians had nagging doubts, even back in those bounteous days. One was de Bortoli. He recalled a meeting he organized with Texeira and a few lumbermen concerned about the future of the state's timber. "We brought him some projects for rational forest management and reforestation," he said. "Texeira listened politely, and then told us, 'Look, what we need in Rondônia is to cut down.' " That was as far as the plan ever got.

Now, belatedly, with the "noble" timber ever scarcer, sawmills laying off workers, and others shutting down altogether, Sulmap was again talking about reforestation. In the early 1980s, fifty lumber companies ran harvesting and sawing operations in Pimenta Bueno. A decade later that number had already slipped to forty-three, and many of them were running on vastly reduced capacity. The hurling down had caught up with the Rondônia lumber industry. With the most profitable wood disappearing, many sawmills moved on to the ignoble "white woods," for plywoods and cheap building materials. Clearcutting was the cheapest method of getting at these less valued species, and the woods of Rondônia suffered all the more. In mid-1990 de Bortoli's company finally began a nursery and sent woodsmen to clear areas in previously logged forests for replanting. Sulmap hired on British forestry consultant Nick Burch, who had already devoted fifteen years to his own reforestation project, to draw up a forest management plan. But Ibama, the environmental agency, had balked on approving plans of forest management. Dozens of companies had to wait while the agency kept their proposals on hold.

By midafternoon the sky had already darkened over Sulmap's woodlot, leaving de Bortoli, and the lot of hulking roundlogs, in purple shadows. "Our business class is interested only in easy profits," said de Bortoli, in a candid moment. "Now they are beginning to respond to the demands for reforestation, but it's a defensive move, more as a result of pressures from the government and the ecologists than as a matter of conscience. They still are thinking in the short term, easy money. I am frustrated," he went on. "Money is what talks here, not sense. The president said it, and I agree. Our business class is a wasteful class."

The crisis of the wood industry still seemed miles away from Gasparetto's spread of pristine forest by the Tapajós. To be safe, though, he had begun on his hundred-thousand-acre spread what few of his colleagues in Rondônia or southern Pará had. Gasparetto had undertaken what the trade calls enrichment planting. The idea, put oversimply, was to enhance nature. In Amazonia a single hectare contains perhaps four hundred species of trees, of which five or at most ten will be of commercial value. Enrichment planting usually means opening a path in a spread of land that has already been logged or partially clearcut for pastures and sowing valuable tree seedlings down a narrow trail. Increasing the number of valuable species will, the argument goes, inevitably raise the value of the timber stand and make repeat logging more and more profitable.

Gasparetto tramped down one "line" with head-high ipê, massaranduba, and jatobá, inspecting his tidy columns of trees. It is an expensive operation, he said. And there are a number of unknowns: How long will it take to nurture these replanted trees to maturity? What will the mortality rate be? "The problem," he confessed, "is we are talking thirty, forty, fifty years from now, and no one knows what the market will do. No one can say what species will be valuable then."

As with most every other strategy for the Amazon, practices such as Gasparetto's have their critics. Many argue that seeding the Amazon forest to induce regrowth is the botanical equivalent of carrying coals to Newcastle. Uhl, for one, has noted that the rain forest is its own best seed bank. In several studies he recommended logging in strips of tens of yards, creating a checkerboard, alternating squares of clearings and forest. Jean Dubois, the forester with four decades' experience in the Amazon and other tropical forests, said similarly that if care is taken to leave intact enough stands of primary forests, then wind and gravity, birds and rodents will do the rest, scattering seeds to the cleared strips.

Such forest management techniques have been followed in Costa Rica and Peru with some success. Malaysia's teak forests have been harvested for three or four generations running, but environmentalists report predation there as well. Though prolonged experience in the far more diversified forests of the Amazon is scanty—most research relies on a single study carried out in Suriname by the Dutch forester N. R. de Graff—many students of forestry believe these techniques eventually will be the key to sustained harvesting of the timber that all civilizations continue to covet.[13]

However, Nick Burch, who is one of the believers, is betting in a big way on line planting. In the late 1980s he founded what he now calls the biggest tropical reforestation project in the Amazon. His Reflorestadora Rondônia today boasts a nursery, replete with 35,000 seedlings of thirty different native Amazonian species, ready for planting. He and his son, Jason, have already planted 100,000 trees, on lands degraded by itinerant farming, and grazing, and reseeded them with the trees that once flourished in Rondônia. Burch had plans to plant 250,000 more trees by the end of 1991.

As a botanical garden Burch's project seemed a splendid effort. As a business venture it looked somewhat less impressive. Burch said he made a fortune from a sawmill in Scotland and lost one in the Amazon. He calculated he had sunk $250,000 into reforesting the Amazon. His wealth was in the ground, but the profits would come only in time for Jason to enjoy them, twenty or thirty years down the road. For now he watched over a handsome nursery, a small forest of young trees, and a wilderness of IOUs that stretched from the local bar to the phone company. Burch himself admitted that his management skills were not up to his forestry.

But reforestation, which is a stated objective of the Brazilian government's new, improved environmental policy, turns vitally on expertise and a reliable stock of tree seeds. Whatever the system, be it line planting or natural regeneration, it is exacting and expensive work, far more so than the simple milking of forests for their best woods that has too often been the fashion in Amazonia. In a country now under heat from the environmental movement for squandering its tropical forests and facing a possibly disastrous timber boycott, Burch himself seems to be a squandered human resource.

But what is to be done once forests are leveled? Though 90 percent of the Amazon's original forest cover is still untouched, more and more has come crashing down in the last three decades. Cattle ranching, peasant farming, and mining are the chief fellers, and often these activities are short-lived. The land they have denuded is often wrung dry, of minerals or nutrients, and then abandoned. All this degraded land might be plowed over and sown with eucalyptus for pulp or charcoal, but that would be ecological imperialism, to borrow Alfred Crosby's term, not restoration. Left to its own devices, this land might regenerate its original flora and forest cover (or something very much like them), but that could take two centuries or more.

Oliver Henry ("Harry") Knowles, a British logger turned forester, has been puzzling over this question for fifteen years. He works for a giant Brazilian government-owned mining conglomerate, Mineração Rio do Norte (MNR), which operates a bauxite mine in the north-central Amazon, along the Trombetas River. When he started at Trombetas in 1978, Knowles knew the deposits of high-grade bauxite were expected to last for perhaps a hundred years. The mining officials were worried about extracting the maximum amount of bauxite from the forest-encumbered earth. Knowles was worried about the next century, when the ore would be gone and the land left a strip-mined waste. Though lately much of the restoration of mined areas at Trombetas has been handed over to others, Knowles personally designed the forestation of some 1,750 acres of scarred and barren mine terrain. His work is still a reminder of what can be done to repair the damage made by one of the world's most devastating enterprises.

On a December day, under a mantle of rain clouds, Knowles coaxed his yellow Volkswagen along the mining project's web of dirt roads, showing his work as he told in bits and pieces his own personal Amazon story. Born in Wiltshire and raised in West Sussex, Knowles came to Trombetas by an unlikely path. It was the tales of the early naturalists and their wanderings along the Amazon and Rio Negro that first piqued his imagination about the tropical forests. "Once I'd read Wallace and Bates, there was no turning back," he said. Talks with his uncle Dick Norris, an oil driller in Peru, who made occasional visits back to England, continued to fire the young Knowles's imagination. Another uncle, Harry, brought back tales of the Peruvian Amazon, where the German company he worked for had struck oil in Aguas Calientes, in 1955.

The Norrises were out of a job when the Peruvians nationalized the oil fields, but the desire to see the Amazon only grew for their young nephew. From then on his career read like that of any number of vagabonds of empire, moving from one colonial venue to another. The Knowles family didn't have the money to send Harry to forestry school, but he learned to tend trees at a plant nursery at Lord Cowdray's forest estate, a thirty-two-thousand-acre spread in Midhurst. Then he was drafted into Britain's National Service and was sent to Egypt, where he learned engineering, surveying, and road building. He did another two years' surveying work back in England and then returned to Lord Cowdray's estate. Finally, in 1954, Harry got his chance to see the Amazon, managing a logging project on the Perené River, in Peru. At the time one of the grandest engineering projects of all time was being carried out: a railroad straddling the three-mile-high peaks of the Andes and plunging down between two cordilleras, eventually connecting the mining town of La Oroya to the old silver mining town of Cerro de Pasco. Until then railroad ties had had to be imported from Sweden. Knowles was hired to run a sawmill and turn the felled hardwood trees from a coffee plantation into railroad ties.

He stayed on until 1960, when the Dutch bought out the railway and the coffee estate. Both were taken over a few years later under Peru's nationalist regime. Knowles left South

America for West Africa, where he worked on a government logging project in Sierra Leone, staying on until the country turned independent in 1963.

That year he applied for and won a post with the United Nations Food and Agricultural Organization and moved back across the Atlantic to Santarém, along the Amazon River. His contract was for six months, but Knowles's enchantment with the Amazon was rekindled. He simply never left. Initially Knowles's job was to advise local loggers and millers (one was Ovídio Gasparetto) on forestry techniques and alternative species of timber. He also began nurturing plans for his long-desired idea of replanting the felled tropical forests.

Knowles eased the VW Bug up a steep grade and bumped to a halt. After hopping out of the car, he pushed aside some saplings and stopped in the middle of a contradictory landscape, divided neatly down the middle like a split TV screen. He waved a hand to the right, over a terrain of rolling red dunes, the color and texture of baked clay, fissured here and there where the rains had carved out a passage. "Mine tailings," he said. "Four years and not a blade of grass has come up here. Maybe in twenty-five years you'll get tufts of grass at the edges. In one hundred fifty years you might see capoeira," the tangled, low-lying bush that often takes over when an area of rain forest has been logged or clear-cut. "In two hundred fifty years you might have a proper forest again."

He wheeled half around and gestured to his left. Rising like a verdant curtain over the wasteland of orange tailings was a thriving young forest. The stand of trees included a handful of native Amazonian species, some of them valuable hardwoods known as sucupira, breu sucuruba, tatapiririca, and tachi dos campos. There were robust sapateiros, whose wood is still used by the footwear industry to make clogs. This forest, where some trees reached a height of about twelve feet, was an experiment of Knowles's begun four and a half years before, with little more than a vague hunch about wooing this spoiled patch of earth and a bit of fertile topsoil to get the tree seed-lings started.

Turning back around to the dunescape of tailings, Knowles wore a sour look. "Had they spread just a thin layer of topsoil, this scene would be very similar to that growing forest." Not all of Knowles's experiments at Trombetas involved replant-ing native species. Some areas were so far gone, their soils so badly compacted that more drastic remedies were required. Though purists may fault him for altering the natural Amazo-nian biota, Knowles believed that landscapes already drasti-cally disturbed required some more drastic methods. So he began to tinker with exotic tree species, like the hardy euca-lyptus and pine, fast-growing and aggressive trees, ideal for getting the clock of natural succession wound again. The exot-ics were the pioneers, opening the way so that the more frag-ile, slow-growing native species could be coaxed into bloom. "Nature does the work," he said, "but man can give it a little hand."

As we drove on, Knowles recalled his own try at sawmill-ing, a business he started up with a partner in São Paulo. Three years and forty-five thousand dollars later, they went broke. He didn't go into details but hinted at falling out over admin-istration and money. "I could have put that money in the bank and retired on the interest," he said. Knowles went back to the consulting business, but not for long. Logging, he admitted, was beginning to get to him. "The logging companies only wanted to know one thing: how much longer we could go on cutting a single species of tree," he said. "I calculated just ten years. So we tried to develop other species, but the markets wouldn't budge."

Back from the mine, we sat now out on the patio of the Trombetas guesthouse. Men in clean overalls with garden shears tended tidy grass lawns under cashew trees, heavy with the ripened red fruit. Hummingbirds flitted from one delicately perfumed flower to the next. The dark rain clouds paraded across a mackerel sky. Knowles's mood seemed to match the heavens.

"Look," he added brusquely, "there's something else. There is no such thing as an honest logger. I know, because I was a logger. You have to deceive people. I sold virola, a cheap timber for plywoods, as cedro. Virola is half the price, but it looks like cedro. I used to be part owner of a sawmill in Belém, and a builder asked me for the cheapest wood possible for housing construction materials. It was for roof rafters! And they didn't care. So I sold him wood that I knew wouldn't last three years. Logging and sawmilling must be some of the most dishonest businesses anywhere. It has been since ancient times."

So Knowles, the repentant logger, bailed out of the timber racket and decided to go to work making amends. With a century of ore lying in the ground, few mining executives might have bothered to ask what would come of the strip-mined land after its minerals were spent. But this was already the Age of the Environment and of loans whose purse strings came tied to environmental impact statements and recovery plans. The World Bank, which funded part of MNR's Trombetas operation, required a staff ecologist, and Robert Goodland, the prominent director of environment at the bank, recommended Knowles. Knowles accepted MNR's "invitation" and began devising a plan to tidy up where man had trodden so heavily.

In eight years Knowles personally oversaw the restoration of half a dozen mining sites, planting 1.2 million trees. The work was enough to win him international acclaim, a plague of visitors and journalists, and a decoration from Queen Elizabeth, who selected him to be a Member of the Empire. It was something less than knighthood, Knowles allowed, but still a pleasant surprise for this logger turned ecologist who had spent thirty years buried anonymously in darkest Amazonia. It had not been all kudos either. "I sometimes feel I'm cleaning up someone else's shithouse," he said, as he bumped along in his old Volkswagen beside the barren red dunes.

Honored in his native England, Knowles suffered frustration in his adopted Brazil. In 1986 his reforesting experiments were virtually halted; a new management team hired two new ecologists, young, university-trained men, who also happened to be relatives of two top MNR executives. Their ideas for the greening of Trombetas parted radically from Knowles's.

The difference was visible, and spreading, all over Trombetas. Atop a bluff that overlooked a bauxite washing plant, Knowles gestured toward a small reservoir of wet reddish claylike earth and the mark of the new regime. This was a "thickening pond," for decanting water from the washing plant. The tailings, a thick oozing of mud, were pumped from the washing plant into a series of such ponds for drying. "In five years," said Knowles, "this mud will be mostly dry and ten to fifteen meters [thirty-three to forty-nine feet] thick. It will take ten years for total drying, and only then will it be ready for replanting."

However, in its hasty excavations, the company had also scraped away and discarded the topsoil. Without the topsoil, and its life-giving nutrients and microrganisms, there was no way to get succession, or the natural return to vegetation and woods, started again. The only plant life in evidence on this site was a meager crown of brittle brachiaria grass, a thick foraging species known for its resistance to invasion by other plants—a living botanical barrier to reforestation.

"See those trees," Knowles said wryly, pointing to a few scraggly stems that clung to the hardened red earth like the lonely strands of hair on a balding pate. "They'll be about forty centimeters [sixteen inches] high in fifty years. If they had spread the area with just fifteen centimeters [six inches] of topsoil, they would be two meters [six and a half feet] tall now."

Knowles has stayed on at Trombetas as an environmental adviser but lately has found that his advice was already counterbalanced by another, quite different notion. For one, the reforestation schemes were swapped for "revegetation." Instead of trees, grass was now being seeded over the spreading areas of mine tailings. As we tramped over the red dunes of Trombetas, the scene that came to mind was both comical and poignant: Harry Knowles, the accomplished forester, for his dedication to restoring the man-trammeled rain forests, decorated a Member of the British Empire on a great green Amazonian lawn.

But even in the torpor of the Amazon things can change. By mid-1991 a new, more ecologically minded president had taken over the mine, and environmental policy had been completely reworked. The new administration named a man to coordinate three important new divisions at Trombetas: work safety, worker health, and the environment. In November Knowles returned from a vacation to find that the two junior ecologists who took his place had moved on, and suddenly his opinions were being solicited again. It was too soon to tell then just how this new policy would play out at the mine site. However, Knowles held out the hope that soon he might be yanking up grass and planting trees again.

CHAPTER 7

STRANGE FRUIT

> And thy seed shall be as the dust of the earth, and
> thou shalt spread abroad to the west, and to the
> east, and to the north, and to the south: and in
> thee and in thy seed shall all the families of the
> earth be blessed.
>
> —Genesis 28:14

The man with a dark beard and cowboy boots patted a pair of gardening shears against the palm of his hand, as an executive might fidget with a ball-point, and strode out the door toward the garden. He led the way past a plant nursery, where kneeling men in shorts and sandals tenderly wrapped seedlings in protective black plastic, and on through the rows of spreading fruit bushes that adorned his small backyard orchard. The leaves were a waxy olive, and the thick branches covered with a reddish orange berry the size and shape of a cherry tomato. Some of the bushes were nearly as tall as trees, and they marched in tight rows straight across the yard. A dozen boys collected fistfuls of the ripened fruit, which dropped with a plunk into plastic buckets. The sun was high now quickly evaporating the haze of morning that swathed the town of Alta Floresta. In its place, dust was swirling as the workday's traffic plied the unpaved streets.

As he walked, Divino Araujo explained about the sour-sweet

acerola fruit, occasionally pruning back the unruly branches in deft lunges, the snip of his shears punctuating his lecture. He was lank and tall, with a jet beard and overalls. His cowboy boots were also tall, and worn and caked with red mud. The acerola, he lectured, was originally from the Caribbean—the cherry of the Antilles it was called—where it was cultivated for its high load of vitamin C and tangy juice. Not long ago it was exported to Africa, where it took well. More recently it found its way south, to Brazil, where it was just beginning to be planted. Most of the crop was now grown in the northeast, a gentle, arid land with sparse vegetation and lapped by the balmy waters and winds of the equatorial Atlantic. Somehow Divino had gotten it in his head that you could grow it in the humid tropics of the Amazon.

Fellow farmers in Alta Floresta, a community of small farmers in northern Mato Grosso, in the southern basin of the Amazon, looked askance as Divino and his wife, Janethe, turned their landscaping company over to the cultivation of this strange fruit. Their small orchard, with twelve hundred trees on a mere five acres, is a monument to Divino's vague notion.

Here, as in many other venues in the Amazon, agriculture had been a punishing vocation. Like the Araujos, a generation of small farmers left the overcrowded lands of southern Brazil for the sparsely occupied north, only to become handcuffed to the mean work and meager returns of farming rice, coffee, cocoa, and kidney beans. These were the crops their parents knew and had sown all their lives. Now the sons and daughters were in charge, and the ways and crops of their past were part of the baggage they hauled across Brazil and transposed onto this new land.

Again and again this has been the case in Brazil. The Araujos are heirs to a restless, often desperate, and incurably hopeful people who have been on the move for generations. Divino's fair complexion and inky beard are features of Portugal, where the Araujos have a long family line. Janethe comes from Ceará, the northeastern state known for its punishing droughts. Her rounded cheeks, burnished skin, and straight black hair were features that told of the mixture of her Portuguese grandfather and a part Indian mother. From their separate corners of Brazil they migrated north, to the Amazon Basin, joining a whole wave of small landholders that was extending the boundaries of Brazilian settlement and agriculture. They met in Alta Floresta and were married a year later.

Divino was born in Minas Gerais but was raised in Paraná, the grassy, fertile country south of São Paulo. This was the home of the sons and grandsons of Poles, Germans, Irish, and Italians as well as immigrant Swabs and Japanese. Driven by a thin promise of land and work in this part of the New World, their forebears came from across the oceans, where farmland was scarce and living dear. First invited during the end of the Brazilian monarchy, the Europeans were summoned to take the place of the slaves. (Abolition came only in 1888, making Brazil the last country on earth to end slavery.) Most of the immigrants went to southern Brazil, the green belt, with rich volcanic soils, gently rolling grasslands, pine forests, and temperate climates. They scraped and saved and carved a life out of that wilderness, and then they moved on.

Only a few decades ago, the lands in the extreme west and north of Paraná were being settled, and the map had to be drawn and redrawn to register the growing crop of new towns. Divino's family settled in one of these old frontier towns, near Palotina, a cattle and coffee region in the west of the state. The Araujos had 125 acres of mint, and Divino grew up surrounded by its inviting green carpet and the heady perfume. But things were changing in Paraná, in all of the Brazilian south, in fact. Frosts devastated the Paraná coffee crop in back-to-back years. The staple of this nation for more than a century was in trouble. On farm after farm, thousands of small landholders were soon yanking up their ice-singed bushes of arabica. Once Brazil's leading coffee-producing state, Paraná by 1990 had slipped to number three and reduced its area of coffee from 49 percent of the arable land to 16.9 percent.[1]

Like the Araujos, many small farmers began to plant wheat and, more recently, soybeans. Soya had been imported from the United States and was gradually taking over the landscape. Unlike coffee and mint, soya plantations required machines, not farmhands, and the small producers of Paraná were soon pitted against executive farmers with great diesel tractors, chemical fertilizers, crop dusters, and gleaming silos. The land became a quilt of soy and wheat and sorghum, miracle crops that created a booming agroindustrial sector, but also a social commotion of unprecedented proportions.

For families grew as well, while the land values soared and property became concentrated in fewer and fewer hands. Many small landholding families had nowhere to go and were soon out of work. Many farmers opted to sell out and become sharecroppers, renting a few acres from a plantation while selling their labor to agribusiness. Many others simply vacated the countryside and built shacks in cities like São Paulo and Curitiba, where the slums, or *favelas*, began to swell. Curitiba, the state capital and one of the Brazil's most pleasant and prosperous cities, underwent the most intensive rate of "favelization" in Brazil. While the state's population grew only 1.5 percent, Curitiba's ballooned 5 percent, mostly at the unkempt edges where *favelas* took root and flourished.

So, like their fathers and their grandfathers, another generation picked up and moved on. In fact, between 1970 and 1990 this coffee-growing state had become an exporter of people. According to a former state secretary of agriculture, Osmar Dias, some 1.5 million Paranaenses left the state after 1970. A majority went to São Paulo, throwing themselves in the industrial caldron of the *bandeirante* metropolis. Another 30 percent went to the Amazon region, especially to Mato Grosso, and the rest migrated even farther, into the northern Amazonian states.[2] Now, some were already returning, having failed in Amazonia, while still others detoured to the arid but mostly empty countryside of Bahia.

These people are the detritus of modern Brazil, the jetsam

of a green revolution that had rendered superfluous the small farmers and their family holdings that were once the mainstay of Brazilian agriculture.[3] In a scant three decades, in fact, Brazil's demographics were stood on their head. In 1960 some 70 percent of the population of 70 million lived in the countryside; today, in a society of 151 million, only 30 percent are country dwellers. And the hemorrhage from country to city continues unstanched.

There is an argument, a passionate argument, that many of the worst distortions of Brazilian society—from overcrowded slums to the falling rain forests—are linked to the unequal distribution of land. The squatter camps in southern Brazil, where hundreds of erstwhile farmers live like refugees under black plastic sheets by the roadsides, fuel such arguments. The situation seems simply to cry out for a radical plan, the taking away of land held by a powerful few to give over to the miserable many.

Lately the fires in the Amazon have reignited this call for land distribution. If only the poor small landholder could be secured on his farm in southern Brazil instead of being shucked by the machines of indifferent agribusiness, then the mad rush north, to the frontier of the Amazon Basin, would be halted. This would, the argument goes, promote a twin justice in a single act. One would be ecological, sparing the magnificent forested Amazon from the landless hordes; the second would be social, by dividing up the land and making Brazil a more egalitarian society.

The distortions that remain in the Brazilian countryside date back to the days of empire. In the first two centuries after Portugal had claimed Brazil, when most of the nation was still a frontier, Lisbon divided up this vast land among lords and barons. This was the system of *sesmarias,* grants of sprawling properties, some of them as big as European countries, that totally covered the map. This was totally different from the pattern of settlement in the western territories of the United

States, where the landless could come and squat and register their claims at a local land office.[4] In Brazil the countryside was all spoken for long before it was occupied.

It took a farsighted emperor, and the imminent end of slave labor, to attempt to crack the encrusted system of landownership in Brazil. Even then the status quo prevailed. Emperor Pedro II, who fancied himself a modernizing monarch, saw the writing on the wall, with the outlawing of traffic in African slaves and Britain's Aberdeen bill of 1845, which permitted search and seizure of suspected slave ships. Pedro introduced legislation to the Congress meant to force some dramatic changes in this plantation nation, where the barons of sugar, coffee, and cattle reigned. The plan included steep land taxes, mandatory demarcation to dispel claims disputes, the cancellation of ancient land grants held by the rural elite, and state expropriations of private land when necessary. At the same time Pedro looked to replace slaves with "poor, young, and robust" immigrants from Europe, who had begun to flood the New World. The idea was to make over the Brazilian countryside into something like an Australia, with plenty of land and a crying need for laborers. "Never," writes José Murilo de Carvalho, a scholar of the imperial period, "had such a radical proposal been presented, nor has there been one since. . . ."[5]

The Law of the Lands eventually passed, in 1843, but it was so heavily amended and its execution was so thoroughly stonewalled that by 1877 it was a "dead letter." Though the land barons of Brazil had no objections to drawing freedmen as laborers, they refused to pay the bill—for passage, settlement, and assistance to the immigrants. They even refused to cooperate with demands for a proper land registry. Brazil's first and "most authentic agrarian reform" plan was thus stillborn.[6]

This frustration would set an ominous tone for future policies of land reform. It also ossified the already skewed landholding system, whereby a privileged few held the lion's share of property. Not only did this land tenure system point to an antiquated economy, where arable land was being left idle to garner value in a heated real estate market, but it also exposed a moral problem: So many Brazilians went hungry while productive land was left unplanted. Land reform seemed not only a necessary instrument of modernization but a commandment.

Francisco Graziano Neto was a young Brazilian agronomist in the mid-1980s, when the call for land reform was riding high again. His job, as a senior administrator with the land settlement office, Incra, was to scour the country for tax evaders and latifúndios, large, unproductive estates that were believed to blanket the countryside. Graziano paid special attention to the south of Brazil, where the land was richest and the disputes were hottest. The idle properties would be identified, heavily taxed, expropriated if necessary, and prepared for resettlement by displaced farmers.

But Graziano and his colleagues searched in vain. In time he realized that the picture he and many people on the political left had of land in Brazil was an illusion. It was not that there were no latifúndios or wanton speculators sitting on idle tracts of land. It was simply that there was not nearly the amount of this land that everyone imagined. But the official statistics were absurdly out of date. For example, the national property registry listed more sprawling tracts of "idle" property in São Paulo, Rio Grande do Sul, and Paraná—some of the most intensively worked lands of Brazil's farm belt—than in the barely cultivated and thinly settled lands of northeastern Brazil. Odder still, supposedly more and more land was left unused, even as Brazil was in the throes of a green revolution. "Some estates on the books had been divided up a long time before. Others simply didn't exist. The point was, there was no idle land in southern Brazil," Graziano said. He concluded that the data that had served as the ammunition for bold land reform programs were totally, and tragically, distorted—so distorted, he believed, that the numbers served only to polarize the debate over a proper land reform.[7]

The left and the church, armed with their damning rural census, called for a total overhauling of landownership, breaking up big estates from south to north to settle the millions of landless. Rural workers' unions representing the landless organized squatter camps occasionally clashed violently with police. This fueled radicals on the right, who drew their pickups into a circle, bought guns, and bombarded Congress with their lucrative lobby. The landowners also managed to play like a fiddle the fears of a population naturally skittish about radicalism.

By the time the land reform act passed in the 1988 Constituent Assembly, which was recasting Brazil's constitution, it was a contradictory proposal, hamstrung by amendments and impossible conditions. One was that no "productive" land, no matter the size, could be the target of expropriation; the all-important definition of "productive" was left to the vagaries of future legislation. It also virtually ensured the financial failure of the policy by stipulating that expropriated land be paid for in "agrarian debt" bonds, essentially government debt paper, which no landowner would readily accept, knowing the financial chaos of Brasília.

Graziano, who is a senior adviser to the left-center Brazilian Social Democratic party, concluded that the error was a political one and that his colleagues on the left were largely responsible. "Breaking up the big estates and handing out parcels of land were seen as the panacea," he said. "It was going to be our own French Revolution." Yet he also came to believe that the Brazil that had inspired these revolutionary notions of land reform had died long ago.

The "distributive" utopia of land reform was one born of Brazilian realities in the 1930s and 1940s, when the latifúndio was still the major model of land tenure. Back then Brazil was supremely an agricultural nation. It was farming that lured people to new lands, and the planting of cash crops, such as coffee, quickly filled the southern frontiers of Brazil. The population of Paraná's north country rose like a helium balloon, from a few scattered souls in 1920 to more than a million in 1960. These were the coffee pioneers, and they were the protagonists of a demographic growth which surpassed that of New York, Illinois, and Ohio during the tumultuous early frontier days of the United States.[8]

Yet even as the calls for land redistribution escalated over the years, the Brazilian countryside was being torn up and remade. The rural population shrank while production of grains and foods soared. The cities swelled, demanding ever more agricultural products, putting ever more pressure on those farmers who remained. The farmers who hung on in the south of Brazil, where this economic revolution was taking place, were no longer lonely families sowing and reaping on their few small acres for private consumption or sale of a bit of surplus to the nearby village. They became small businesses, using tractors and silos and fertilizers and pesticides. They produced, often, for big agricultural conglomerates and formed part of a chain of production that stretched from farm to industry to city markets. Brazil is the world's second-largest supplier of frozen chickens, but it is small farmers who produce 80 percent of these chickens for large agroindustries. Instead of the hoes and the strong arms of many sons, what counted more and more was technology and finance. There was less and less room in this landscape for Tolstoy's Levin, stripped to his shirt sleeves and wrestling a plow through acres of some rude and fecund piece of land. Arcadia was a business, a big business now, and amateurs got swallowed up in its machinations.

Geraldo Müller, a São Paulo agronomist who has plotted the transformation of the Brazilian countryside, called this the twin-edged sword of modernization. "Those farmers who modernized along these molds survived," he said. "Those who did not failed. They turned into the poor, the modern poor." Rural unions call these people the *sem-terra* (landless). In the argot of rural sociology, they became really a farm proletariat, "eventual" labor, roaming the countryside to work during the harvests of sugarcane, oranges, and manioc, which were being planted by the firms that succeeded them. As in the United

States green belt, the family farm was fast disappearing.[9] Machines had taken over. In Divino Araujo's adopted home state of Paraná, there was a tractor invasion. In 1970 there were 17,000 tractors in the countryside; twenty years later there were 99,140. Accordingly, it was better hours and better wages, not plots of land, that more and more rural workers wanted. The rural struggle became a union struggle.

"The tragedy is that Brazil put twenty million people out of the countryside in thirty years," said Müller. "Brazil could push its production of grains from the current level of seventy million tons to a hundred million tons without adding a single rural job."

This was a fact that the left had not fully assimilated, Müller said. "Just as modern industry doesn't depend on the number of laborers, agriculture doesn't depend on land anymore. It depends on biotechnology, which doesn't create jobs. And it depends on money. Distributing land is not the same thing as distributing wealth. We need to stop seeing rural land as a solution for employment. It's just the opposite. That's why the so-called progressive church is reactionary. They want to go back to a Brazil that doesn't exist anymore. Rural culture in Brazil is over."

Divino Araujo hung on for a time even as the floor of the south shifted beneath him. He heard a German family was hiring field hands and went to work on a large farm near Palotina. Here, again, the crop was the pervasive soya and the work seemed less like farming than tending an assembly line. Divino took the graveyard shift, driving a tractor from midnight to dawn through the artificially lit fields. Here fieldwork had become a factory. "It wasn't agriculture at all," Divino said as he pruned acerola. So Divino punched out and drifted into Palotina, where he got a job at a small hotel. There he was a bellhop by day and a student by night. He struggled through a few grueling semesters and found he had enough time for class and hauling luggage, but none for homework.

A family on a river boat, southeast of Manaus.

A Yanomami boy in the forest of Roraima.

The burning of cleared land in Rondônia.

The Brazilian explorer and writer Euclydes da Cunha.

The positivist explorer and indianist General Cândido Mariano da Silva Rondon.

Amazon tribespeople gathered at the Altamira meeting.

Two Kayapó indians in Altamira.

A lumberman cutting an "angelim vermelho" tree.

Three charcoal wood cutters in Agailandia, Pará state.

Scuba diver, with underwater chain saw, harvesting trees from Tucuruí lake.

The Serra Pelada gold dig ("garimpo") in Pará state.

Cows and a cowboy in Acre state.

Japanese dancers keeping traditions alive in the Amazon in Tomé-Açu, Pará state.

After a few months he picked up again and moved to Brasília, the nation's capital, seven hundred miles to the northwest.

With the equivalent of a high school diploma and no skills that didn't involve hoeing rows or steering a tractor, Divino found himself in a hardscrabble city. Brasília then was still seen as a Mecca for migrants, especially the *sertanejos* (backlanders) out of land and out of work in their home regions. The city had been built, brick by brick, by the northeasterners, the squat, sturdy people of Bahia and Ceará, with complexions of brown, black, and slate. Divino was taller and lighter-skinned than most of the migrants. These traits are advantages in much of Brazil, but by pedigree and birthplace he was really only one more hillbilly in the metropolis.

A friend wise in the ways of the capital got Divino a job— one for which he was utterly unqualified: bus driver. Till then the largest vehicle he had ever driven was a pickup, and then only on the dirt roads of farm country. He didn't have a driver's license and hadn't the faintest idea how to get around in Brasília. In the Brazilian capital that can be fatal. The city, an architect's fantasy of order and progress and a monument to the futurism of forty years ago, is a wilderness of cloverleafs, viaducts, one-way lanes, and dead ends. Stoplights are rare, and addresses look like higher math: 403 SQS / Bloco B / 102.

Miraculously Divino passed the test. His first rush hour was a near disaster. He was assigned to a particularly decrepit Scania bus and a typically overcrowded route. "I spent fifteen minutes trying to get the thing into first gear, and when I did, I hadn't the faintest idea where to go," he recalled. "I had to ask the passengers."

They were understandably startled. "You don't know?" The packed bus gasped in unison. "Okay, go ahead, we'll teach you the way."

With their guidance and the adrenaline of sheer panic, Divino made his run, and many others. In a few weeks he was one of the best drivers of the fleet. But he had no stomach for diesel fumes and nine-hour days of punishing driving. So Divino quit

and started combing the classifieds. He answered one ad
announcing a chauffeur's position at the Filipino Embassy. He
nearly decided to abandon the whole idea however, when the
groomed and lotioned man with the polished leather shoes and
three-piece suit at the embassy turned out to be not his pro-
spective employer but a rival candidate. "I was twenty and
looked five years younger. I looked like a yokel in jeans and
rubber sandals."

Somehow, Divino got the job, only to find out his passenger
would be no one less than the ambassador herself. He swapped
the stubborn gearbox of the Scania for a Mercedes Turbo and
the jeans for a navy blue suit and bow tie.

The job ended abruptly eight months later, when he was
stopped for a minor traffic infraction by a young cop, eager to
exploit the power his uniform bestowed. Divino refused to hand
over the Mercedes keys, however, and the whole affair ended
up at the police station and, finally, the hospital. Divino's injury
was minor—a cut finger when the cop yanked the key chain
away—and the matter was handily put to rest when the ambassador herself barged into the hospital, whose director was a
close friend. But the altercation brought home a crucial lesson
on the ways of life in the Brazilian capital, where social station
was paramount. There one's fortunes were determined not by
some respected code of laws and civil rights but by the clout
of your public godfather and his ability to distribute and extract
official concessions and privileges. Had it not been for his
prestigious employer, Divino could easily have ended up behind
bars or worse. Such was only the routine code of Brasília. But
Divino, a farmer's boy in a bow tie, thought the prestige of
one's boss a fairly flimsy life insurance policy.

So Divino enrolled in agricultural school, was graduated two
years later as an agricultural technician, and decided to go back
to the farm. There was no room left for him in Paraná, where
the eight Araujo brothers had only 125 acres between them and
where mechanization had remade the rural map. Divino turned

his back on the south and, like so many other Paranaenses, headed north to Amazonia.

The experiences of these migrant settlers have often been brutal ones; they have generally taken up agriculture with the fury of those who burrow after gold. "Here in Brazil the soil had first been violated, then destroyed," Lévi-Strauss commented on his way through the southern backcountry in the 1930s. "Agriculture had been a matter of looting for quick profits. Within a hundred years, in fact, the pioneers had worked their way like a slow fire across the State of São Paulo, eating into virgin territory on the one side, leaving nothing but exhausted fallow land on the other."[10] They kept going, and by the 1960s the agricultural frontier had spread from western Paraná to Brazil's "far west," the marsh and grasslands of Mato Grosso do Sul. Soon the migrations became a stampede, and the settlers spilled into Mato Grosso, Rondônia, Amazonas, Acre, and Roraima. The slow fires were now a conflagration.

I once spent two hours in a droning twin-engine plane, circling endlessly over the airport of Alta Floresta, waiting for the smoke clouds to clear for long enough to allow the plane to land. Many Amazonian airports shut down for days between July and September, for the annual *queimadas* (burning season). In fact, the felling and burning of forests in Mato Grosso jumped fourfold, from 8,000 square miles in 1978 to 31,837 square miles in 1989. Farther north, in Rondônia, the felling was even more intense. By 1989 Rondônia had lost 10,893 square miles of forest—an area the size of Maryland— or almost seven and a half times the amount deforested before 1978.[11]

Divino Araujo was part of the human wave that swept north. He left Brasília and took the Cuiabá–Santarém highway, stopping seven hundred miles north of Cuiabá in Alta Floresta. His romance with acerola was a small, but promising, experiment, a jet of water, perhaps, against the all-engulfing flames of Amazonian agriculture.

To drive to Alta Floresta, you take the highway north from Cuiabá, a grueling seven-hour journey over rutted and semi-paved road, and then cut west for another two pounding hours' drive. By air it takes slightly less than two hours. The twin-engine Fokker traverses some of the most promising agricultural land in Brazil, the *cerrados*. The slim line of the dirt top roads below slices through miles and miles of fields, brick red or rust-colored, freshly seeded and waiting for the winter rains. Occasionally the land is terraced and green with new corn, soya, sorghum, and pasture.

The original vegetation, where it survives, is mostly gnarled brown scrub, like rusting steel wool. The Peixoto de Azevedo River loops lazily to all points on the compass, wending north to the Teles Pires, which empties into the Tapajós, which finally decants into the Rio Amazonas, seven hundred miles away. Gradually the landscape of tamed fields and paved roads gives way to dense forest, seamed by occasional dirt roads and dotted here and there by lonely farmhouses. Just half an hour in the air out of Cuiabá, the landscape is already a near-solid carpet of forest, reaching all the way to Alta Floresta.

The town lies between the ninth and tenth parallels, well within the band of the humid tropics. In May 1976 a truck weighted down with bricks became mired along a muddy dirt track. The mud reached up to the chassis, and to get the truck unstuck, the bricks had to be unloaded. This became the spot where Alta Floresta began. Yet this town was no accident. Unlike many frontier villages, which erupted willy-nilly along the newly built roads to Amazonia, or the ill-planned government-sponsored settlement projects, which quickly spun out of official control, Alta Floresta was a totally planned town.

One company, run by a single man, was responsible for shaping this settlement. His vision, his purpose, his caprice and errors are stamped all over this community of farmers, merchants, gold diggers, and cattlemen that sprang up whole from the bush and jungle. Integration, Development, and Colonization (Indeco) was the brainchild of São Paulo developer

Ariosto da Riva. The company had painstakingly prepared the way. The land was surveyed by engineers, explored on foot by topographers, laid out on blueprints, and built brick by deliberate brick. Indeco bought up 2.5 million acres, divided it into small farmers' lots, and carefully selected the colonists. Almost all, like Divino Araujo, were from the south. Some had been displaced by mechanization. Others had lost their lands when the dam of the great hydroelectric station Itaipú closed over the Paraná River, flooding tens of thousands of fertile acres. All were traditional farmers.

The lots were subsidized but never given away, as in the grand populist land reform schemes of neighboring Rondônia. The da Rivas—Ariosto, two sons, and a brother-in-law, Sidney—built the town from the bottom up. They measured the settlers' lots and yearly took aerial photos to monitor deforestation and the growth of the town. Today Alta Floresta is both sprawling and orderly. In fifteen years the population grew by startling proportions. From a few intrepid settlers who braved the dense forests and mosquitoes and the heat, the population had reached two hundred thousand by 1990.

The da Rivas built everything: schools, streets, electrical generating stations, even the church. Fittingly the family name adorns the two main streets, several schools, and the gymnasiums. For several years Alta Floresta progressed, like a beacon in a fog of pioneer settlements, a struggling but solid community. Except for a few privileged pioneers and herdsmen, the people here were not wealthy; they rarely were in Amazonia. The main crops were the familiar coffee, cocoa, rice, beans, and corn—providing enough to get by on and not much more. Then everything changed. Gold was found in a nearby river, and overnight a huge encampment emerged. They called it Novo Planeta (new planet). Suddenly gold began to turn up everywhere, especially on the Juruena River and the streams threading through a town a hundred miles to the east called Peixoto de Azevedo. Quickly Alta Floresta and Peixoto de Azevedo became a Dickensian portrait of the Amazon: the first a place of order and a modicum of progress, the second a raggedy settlement driven by greed, desperation, and burning ambition.

But soon Alta Floresta also fell under the spell of El Dorado. Ten years after the gold rush began, the emblems of prosperity were all around: eight banks, a department store, two discotheques, and an airport with interstate flights several times a day. This was wealth that could come only from the subsoil, not from topsoil. But the effects in Alta Floresta were a mixed blessing. Money flowed. So did liquor. Farmers abandoned the servitude of agriculture for the adventure of gold. Prostitution, that inseparable institution of gold country, burgeoned. All manner of shops opened, selling everything from semiautomatic carbines to bikinis. Soon, though, many of the instant merchants were in trouble. Every wet season, when the waters rose, washing under the nuggets of gold hidden in stream bottoms, the nomadic prospectors, or *garimpeiros,* moved on, and the commerce of Alta Floresta went into panic. Ariosto da Riva had a long duel with the miners. Suddenly this company town was threatened by a rogue culture whose rhythms owed nothing to the growing season or the requirements of husbanding the soil and everything to the glint-eyed pursuit of instant wealth.

Herles de Mattos, an independent planning consultant who spent a decade compiling statistics on Alta Floresta, surveyed the booming town in the mid-eighties and warned that a day of reckoning would soon come—as soon as the gold wealth began to disappear. "Everything revolved around gold," de Mattos said. "Gold built many things that agriculture couldn't, but it distorted the whole economy." The planted area of cocoa, a staple from the beginning in Alta Floresta, plunged (from 12,500 acres to 5,700 acres), as farmers lit off for the gold digs. Then the gold sites began to give out near the town, and the placer deposits moved out in concentric circles to the surrounding villages and outposts. In time the gold merchants were in trouble. By late 1990, when I last visited the town, the shake-out had begun. Shops were closing down and merchants moving out.

Many townspeople believed this crisis was for the best. In a few years Alta Floresta would be back on track again. A few of those who had been lucky in the gold mines were now investing in cattle. The ebbing of the gold culture also opened the way to the return of agriculture, and many overnight prospectors were heading back to their fields. De Mattos predicted that Alta Floresta would soon be in a position to be a center of agroindustry, with meat-packing plants, sugarcane rum distilleries, and maybe even a chocolate factory. But so far these were still dreams, spun out over beer in mostly empty hotel bars. Alta Floresta's problems were far from over. Free of the tumult of the gold culture, the town confronted the daunting elements of the tropics, a national recession, and the more daunting jungle of government bureaucracy that hamstrung farming. Yet de Mattos, looking beyond the immediate crisis, believed Alta Floresta could be retrieved and remade. Now, at least, the feverish dreams of El Dorado had given way to a gentler pastoral one of living off the land.

Divino Araujo was a part of the new dream. He had been graduated as an agricultural extensionist and moved to Alta Floresta to help the small landholders and start a farm of his own. Divino and his Janethe were first hired on by the da Rivas to do some landscaping and set to work on restoring the green to this bare and dusty town. They had plenty to do. In its early years Alta Floresta's streets were unpaved, and traffic filled the air with a haze of choking red dust. In the rainy season the streets turned to bogs of red mud. The Araujos set about planting, and today the town is appointed with royal palms, orchids, great ferns, and trees from all over Brazil.

The idea of planting acerola was the work of an unlikely union. One of the conspirators was Paul Vaes, a Frenchman who had spent a good deal of time in tropical Africa, the Caribbean, and southern Brazil. Divino had the green thumb, and Vaes the wisdom of markets and industrializing agricultural wares. I met Vaes at Divino's house near the center of town. A man built like a barrel, he came puffing through the heat and extended a large, moist hand. His T-shirt, stretched tightly across his girth, was dark with sweat, and he seemed likely to collapse under his own bulk at any moment. But despite his occasional wheezing and his sixty years, Vaes appeared remarkably fit and even jolly in the punishing weather. He had a full head of hair the color of wheat and thick tinted eyeglasses that framed impish blue eyes. The voice, like his laugh, was vivace and rose to booming, as he told of his repeated adventures. He spoke a serviceable Portuguese, replete with the current slang, though pronounced with an indelible French accent, despite his twenty years in Brazil.

His story sounded like something out of one of the lower-brow Graham Greene adventures. Vaes is something of a self-made agronomist, and his specialty had long been making papain, the powerful enzyme from the papaya used to break down proteins. Over the years papain had been harnessed for a wealth of uses: to tenderize meat, to clarify beer, as a filler for bologna, and even for beauty products. He began his colonial duties in the French police force in Algeria, leaving just before the Battle of Algiers ended that chapter of empire. Later he met and married a Belgian and became a naturalized Belgian. He managed a papaya farm in the Congo for a large Belgian company, Boudart, until Patrice Lumumba had different ideas about who should run things in Africa. Vaes hung on for another year, until a group of young nationalists discovered this French-speaking white man in their bosom and hung him up by his forearms for a day, or so Vaes told it. He then swam the Congo River to Uganda and hopped a freighter back to Europe. From there he served a short stint in the Caribbean, based in Nassau, where he tended the papaya groves by day and the slot machines by night.

But at that time he found the Caribbean island entrepreneurs far more fascinated by the burgeoning drug trade than by papaya, so he decided to move again, this time to São Paulo, where a doctor friend had some farmland that needed professional attention. He managed an orange grove for several years, until he got the itch to go back into the papaya business. So he saved up his salary, bought a tract of land up in Mato Grosso, and moved to Alta Floresta in 1976, the same year Divino arrived.

Vaes, the town's first foreigner, felt welcome in the north country. But later he had a couple of scrapes with the bosses of this company town that have since become part of the folklore of Alta Floresta. The biggest run-in was over coffee. The Paranaenses who colonized Alta Floresta brought with them the habits from their native south. "They came with everything, kids, pigs, seedlings, and God only knows what else," said Herles de Mattos. The problem was the type of coffee: arabica. Da Riva at first encouraged the *colonos* to plant the familiar arabica, which fetched higher prices, but took poorly to the acidic Amazonian soils. Vaes told them of the error and, so the story goes, was practically run out of town for this indiscretion. The da Rivas and Vaes seemed to have made their peace when I last visited town. "You could say he is a colonel." Vaes smiled. A colonel is the traditional patriarch of the Brazilian backlands, who runs his territory with an iron hand and, often, an iron heel. "A gentle colonel," he amended.

Vaes had his own share of setbacks in Alta Floresta. He built a papain factory and began to buy the fruit from the surrounding small landholders. A number of farmers signed on and delivered him plenty of fruit—at least until the *garimpo* (gold dig) beckoned them to the promise of greater fortunes. The papaya crop was good, but the price disastrous. He survived until 1984, and then Africa, with its cheap labor and rich volcanic soils, took over the papaya market. "We managed to produce papain at forty-six dollars a liter, while the international market was paying eleven dollars and twenty-eight cents." He wagged his head back and forth. "Now there is a world glut of papain."

Vaes had learned about acerola in the Caribbean, and in

1984, when he shut down his papain factory, he began tinkering with the Antillean cherry. He teamed up with Divino, and the two of them began to plant acerola. In eighteen months the first trees began to produce. To their delight, they took well to Amazonia's acid soils, which have been the ruin of many traditional food crops, such as rice, beans, and corn. They approached a São Paulo factory, which immediately wanted five hundred tons for producing vitamin C tablets. Just to fill that order, however, they needed to have half a million trees in the ground. Divino set to work producing seedlings, selecting out the best plants, and reproducing them in his backyard nursery.

In a year they had distributed ten thousand seedlings to small producers. But in the Amazon agricultural evangelism is slow work. "No one believed this would work. We need to popularize the acerola," said Vaes. "The problem is, the small farmer is totally decapitalized." The reluctance of Alta Floresta farmers also lingered, despite some obvious advantages. One hectare (2.5 acres) can be planted with 625 acerola trees, and a family with 1,000 trees could earn the same amount as one with 30,000 coffee bushes. Unlike most other fruits and crops, acerola flowers and bears fruit all year long and needs little tending.

Work at the Araujos' started early. The pickers were out in the groves by sunup, and by eleven o'clock they had gathered two hundred pounds (the Araujos regularly hired children from a local orphanage, paying them about five cents for two pounds). Janethe Araujo, commanding her small kitchen, daily made two hundred pots of acerola jelly and fifty quarts of juice. They sold all they could produce at the local supermarkets and vegetable fairs. The "factory" was a small, family-run affair, and the production method low-tech but lovingly done. In place of a centrifuge, Janethe used a standard blender and filtered the pulp through a spaghetti strainer. Sugar was added and then mixed into a great copper basin used in Janethe's native northeast to make *rapadura*, a sort of hardened molasseslike sugar candy. The pan was heated by a wood fire built under a home-made brick oven.

She and Divino were perfect foils. While he was tall, deliberate, and quiet, she was petite, bubbly, and driven by a boundless nervous energy. I spent nearly two days with the family collecting acerola and stirring jelly and was exhausted long before Janethe's day was done. Janethe took time out only when the mail came bearing a brochure for the Brazilian book-of-the-month club. In Brazil, where television is supreme and authors go hungry, avid readers are a minority. In the Brazilian backcountry, where illiteracy is the rule and leisure time almost unheard of, to be reading at all was a rarity. In a house with three children, a dozen in-laws caroming, and a juice and jam factory to run, it seemed acrobatic. In rubber gloves and an apron, Janethe beat pitcher after pitcher of juice and talked late into the afternoon about potboilers and gothic romances.

Slowly, cautiously, Alta Floresta had begun to show interest in the Araujo enterprise. A handful of adventurous peasants had planted acerola both to eat at home and to sell to the Araujos. (One man even proposed a partnership.) And now Paul Vaes was hatching plans to retool his papain factory to make frozen acerola pulp for juice and, eventually, to freeze-dry it for vitamin C tablets. Despite his contretemps with the da Rivas, he had also struck a deal with Indeco to buy and distribute seedlings about town.

Of course, acerola is no panacea for the struggling small farmers of Amazonia. Even a global plague of head colds would not produce enough demand to handle the megatons of vitamin C that could be coaxed out of the soils of the Brazilian Amazon. On the other hand, if demand suddenly took off, the remotely placed rural communities like Alta Floresta—with poor roads and communications, no industrial base, and subsistence-crop farmers—would be hard put to meet industrial-scale production quotas. But this novelty crop had already served to point a way toward an alternative for this community of farmers, as it worked out its own strategy for survival in this corner of the humid tropics.

For the moment, Vaes figured, the only real catch to producing acerola on an industrial scale was a marketing scheme persuasive enough to win over chary growers and consumers to the charms of this strange fruit. But Vaes had some ideas. "Acerola is not exactly an aphrodisiac," he said, "but, well, it invigorates the blood. I am a happily married man, but at my age, you see," he said, leaning close now and hoisting a sandy eyebrow, "it's not much more than, you know, once every fifteen days." He lifted his chin knowingly. "With the acerola it's once every five days!" His laugh vibrated throughout the kitchen.

"ADVENTURERS, MADMEN, AND STARVELINGS"

> The fascination of the mine . . . invaded all of Brazil. The obsession was unending, spread among all the classes, like a collective madness.
>
> —Paulo Prado, *Retratos do Brasil*

> What wealth, Holy God! It is this whose possession drives the State to ruin.
>
> —Marquês de Pombal

The road east of Alta Floresta is a pitted but passable dirt track, flanked on each side by spreading fazendas. This was November, and the rains of the season Amazonians call winter were already falling, leaving the pastures thick and invitingly green. But after a few miles the pleasant landscape soon faded; in its place came a bare and scarred terrain that told a mute tale of pillage. This was gold country, and the signs of that ancient and chaotic vocation were all about. Every river was opaque with silt. Each stream bank was denuded, the bare mud left to crack under broiling sun and dissolve with each rainstorm. Here and there the land was pocked with man-made craters, full of still and fetid water, the color of wet cement.

This was the road to Peixoto de Azevedo, a decade-old gold rush town that had grown like a fever blister in the middle of Mato Grosso. I went with a colleague, Paul Knox, from the *Toronto Globe and Mail,* to see up close the place that had so often figured in the Brazilian headlines for its bounty and bustle and the legendary violence that goes with gold country.

Our driver, Ramiro, knew Peixoto well and was eager to show us about. Since 1979, when the first gold nuggets were unearthed there, he had frequently been called upon to ferry gold merchants, the occasional reporter, and even tourists to and from the *garimpo,* a placer mine or gold dig. Ramiro was elegantly dressed for his sweaty métier. A cherry polyester shirt with bloodred buttons flashed blindingly in the white sun. White denim jeans clung rather too snugly around the hips and bulging crotch, tailoring which seemed less defect than affect. Below, cream leather shoes culminated in acute points. A fat gold ring, a memento from his days in the *garimpo* on the Juruena River, was his only jewelry. In the fashion of some Latin men, the nail on his right pinkie protruded nearly an inch past the tip of his digit, standing startlingly erect when he drew on his cigarette. The whole portrait was somehow endearingly macho.

Ramiro had spent a few years amid the *garimpos* of Mato Grosso, somehow avoiding malaria yet finding a good amount of gold. In the end he had dug up enough to buy his own cab and three houses in Alta Floresta and yet another back in his home state, Minas Gerais.

After six hours of driving, we pulled slowly onto the wide main drag of Peixoto de Azevedo. If it had been laid with cobblestones, this might have been a fine, broad boulevard like those of the elegant seventeenth- and eighteenth-century gold rush towns of Ramiro's state. But Peixoto is part of the new gold rush, where towns are slapped together with brick, sheet metal, and clapboard, by people in a terrible hurry. Peixoto's main street was dirt and during the heat of midday veiled in a cloud of fine rust red dust. Flophouses, open-air vegetable stalls, greasy spoons, and tire repair shops crowded the way. Mules were parked alongside new four-wheel-drive pickups. There are no honest sports cars made in Brazil, but often simple sedans are done up with shiny magnesium wheels, dangling tassels, and haughtily raised chassis. Peixoto's steamy torpor was pierced from time to time by the apparition of one of these numbers, rumbling past with its motor low, radio high, wheels flashing. I imagined this sort of promenade happened with a certain frequency in Peixoto.

This was one of the largest of that special breed of village the Amazon has sired—outsize, loud, scruffy, and chaotic. Like so many frontier venues, it was overgrown and fairly bursting with migrants who arrived by the busloads. These were tough times in Peixoto. The gold, once bountiful, was scarce now, and though the migrants were still coming, they found slim takings. Each of the shops of gold merchants, which lined the side streets, was an identical and disconsolate portrait: A Formica countertop supported a precision scale and a pair of elbows, which in turn propped up a frowning face. Some were calling it quits. *"Peixoto acabou,"* said one idle buyer. Peixoto is history. Yet dim hopes of a sudden turn of fortunes still seemed to tease those who remained.

There is nothing exotic about these towns, which carom from prosperity to perdition in a flash. We know them from the chronicles of the last century's gold rushes, from Witwatersrand to the Klondike, from eastern Australia to Vancouver Island. Wherever and whenever the special ingredients of geology, poverty, and burning ambition mingled, another gold boom was born in yet another of the "waste places of the earth," as W. P. Morrell has written.

The *garimpeiros,* or prospectors, are nomads, wandering for hundreds of miles, wherever there is a *fofoca; fofoca* means "gossip" in Portuguese and in *garimpeiro* parlance refers to the newest gold find. Along the way they spawn boomtown after boomtown. They rise like mushrooms after rain. Some vagabond miner dips his pan in a stream, swishes the debris away to find a few grains of gold dust. He gets drunk and tells the world, and in short order, the world is on its way. In a week *garimpeiros* are streaming in from distant corners of the country. In two weeks a tent city has bloomed. In a month the tarpaulins are replaced by plywood planks, and then by solid brick and aluminum, as merchants, beer sellers, and gasoline distributors set up store. Bars and dance halls blossom, followed by prostitutes—and closely on their high heels, the pharmacies. There is a book still to be done on the pharmacy in the frontier zones.

Since at least the times of Eureka Stockdale, who organized the Australian claims takers, gold prospectors have been viewed through the gauze lens of romance. Like the hunters and trappers of the Canadian west or in the east of Russia, the gold diggers are painted as the living, pulsing symbol of man's contest with nature, the vanguard of defiance against government ordinance, and the seed of a rough backlands democracy. Such visions inspired the frontier paeans of the likes of Frederick Jackson Turner and Brooks Adams, enriched by legends down through the decades, tumbling finally into the alluvium of popular imagination. In Australia, in fact, the rabble of gold prospectors who rallied behind Stockdale were instrumental in the founding of that country's powerful Labour party. Thanks to the pilgrims of the two feverish American gold rushes, in 1849 and 1857, California and Oregon were peopled and secured as U.S. territories. Likewise, the prospectors who swarmed to Vancouver Island and were whipped into an orderly society by the firm hand of James Douglas successfully occupied and defended that important territory for the emerging dominion of Canada.[1]

Yet there has always been a terrible toll to these gold booms. Aborigines have been pushed off their land, murdered, or pressed into service. Until African slaves arrived, the Indians of central Brazil were captured and forced into the mines to labor for the Portuguese gold merchants during Brazil's seventeenth-century gold rush. John Hemming, in *Red Gold,* his first volume on the embattled Indians of Brazil, says that very little is known of the fate of the Indians whose lands were invaded in the seventeenth century by the gold prospectors of Minas Gerais. The only certainty is that the ones who escaped forced labor had to flee from the miners' mob, which gutted their forests, despoiled their streams, and flushed out fish and game.

Next to the hunt for spices, the getting of gold has been vital to the shaping of most frontiers, starting with the greatest one of them all, the New World. Indeed, Columbus was never one to let discovery get in the way of acquisition. "The islands are very green and fertile, and the breezes are very soft, and it is possible that there are in them many things, of which I do not know, because I did not wish to delay in finding gold, by discovering and going about many islands. . . . I cannot fail, with the aid of Our Lord, to find the place whence it comes."[2]

Peixoto de Azevedo and the dozens of other gold towns and camps that have cropped up all over the Amazon Basin are fruit of Brazil's second massive gold rush. The first was touched off at the tail of the seventeenth century, when the *bandeirantes* of São Paulo stumbled upon gold in the hills of Minas Gerais (general mines). The discovery came none too soon, for the sugarcane plantation economy was flagging before competition from the highly mechanized mills of the Caribbean. Soon word of the gold veins in Minas Gerais had raced to Rio de Janeiro and across the Atlantic to Lisbon. By the beginning of the 1700s the world's biggest gold boom was under way, drawing adventurers, financiers, and finally settlers in tow. The population of that severe and mountainous terrain grew from a few scattered souls in 1700 to thirty thousand three decades later and half a million by the century's close. Towns like Ouro Prêto (black gold), Diamantina, São

João del Rei, and Mariana became the seats of fabulous wealth, appointed with rococo art and resplendent with imported luxuries.

Gold drew adventurers farther into the interior. Some four thousand men poured into western Brazil, near Cuiabá, in 1718, when gold turned up in the Paraguay and Cuiabá rivers, and the old river entrepôt grew to seven thousand people in less than a decade. Goiás, in central Brazil, was the next gold town, booming from the moment the first nuggets were unearthed in 1725. So alarmed was the Portuguese crown with this mad rush to the interior that Lisbon passed an edict in 1730 seeking to curb the advancing gold front, which was draining agriculture of its labor force. With all this burgeoning treasure, Portugal hastened to spread its kingdom by way of capitanias (provinces) throughout the empty interior. It also tried to control the gold boom by issuing mining permits, favoring wealthy financiers who had large numbers of slaves. This immediately stimulated clandestine prospecting, and soon Lisbon was fighting a rearguard action against massive contraband.

It was the gold of Minas Gerais that sustained the Brazilian mining boom. The take was spectacular, thirty-two million ounces in a century, or an estimated 80 percent of the total world supply. But neither the Brazilian magnates nor the Portuguese crown knew how to convert treasure into wealth, and the gold bounty was squandered on leisure, ornaments, and frivolous imports. A lopsided trade pact with London, the Treaty of Methuen, didn't help matters. By its term, Lisbon committed itself to buy British manufactures in exchange for Portugal's farm produce and wines. The result was a gaping trade deficit in London's favor, which the Portuguese crown promptly paid off dearly, in gold. "Brazilian gold mined by African slaves financed English industrialization" is the old but accurate saying for the first Brazilian gold rush. Historian E. Bradford Burns even concludes that per capita income during the Brazilian gold cycle was, in the end, actually lower than during the previous period, when plantation agriculture reigned.[3]

Today, virtually everywhere, the mass gold rushes have become the stuff of dusty museums. South Africa, Canada, the Soviet Union, and the United States long ago left behind the pick, pan, and sluice table. Today gold is gotten mostly by geologists and engineers wielding computers, satellite photographs, fine chemicals, and advanced degrees. In the Brazilian Amazon, however, new gold strikes are stirring forgotten history. A century after the assault on the Klondike, the Amazon forest is the setting for one of the world's most massive gold rushes, maybe one of the last. All these historical themes—the boom, the contraband, and the skewed rural economy—echoed like a leitmotif two centuries later in the Amazonian gold rush.

Under much of the two million square miles of Brazilian Amazonia run ample strata of Precambrian rock, the most ancient and mineral-rich of the earth's layers, dating from one to four billion years ago. Slowly, after millions of years of erosion, the Brazilian Shield rose, virtually unperturbed by volcanic thrusts, glaciers, or faults. The steady work of tropical weather, leaching, and decay gradually left exposed and accessible to humans large concentrations of some of the most valuable materials known: iron, manganese, nickel, petroleum, diamonds, emeralds, niobium, bauxite, cassiterite, and especially gold. Although Brazil's current annual production of about ninety tons represents less than 5 percent of total world gold output, it has increased dramatically in recent years (thirteenfold from 1970 to 1990). What is more, the finds, especially in Amazonia, are only just beginning to be plumbed while output in South Africa, Canada, and the United States is beginning to decline.

Thanks to nature's unfailing clockwork, these riches are constantly and abundantly replenished yearly when the warm weather melts the snows of the Andes and the rains of the wet season "awaken a thousand streams," in the words of Norman Gall. The waters swell and tumble east, into the rain forest, disgorging the minerals into the gravelly riverbeds, banks, and deltas of the Amazon Basin.

Across the Amazon Basin, *garimpeiros* have scattered in search of these riches. Thousands work the muddy Madeira River, the Amazon's largest tributary, where they brave the violence of the currents, and of fellow workers, to dive for bits of gold buried in the muddy bottom. Claim stakers work the alluvial deposits of more than 427 placer mines along the Tapajós River, in Pará State. In 1991 miners and government officials had counted over 1,850 gold digs in Amazonia and 1,000 air-strips carved out of the jungle.

No one has a precise figure, but at the end of last decade the National Department of Mineral Prospecting estimated there were 290,000 *garimpeiros,* or free-lance prospectors, working in Brazil. Prospector organizations, which are often at odds with the government tallies, inflated the number to a million or more. (The Union of Garimpeiro Associations in the Legal Amazon [Usagal] claimed that 1.3 million *garimpeiros* were working northern Brazil in 1991.) Counting those who depend on the prospectors, the *garimpo* population would soar to as many as 4.5 million.

Some of these *garimpeiros* are small-time entrepreneurs, who, like the grubstakers of the Old West risk their money and sav-ings on a distant shot at future riches. The vast majority are the poor and the desperate, refugees from the drought-stricken northeast or the sated city slums who are trying to find gold because they have nothing to lose. A few become rich, buy farms, settle down, and support families. Most others remain poor but keep trying anyway, against all odds.

They are a little like the lonely pioneers Claude Lévi-Strauss encountered half a century ago, strewn along the path of Ron-don's telegraph line in the lonely outback of Mato Grosso and Rondônia—a band of "adventurers, madmen and starvelings . . . swept into the interior on an impulse of high enthusiasm, only to be abandoned, forgotten, and cut off from all contact with civilization."[4] Yet that may be only half the portrait. The British anthropologist David Cleary, in a doctoral thesis that became a book, *Anatomy of the Amazon Gold Rush,* takes careful stock of the Brazilian gold country. After spending two years researching Amazonian *garimpos,* Cleary found that the *garimpeiros* are neither fearsome desperados nor hapless victims but are instead hardworking laborers making calculated gambles.[5]

Much has been written in Latin America of the blooming of the informal economy, as a likely safety valve for the unemployed and underemployed urban workers as well as a font of entrepreneurial creativity in a bureaucracy-bound marketplace. The *garimpo* is, indeed, an irregular economy, yet it is more than that. Most *garimpos* spawn an entire informal society and culture. Laws against theft, claims jumping, and violence are already on the official books, but the law keepers are generally assigned to remote posts, or else they cannot be bothered with the dirty work of regulating life in gold country. In the absence of recognized authorities, they have been forced to rely upon their own devices and build their world from the dirt upward. Their world turns more on unwritten, often unspoken codes of work and of honor. Still, this is no perfect frontier anarchy. The lack of a mediating force, such as the police or an impartial and reliable justice system, leaves most of these gold societies in the hands of the powerful and the wealthy.

One day in 1979 Genésio Ferreira da Silva, rolled around a few mottled bits of dirt in his palm and thought he was a rich man. Some say a farmhand had stumbled on the gold. Other stories have it that Ferreira had hired the prospectors. Whatever the truth of the matter, in gold country, events take on their own, lightning volition. In a matter of weeks Ferreira's farm, in southern Pará, was overrun by a stream of *garimpeiros* who eventually numbered eighty thousand men. They were to take this land, the Serra Pelada (bare sierra), and make it a hole larger than the Orange Bowl. They were the protagonists in the single largest *garimpo* in this century. Ferreira got nothing in the end but trespassers. So raucous was this gold rush that Brasília even expropriated the part of his farm that harbored this wildcat gold dig in the eastern Amazonian state of Pará.

Serra Pelada has furnished us with the enduring images of the Amazon gold rush: Wood and rope ladders snake down the man-made canyon, where men and boys hack away at the little blocks of claims. Blacks, whites, Indians, and swarthy caboclos work side by side. Some are physicians and lawyers; others, illiterate and unemployed. In Serra Pelada they briefly become equals in the democracy of dirt, a uniform of mud cloaking them from hair to the rubber sandals. Parity ends at the cashier, as the *garimpo* is a complex and hierarchical society, where a moneyed few are in command and the many toil for salaries, day wages, or percentages. Yet even though most will stay poor, the *garimpeiros* of Serra Pelada are diehard individualists. They, not the *donos* (mine bosses), dictate work schedules, and the prospectors can pick up and move on whenever they want. It may seem a paltry freedom, but the *garimpeiros* are far freer than their peers working the farmers' fields or the assembly lines. Still, their work is grueling. The lot of them descend into the gaping pit to dig and scrape and to rise again, laden with bags of earth and rock debris, in labor that recalls the cruelty of an apocalypse by Bosch.

Mining companies, which have often seen their claims overrun by *garimpeiros,* charge that the latter are the scourge of mining. They accuse them of skimming off the best ore, leaving uneconomical deposits behind. Their trade, so goes the mining mogul's lament, is closer to pillage than extraction. Once again Cleary challenges that myth.[6]

Vivid as it is, the primitive scene at Serra Pelada is more the anomaly than the rule in Amazon gold country. In the *garimpo,* conditions are almost always rude and harsh. But lately the business has grown far more sophisticated. Diesel engines run pumps that suction water out of rivers and jet it against the ore-streaked embankments. The debris is suctioned up and run through a sluice table, passing one, two, three times, if necessary. In the end, Cleary says, the gold traces that may still be left behind are not much more abundant than those left in the tailings of the industrial mining operations. Far from being a parasitic trade, *garimpagem* has become a "formidable competitor" to the industrial mining sector and "emerged as an extremely effective form of gold prospecting."[7]

In truth, the mining companies have just as often muscled *garimpeiros* off goldfields as the other way around. *Garimpeiros* have always been the ones to find and produce the vast majority of gold in Brazil. In 1990 authorities reported that *garimpeiros* were responsible for producing fully sixty of the ninety tons of gold found in Brazil. In 1991 the mining companies had gained ground, but *garimpeiros* still accounted for forty-seven of the estimated year-end total of eighty-four tons of gold produced in Brazil. (However, the decline in production by prospectors was expected to continue in the years ahead—a sign that the great Brazilian gold rush may be dying out.)

For all the efficiency, the *garimpo* technology is, surprisingly, much the same as it has been for centuries. The principal tools are: the pan, a conical metal disk that looks like a slightly flattened wok; the sluice table, known locally as *cobra fumando* (smoking snake), which comes in a dozen versions, in place of the sheepskins (the golden fleece) used in ancient times on the Black Sea to trap gold particles; and, the most essential ingredient, water, for washing the mineral ore away from the debris. Lately methods have become more sophisticated. The internal-combustion engine has been added to pump water through hoses, to blast away the stream banks that imprison strains of gold.

On many deeper rivers, *dragas,* or great barges, equipped with huge motors and pumps, are utilized. On the way to Peixoto we boarded one elaborate barge, a two-story affair, with a giant engine room, a web of hoses, a built-in kitchen, and even an air-conditioned bedroom suite. But none of this equipment is so sophisticated that an illiterate peon couldn't operate it or break it down and set it atop a pack mule. Cessnas, Piper Cubs, and the sturdy Brazilian twin-engine Bandeirantes are the pack mules of the Amazon, flying *garimpeiros* and their supplies in and out of the most remote gold digs. The transistor radio brings the gold quotations issuing from the London Stock Market. Direct-dial telephone, available in even the most forlorn of gold towns, connects these men to family and friends all over Brazil.

But as in the eighteenth century, the new gold rush is fraught with contradictions. Once again gold diggers are leading the way in the renewed Brazilian thrust into a rugged frontier—a kind of raggedy vanguard of a great popular migration. Yet with the *garimpeiros* have gone price-gouging merchants, diseases, conflicts with indigenous groups, and a social order maintained by the barrel of a gun. Contraband is again rife, and once again Brazil faces the dilemma of watching vast treasures turn into someone else's wealth. Despite a policy to price *garimpo* gold at the international market level, contraband still flourishes. Some bootleg gold buyers still prefer to run the risks of avoiding taxes by sneaking the gold over Brazil's many borders. Uruguay, which has no gold mines, registered exports of thirty tons in 1990.

The social costs are not so hidden. Some Indian groups, like the Kayapó of the Xingu region and the Mundurucú of the Tapajós River, have actively participated in gold digging and seem to have worked out a modus vivendi with this tumultuous trade. (The Kayapó even charge royalties for the twelve hundred *garimpeiros* working placer mines on the Maria Bonita.) Yet others, like the Stone Age Yanomami, the tribe of nine thousand Indians whose lands sit upon some of the richest gold and tin deposits of South America, have been besieged by illegal miners. At one point, in 1989, as many as twenty thousand *garimpeiros* (some claimed there were as many as forty-five thousand, though that figure appeared to be exaggerated) worked finds on the Yanomami lands. The result has been a proliferation of the white man's diseases—malaria, syphilis, tuberculosis—that claimed thousands of Indian lives.

Yet here again the portrait of ruin and ghost towns is incomplete. Even after the bust, Brazil's first gold cycle left behind more than gilt memories. Minas Gerais, though old and crumbling in parts, is dotted with old gold towns that are thriving communities. Industrial mining has taken over in some areas, while farming, commerce, and industry have spread to others. The gold of Cuiabá quickly vanished, but the town remained and, with 750,000 inhabitants, is today the third-largest city in the Brazilian Amazon. The spectacular wealth of Serra Pelada, which produced thirteen tons in 1982 has slowed to a trickle, but the nearby town of Marabá remains and grows at a mind-boggling rate. In many areas the *garimpo* continues to exist alongside other forms of economic activity.

A visit to the Brazilian gold country is an immersion in this maelstrom. All the ingredients are there: the violence and the vigor, the ingenuity and moral blindness, the rape of nature and the entrepreneurship. Cruelty rubs up against bonhomie, and the absence of written laws makes for surprising deeds of honor and decency, but also episodes of swift, brutal justice.

By the time we arrived in Peixoto, the *garimpo* had moved to well beyond the town limits, so we left the din and dust of main street behind. A few miles past the center, by a long wooden bridge, three men stood thigh-deep in a pool of opaque brown water. One man held the end of a thick hose under the muddy water while a second struggled to secure another hose that writhed like a livid serpent as water gushed out of its mouth. A diesel engine provided the counterpoint, popping and gurgling as the men wrestled with their tasks. The jet of water bit into a fifteen-foot stream embankment, which disintegrated like sand dunes under a breaker. A third man stood by surveying the operation. He was gaunt and caked with mud, yet somehow compellingly authoritative as he stood, arms akimbo, surveying the excavation.

This man acknowledged his visitors with a nod and, in a

touching sartorial gesture for these rude environs, signaled for a blast from the water hose to make himself presentable. He then scrambled up the steep embankment. Dionísio Francisco Gecazoni was fifty and as thin as a twelve-year-old boy. Sinewy arms and elbows protruded from large short sleeves. His hair was the color of sand, and his face rouged in the cinnamon silt from the fosse he had been working. His smile revealed a troubled landscape, made more of space than teeth.

We all were a bit apprehensive at first. After all, in gold country strangers often mean the law, the environmental inspector, the claims jumper, or just plain *malandros* (ne'er-do-wells). Yet as so often happens in the Brazilian countryside, guardedness melted away to a gracious reception, belly laughs, and, predictably, a colorful biography. Gecazoni was the grandson of an Italian who late in the last century had migrated to Santa Catarina, in the far south of Brazil. There he worked as an auto mechanic until he hit the glass ceiling of circumstance imposed by a rigidly cast urban society. "There," he said succinctly, "whoever made it made it." The rest knuckled under and took what was left over or, like him, got out.

But Gecazoni didn't seem to see himself as an exile. "Here we came for adventure. Even though it's dirty work, it's my work." The thin man's eyes began to warm as he spoke. And his story lapsed into the braggadocio of the frontier. "Didn't catch too many malarias." He frowned with effect. "Only about ten!" He loosed a wide, gap-toothed laugh that shook his entire bony frame.

Gecazoni came alone to Peixoto de Azevedo, sending for his wife and seven children only fifteen months later. He did well, at first, turning up 300 to 400 grams (10.5 to 14 ounces), working three pairs of machines. Then along came Fernando Collor de Mello and a stinging monetary policy that confiscated bank accounts and money market funds amounting to close to 80 percent of the country's currency. The idea was to stanch the hemorrhage of cruzeiros that fed the country's inflation rate, edging toward 80 percent a month, when Collor took office in March 1990.

The Collor plan helped stun, but not kill, inflation at first, but the scarcity of cruzeiros forced those holding gold and dollars to cash in. Never in Brazil—perhaps in the world—had hard currencies gone so soft so fast. Suddenly gold and dollars were trading at half their purchasing power the day before. As yesterday's wealth suddenly turned into today's loose change, miners poured out of the *garimpos* and into Cuiabá. Alta Floresta, Peixoto de Azevedo, and dozens of other gold country towns.

(A year later Collor's policy began to falter. Monthly inflation crept back up to double digits, driven in large part by free-spending state and local governments, but also by Collor's failure to streamline the outsize bureaucracy. With prices heading skyward and his credibility toward the floor, Collor, in the fashion of so many presidents past, tore up the script and started again. Collor II, as this plan was called, resorted to something the young president said he never would turn to: a price freeze. The "desperate tool of weak governments," Collor had called it during his fiery campaign.)

Despite the stumbling, Collor remained remarkably popular in the Brazilian interior, known for its poverty and near-total abandonment on the part of the government. Even in gold country, where fortunes melted overnight before artificial exchange rates, Collor enjoyed surprising support. "Something had to be done," said Gecazoni. "You put money in the bank to buy a machine, and the next day the price had doubled." He was still faithful to the flagging president. "I lost a lot of money; everybody did. But I voted for him. I'd vote for him again," he said firmly.

Gecazoni may survive the government, but not the vagaries of geology. The rich surface deposits had begun to give out; his weekly take of 300 to 400 grams was down to 80 or 90 grams (2.8 to 3.2 ounces), barely enough to keep the diesel pumps and the work crews running. Of three pairs of machines, only one now remained in operation. The diesel engine still rumbled away, but a kind of torpor had settled over his encampment. In his "home," a lean-to capped with a perforated sheet of black plastic, a man with malaria was wrapped up in a hammock, taking saline solution through an intravenous tube and sleeping out the fever. Gecazoni's wife, a sturdy woman with jet black hair and a brilliant gold front tooth, scraped leavings of lunch—a crust of rice and beans—from a blackened pot.

The scene did not evoke an image of success, but Gecazoni seemed to take a long view. Though *garimpeiros* are notoriously closemouthed about the exact extent of their wealth (until they blow it all in the nearest bar and brothel), he let on that he had found enough gold to buy a house in Guaratuba, a port on Brazil's pleasant southern shore. He also said, when asked, that yes, he was proud to be a *garimpeiro,* though he seemed a bit alarmed at the ruin his trade had wrought. He surveyed the landscape around his tent, of dunes of sand and piles of detritus from the mine excavations, appointed by fetid pools of water. "It's a crime, isn't it?" he said. "This here"— he lifted his chin at the wasteland around us—"this won't produce anything anymore."

Gecazoni also had some thoughts about mercury pollution, that most insidious threat of the gold rush. Gold miners use this heavy metal to separate gold from the debris dredged up from gold-laden stream bottoms. The gold, gravel, and sludge are generally poured into a bucket containing liquid mercury. The mercury binds the gold, and the lighter debris is poured off. The *garimpeiros* then burn the amalgam in a simple crucible, evaporating the mercury and so freeing up the gold particles. Roughly one ounce of mercury is needed for every ounce of gold. But little care is taken in this process, and much of the mercury escapes into the streams as quicksilver or, worse, as vapor, entering the lungs of gold prospectors or dissipating into the atmosphere.

The vaporized mercury falls with the rains, now as a super-concentrated compound called methyl mercury, which is a hundred times more toxic than the quicksilver. The methyl mercury seeps into plants and streams and is ingested by fish, which eventually are consumed by humans. The metal accumulates in the bloodstream and eventually attacks the nervous system. Researchers are investigating the extent of mercury poisoning in the Amazon, but in some areas scientists have tested hair and urine of riberine populations and found twenty times the safe levels of mercury. Though no one has exact numbers, researchers have estimated that in the last twelve years some twelve hundred tons of mercury have already been dumped in the rivers and streams of the Amazon. Some scientists believe this could turn the gold sites in the Amazon into a tropical Minamata. In that industrial Japanese city, of course, the dumping of thousands of tons of mercury-laced industrial waste by an acetalhyde synthesizing plant fouled the bay, provoking forty-seven deaths and thousands of illnesses. The Brazilian government, in a ham-handed display of authority, passed a law banning the use of mercury in gold prospecting. However, the idea of policing half a million or more *garimpeiros,* who dig up sixty tons of gold a year, was a total fantasy.

In an unprecedented venture a major Brazilian gold buyer, Goldmine Foundation, together with Brazilian scientists, launched its own cleanup campaign. The idea was to install exhaust and mercury recovery equipment—called retorts—in *garimpos* throughout Brazil. Though the campaign had just gotten under way in 1991, the Rio de Janeiro-based bank hoped to attract international lenders to finance the purchase of the equipment (each retort unit costs about $240) and an educational program to reach the tens of thousands of *garimpeiros* in the Amazon. It seemed a staggering task, one that ecological groups might balk at. It would be hard to imagine Greenpeace or the World Wide Fund for Nature assisting this unruly trade, which has so often meant intrusion onto Indian reserves and the spoliation of land and waterscapes.[8] Yet eliminating the threat of mercury poisoning would seem to be a vital step in avoiding a potential tragedy. And in these times of ecological choler the initiative seemed a brilliant stroke of enlightened self-interest for a company whose very lifeblood was Amazon gold.

Gecazoni told us he had given up the use of mercury for sand, a special kind of sand, it seemed, which he claimed worked even better to draw gold away from the gravel and dirt particles. Perhaps he had stumbled on some miracle remedy. (Geologists everywhere agree that there is really no viable substitute for this heavy metal, which readily binds the loose particles of gold.) His answer smacked less of backcountry chemistry than a sophisticated awareness of the agenda of the ecological decade. It was the makers of that agenda who were increasingly scrutinizing the predation of Amazonia of late, and Gecazoni's class of laborers was feeling the heat.

Did he want his sons to follow in his trade? "Ah, no." He smiled. "That's the last thing we could want." Gecazoni took a last look around the ruined land, waved a heartfelt good-bye, and clambered back down into the pit with his workmen and the growling diesel machines.

If this pair of machines and their trio of workers caused surprising damage, the scene on the sandy terrain a few miles down the road was difficult to comprehend. High on a bluff, one of the rare elevations in this monotonous flatland, one had a good idea of what had happened. Off to the distance, a deep blue line of rising earth massed on the horizon like a great frown. This was the Serra do Cachimbo, a twenty-three-hundred-foot escarpment that traversed much of the central Amazon Basin.[9]

In the foreground, *garimpeiro* huts, covered with the same flapping black plastic wrap, punctuated the raw beige earth. The goldfield was a shallow crater of sand and mud, like the bed of a recently dried-up lake. All about were trios of men with their pairs of diesel pumps, spread out like a heat rash. They worked on an abandoned cattle ranch, owned by a São

Paulo farmer, who had given up ranching for royalties. Now that his herds had extracted all the nutrients out of the topsoil, the *garimpeiros* were busy ravaging what was below. He pulled in 10 percent of the gold take from this arrangement.

Just three decades ago this place was part of the traditional hunting and gathering grounds of the Kreen Akrore Indians, a prelithic people who were practically unknown to white society until the 1960s. After thirty years, and the discovery of gold, there were no signs of the Kreen Akrore. What remained of them had fled deep into the Brazilian hinterlands. The nomadic tribes of gold country and their growling pumps and smoking snakes had seen to that.

After a pausing climb up the steep bluff, a man in shorts and rubber thongs stood beside us now, and we watched together the terrible industry under way below. His shirt, a wisp of a thing, hung loosely over an indefinite frame, and the eyes were yellowish, from hepatitis, perhaps, or maybe just another bout of malaria. A short conversation revealed his occupation: He drove a frontloader for a *garimpo* boss, from dawn to sunset, scraping up mine tailings for a second filtering for gold remnants. "I didn't used to have the body you gentlemen are looking at," he said. He didn't gesture to his gaunt frame but looked straight ahead. He seemed not so much ashamed as astonished by his condition. "When I came here, a year ago, I weighed seventy-five kilos [165 pounds]. I was a strong man." He looked as if he would barely weigh in at 145 pounds now, and all about him brown skin was giving way to sallow.

He didn't want to give his name. "The company said if we squeal to anyone that we're poorly paid, we'll be fired. And you can never know." He eyed us. "Here someone turns up dead by the roadside, and no one ever knows anything about it."

This man, what was left of this man, who would not give his name or look these strangers straight in the eye, had come to the Amazon from Piauí, the poorest part of the poor, parched northeast. He'd worked for thirty-three years on construction jobs all over the eastern seaboard until he heard from friends that the *garimpo* was "good business."

There, from the top of the rounded bluff, we stood together, surveying the fazenda of *garimpeiros* below, scratching away in trios as far as the eye could see. Two, four, maybe six pounds might still be urged out of that scarred earth, and the wealth of a lucky few would whet again a thousand dulled ambitions. But this man wanted nothing more of it. "Now I just want to get a bus ticket and to get out of here.

"For thirty-three years I punched the clock every day. You didn't earn much, but at least it was something. I always got by and even had enough to fill up the tank of my old car and still bring food home to the family. Here, no. It's not like that. Either they don't pay you, claiming they didn't find any gold, or they tell us to wait, and wait a little more. So we wait until we can't take it anymore. Then we go away."

We left him in his vigil on top of the bluff and drove down the bare slope, back through the goldfields, and out to the highway to Peixoto. On the way a knot of people had gathered at a house by the road, and they seemed excited about something. One man flagged us down. The crowd was mostly taxi drivers, and just an hour before it seemed that one of their number had been ambushed while driving in a quiet area at the city limits. The assailant had carefully chosen the spot, a rough stretch of road, where cars would be forced to slow down. There he had lain in wait. From nearly point-blank range the bandit had fired his shotgun at the driver's temple, killing him instantly, and started to make off with the car. However, he was surprised by another cabdriver, who had witnessed the whole scene and arrived in time to wrestle the man into submission. The assailant was now in custody, but passions burned, and lynching was on everyone's mind.

This time the coolest heads prevailed. But that had not always been the case in these parts. Though the story surfaced only months later, almost exactly the same time we passed through Peixoto, the adjacent town of Matupá was shaken by another hideous murder. Three unlucky *garimpeiros* had tried break-ing into the ranch of a wealthy *garimpo* boss. They were caught in the act and, in desperation, attempted to take two women and three children hostage. They were no better at kidnapping than robbery, and soon the farmhouse was surrounded by a mob, boiling mad.

Often in Brazilian backcountry—and not infrequently in the big cities—crowds like these have gathered and worked their awful justice. This is the uglier side of the coin of the self-regulating society that has often been described on the world's frontiers. Lynchings dot the crime pages of newspapers across the country. Though the police eventually showed up and arrested the criminals, they released the prisoners to a mob that had tailed them. Among the crowd were two city councillors, seven policeman, and a prominent local businessman. The "mob" of solid middle-class citizens and public servants took charge, and in short order, rough justice was done. The pris-oners were shot, kicked, pummeled, and finally doused with kerosene and set aflame. Even as they burned, their torturers sought to pry out a statement of repentance. It happened that on hand was an amateur photographer who got most of the grisly scene down on videotape. Terrified, he handed the tape over to a Catholic priest, who turned it over to a São Paulo television station. In January 1991, three months later, the lynching aired on national TV, to some fifty million viewers. "Just let us die in peace," one man moans on the air as his body is consumed in flames.

Ramiro, who had already informed us that this sort of crime was all too common around Peixoto, seemed less shaken than aroused by the news. "Maybe a story for you, huh?" On our way to Peixoto he had pointed out the stream named for the cabby who, a few years before had been murdered in a nearly identical incident and then thrown into the water with a stone tied around his neck. In his five years as a cabby, he contin-ued, nothing, *graças a Deus,* had ever happened to him. He had always taken care to take only those clients recommended

by the hotels in Alta Floresta. *Só gente boa,* he said. Only
good people. And suddenly it occurred to me that in the frontier that phrase was no idle tribute. *Gente boa* meant people
who won't rob you blind, shoot you in the head, and leave you
in the ditch to die.

The mayor of Peixoto seemed like a man who had little
stomach for grisly business. We found him at a filling station,
his sky blue Ford Del Rey, an expensive car in Brazil, mantled
ignobly in a cloak of fine red dust. The initial impact of three
strangers in an out-of-town cab must have rattled him, for he
seemed to tremble slightly as we talked. It was a tremor that
seemed to hint at secret trepidation—bad debts, unsettled scores,
dealings with those other than *boa gente*.

It was Saturday, so instead of visiting city hall, an annex to
a tire store, we crossed Peixoto's boulevard and pulled up plastic
bar chairs around a table at a dingy luncheonette. After a few
awkward but harmless questions and the fourth Antártica beer,
the mayor dropped his guard some. A pharmacist by trade, he
had been elected a few months before to the post of mayor.
By the standards of most any other land, Mayor Aniceto Bon-
Ami Roçante ought to have been basking in political glory.
Only three and a half years before Peixoto had won "emanci-
pation." This happens when a neighborhood or suburb out-
grows itself, turns into a city proper, and wins political and
administrative independence. This is a frequent rite of passage
in the Amazon, where entire towns spring up in the span of a
single dry season, explosions of clapboard, asphalt, and beaten
earth.

A little more than a decade before, Roçante explained, Peixoto de Azevedo was no more than a few ranches, stretching
out along the highway that had opened in the late seventies,
connecting the regional capital of Cuiabá, in Mato Grosso, to
Santarém, in Amazonas State. Then, in 1979, gold turned up
on a spread of bottomland, and soon the *garimpeiros* came
storming in from all corners of Brazil.

As long as there was gold, there was prosperity or at least

the hope of it. At first the *garimpeiros* pulled in fabulous fortunes, up to 1.5 tons of gold (52,500 ounces) a month, worth nineteen million dollars in mid-1991. Some three thousand pairs of pumps were blasting away at the riverbanks, turning clear streams to mud and filling the air with their diesel roar. Roçante moved from his home state of Paraná to Itatuba, farther down the highway toward Cuiabá, and in 1981 he moved farther north to Peixoto. On the frontier, and especially in gold country, social diseases make rich men out of druggists, so soon Bon-Ami and his apothecary became important institutions about town.

He served once as the appointed deputy mayor, taking over the top position when the mayor died. Later he won the first direct elections in independent Peixoto, just in time to take over a town on the skids. Not only had the town grown too large too fast, but most of the gold bounty had slipped through municipal fingers. The ore was spirited away as contraband, peddled elsewhere by the nomadic *garimpeiros* or was allowed to slip through the diaphonous tax nets. Only the problems remained. "For the first few years, the population doubled every year," said Roçante. "For the last several years it has grown twenty-five percent a year."

What does the town need? "Everything." He laughed at our question. And he began a litany. The six schools had 7,984 students enrolled, but another 8,000 school-age children were still outside the classroom. There was one hospital with twenty beds (thirty, if you counted the fold-up cots) for a population of 110,000. Six private clinics tended the spillover, but only for those who could pay their steep prices. Taxes still accounted for only 10 percent of the city budget; the rest came from federal handouts. And virtually all the money allocated for 1991 (about six million dollars) would go merely to pay the city's bills and salaries for the 178 people on the public payroll.

The city's finances were a shambles because its record keeping was a shambles. Statistics was a giddy guessing game in Peixoto. The census was out of date by ten years, an eternity in gold country, and tax and voting records were not much better. Everyone had his own wild opinion on the most basic of numbers. "To give you an idea," said Roçante, loosening up as his lament proceeded, "we have, officially, only seventeen thousand nine hundred inhabitants. But fifteen thousand people voted in the last elections." Collection of property taxes was, likewise, a disaster. "This is one of the largest counties anywhere in Brazil. Thirteen thousand eight hundred square kilometers," he said. (That number didn't sink in until I checked the atlas and found that Connecticut was slightly smaller, 13,520 square kilometers, or just over 5,000 square miles.) "And no one pays taxes. We have twenty-five-hundred-hectare [6,250-acre] fazendas that aren't even on the property registry.

"The federal government has to come in and inspect this situation. There are towns with a lot of 'maharajas' on the payroll. We've got to work." The mayor shook his head. "No one produces. We've got to go through these hard times." This was becoming familiar vocabulary in Brazil. Many people were embittered at the "abandonment" (a favorite word) by the federal government yet, at the same time, tired of those who looked only for government handouts. It was this rhetoric, especially the tirade against maharajas, the supersalaried and underworked public employees, that got Collor elected president in 1989. Collor may have failed to deliver, and maharajas continued to lord over the halls of government well into his term. But the message struck a resounding chord throughout Brazil.

As scruffy and wild and peculiar as Peixoto seemed, then, it was nothing so much as a snapshot of an ailing Brazil. Too much government here, too little there. An economy that swooned between boom and bust. A population adrift, the desperate and determined, patching together their lives out of the rubble left over after the collision of official promises and private dreams.

By late afternoon Roçante seemed to have shed all his initial timidity. He personally escorted us to our next interview, with a Bahian doctor who tended to the myriad infirmities that prospered in Peixoto. Malaria, of course, was rampant, despite the frequent blitzes of DDT. Three in ten patients tested at this clinic showed the parasites of malaria in their blood. There were dozens of cases of mercury poisoning; *garimpeiros* became routinely intoxicated after inhaling fumes from crucibles in which the metal was burned away from gold bits. Vomiting, dizzyness, and visual impairment were the first result. Madness, impotence, and death could follow.

Worse, however, were the numbers of cases of gastroenteritis, malnutrition, and hepatitis—the ailments of poverty, fed by open sewers, fouled water, and stunted opportunity. Then there were the classical maladies: syphilis, gonorrhea, and condyloma, as old as the oldest profession. By late 1990 two cases of AIDS had already been recorded in Peixoto. So it was that in a scant decade the symptoms of modern civilization had already rudely arrived on the frontier.

It was dusk as we left the Clínica Bahia. Roçante now escorted us to dinner. The night was almost cool, and the moon shone dully through a film of particulate matter. A faint breath of wind stirred the heavy air of downtown. Relaxed now, Roçante began to talk about his visions for Peixoto's future. He spoke with the iron conviction of someone who believed that improvement was not only possible but inevitable. It seemed he hadn't had the opportunity to spin out such visions, at least since the campaign. He spoke about chasing down tax scoundrels, streamlining the administration. He even predicted a great economic reckoning that the end of the gold boom portended. Like Alta Floresta, he predicted, the *garimpo* would die, and with it all the parasitic trades that fed off it. Then, perhaps, Peixoto could get on to the business of a progressive and decent society: farming, schooling, cattle raising, even reforestation. The bare and ruined land left by the *garimpos*, he said, would all be reforested one day with citrus fruit trees, which would in turn supply a juice factory, which would sell to cities near and far. If only the government would give a hand.

It was nearly 10:00 P.M. when we said good-bye. Only then

did we realize that the mayor of this city the size of Connecticut, who presided over 110,000 inhabitants, had spent the best part of his weekend pounding the dusty streets of Peixoto, escorting a couple of unannounced and demanding strangers. Roçante, it turned out, had recently separated from his wife and was lodged in a modest truck stop hotel. For the while, at least, the mayor would dream his dreams for Peixoto alone.

The next evening, back in the orderly comfort of Alta Floresta, another personality from gold country turned up at the Hotel Floresta Amazônica. His name, as much as he cared to give of it, was Santos. Ramiro had driven him to Peixoto and back in a single day, a ten-hour round trip. It was past 8:00 P.M. when they returned, and both men looked at once weary and happy as they settled down at the patio bar. Ramiro introduced us to his newest client, a representative from a major gold buyer, who had some urgent business in Peixoto.

This seemed to me a stroke of luck. Beyond the grumblings over bad prices and scarce ore, I had not yet gotten a clear idea of just what was happening in the Brazilian gold markets. I and Paul Knox of the *Globe and Mail* began to ply Santos with the usual questions. How much gold was being produced? Did the *garimpeiros'* union have the support of the miners? Who were the biggest buyers in Peixoto? The answers came back laconic and vague. Santos talked obliquely about renegotiating a loan to a buyer in Peixoto. At first I wrote this evasion down to tactics, the obligatory discretion of the high-ante trade that is gold dealing. Ramiro soon corrected me.

Santos, he whispered, was really a cop, moonlighting clandestinely as a debt collector. This was, he confided, a matter of some delicacy, and we weren't to let on that we knew. But Santos had already abandoned his wariness. His mission was to trace a buyer who was fronted money a year before to purchase gold in Peixoto but never paid it back. It seemed that the buyer had squandered the loan, worth 2.4 kilos (about 5 pounds) of gold, on property and automobiles. "He didn't even have an office to meet in, so we talked in a luncheonette." Santos chuckled.

It wasn't difficult to convince the debtor, however. Santos pulled out a blue nylon zippered *poché,* the sort that Brazilian men often tote over a shoulder. It made a clunk on the table. He opened it and tenderly removed a 9 mm Browning semiautomatic pistol, mat black with a dull brown handle. It was one of three guns he carried. But negotiations went smoothly, and no such persuasion was required. Santos came back with 2 kilos (5 pounds) of gold and a new $25,000 air-conditioned Volkswagen Santana. Goodwill must have overwhelmed him in the end because he even conceded the profligate a 300 gram or 9.5-ounce (or $3,850), debt discount.

The job done, Santos was jolly now and, despite the bone-jarring journey, in the mood to celebrate. So he drove us in his newly won climatized Santana, with Ramiro's yellow cab in tow, to the far edge of town and a bar called Saramandaia. This was a boîte, that local rendition of the French night spot which in Brazil can mean anything from the most innocent of discotheques to a brothel. The discreet venue and the throbbing neon sign pointed to the latter. This was the sort of place that always sprang up in gold country, built to relieve *garimpeiros* of the day's tension, and wealth, where too often passions turned ugly.

The ambience at Saramandaia seemed peaceful enough that evening, but Santos had brought his nylon *poché,* just in case. He flashed his police ID at the door so as not to pay the eighty-cent cover charge. The doorman seemed only mildly impressed and knocked off only 50 percent. Inside, disco, rock, and Brazilian lambada blared from a powerful sound system to a half-filled room. The crowd was a mixture of *garimpeiros,* ranchers, and drifters. A few couples danced, mostly older men with adolescent girls. A Brazilian-Japanese man who had had too much to drink did his own lurching solo, spinning around and around the circular floor.

Santos was not a dancer. He had more pressing matters to

tend and quickly found himself a young companion in a frilly
spandex tube dress. Politely he excused himself to repair to
the motel rooms, located conveniently behind the boîte. "Be
right back," he announced, and he was. A sort of blonde pulled
up a chair and proceeded to stare intently at Paul's neck while
Paul stared unshakably straight ahead. A lithe black girl with
a glorious Afro came up behind me and rubbed her fingers
through my hair. "Thin," she reported. "Want some of mine?"
She snorted a laugh, bent over, and shook her wealth of locks
in my face. Then she ran a hand down my shirtfront and
inquired, *"Cadê a maquinha quente?"*

"What?" I started.

"Where's the hot machine?" she snorted again, and broke
away.

It was really the jet black scorpion marching up the wall
towards the urinal that helped convince me I'd had enough of
Saramandaia and everything else about gold country. Back at
the dance floor, Santos was already yawning, Paul had out-
stared his suitor, so we filed out and into our small fleet and
roared back to the safety of the hotel.

REPAIRING RONDÔNIA

LET'S PAVE RONDÔNIA

—Sign along Highway BR-364

North on BR-364, a few miles out of Pimenta Bueno, the sawmill capital of Rondônia State, traffic slowed to a near crawl. The sluggish procession wasn't due to a bridge out, a flash flood, or one of the scenic cattle crossings where cowboys drive their herds across the asphalt. What waylaid the traffic on this November afternoon was craters. Cars, tractors, buses, and semitrailers formed a long line and, one after the next, descended gingerly into holes the size of small houses that pocked the Amazon superhighway. Some of the holes were dry and bare, reduced to the bare orange earth that underlay the asphalt and gravelly roadbed. Some were small lakes, filled with muddy water. The procession of vehicles crept in and out of these holes, like pack mules picking along a treacherous mountain switchback.

It was only six years before that General Figueiredo had snipped the inaugural ribbon and smiled for the cameras on the gleaming tarmac. Back then this spanking Mato Grosso–Rondônia highway, the "backbone of the west," was already living up to its propaganda pitch. Even before the pavement, the grated highway had become a fast lane for migration. In 1978, when the road was still a packed dirt track through a mostly jungle terrain, some twelve thousand migrants checked in at the vaccination post at Vilhena, the old telegraph station where in 1960 Kubitschek toppled the final tree blocking the way. They piled out of buses and trucks, lined up for a yellow fever shot, gave a brief interview with a migration officer, and then took a deep breath and plunged into the Rondônia frontier. Six years later, when the dirt top became asphalt, the same number of migrants were coming each month.

The settlers hailed from the south or the northeast, like Okies fleeing the Dust Bowl, whole families and their belongings piled precariously atop flatbed trucks called parrot perches. They were squat, hardy northeasterners, chased out by drought and dried-up opportunity. Two, sometimes three times a day the União Cascavel Company sent its buses on the seventeen-hundred-mile trip from southern Paraná, Divino Araujo's former home, to northern Rondônia, dispensing families of small farmers along the way. A good many were descendants of Poles, Germans, and the Irish, and they cut odd figures in this landscape of Indians and mixed-blood river dwellers. Many of them blond, some blue-eyed, and nearly all bewildered, these southerners climbed down from the buses and trucks and started making the jungle into a home.

They came often with little more than their clothes and a few garden tools, streaming into a territory whose map read almost like a frontier parody: Colorado of the West (Colorado do Oeste), Dawn of the West (Alvorada do Oeste), Skyscraper of the West (Espigão do Oeste), Black Gold of the West (Ouro Prêto do Oeste). Everything about Rondônia, the opportunities, the hardships, the land grabbing, the violence, spoke to this one point on the compass. The flood of migrants peaked in 1986—when, in twelve months, a staggering 167,000 newcomers entered Rondônia with a view to settling down—and then declined to a dull rush in the next few years.

In no small way they managed to settle and secure this Brazilian west. George Martine, a Brazilian sociologist and demographer who has spent years tramping through Rondônia, reported that the state, which had produced next to nothing beyond subsistence crops, by 1989 was contributing 7 percent of the Brazilian harvest of cacao and bananas and up to 3 percent of rice, beans, and manioc.

Yet the migrant tide quickly overburdened the land. These settlers soon alarmed the world with their destructiveness and their suffering. Martine says that in 1985 fully 42 percent of all cases of malaria in Brazil were recorded in Rondônia, with less than 1 percent of the national population.[1] Ill health and poor soils forced thousands of peasants to sell out and move on, often into the slum-choked cities of Porto Velho and Ariquemes. More and more, ranchers and speculators gobbled up the 100-hectare (250-acre) plots the government had handed out in what had only just been touted as the scene of "the greatest land reform program in history." The checkerboard paradise of small landholders was now reverting to a carpet of pastures and spreading soy plantations.

The forests fell with the fortunes of the ailing peasants. The peak years of migration also were the worst years of burnings in the Amazon, and the world began to take notice. Soon the World Bank was pressured into suspending its loan to the Brazilian government, for Brasília's failure to safeguard forests, watersheds, and Indian reservations. In 1985 the bank, which had lent five hundred million dollars for BR-364, did hold up funding, but already much of the damage was done.

In forty years Rondônia's population grew from a mere 37,000 in 1950 to just under 1 million in 1985, a startling 2,400 percent increase. By 1990 the population had climbed to 1.2 million and was growing still, despite the hard times for newcomers. But feeble soils coupled with epic bouts of malaria forced tens of thousands of small landholders to sell out or move on, slashing and burning their way deeper into the forests. In twenty-five years Rondônia had lost a Massachusetts and a half rain forest.[2]

By 1990 Brasília was strapped for funds, both foreign and

domestic. The great land giveaway that Figueiredo and his merry deed dispensers promoted had ceased. Even rudimentary maintenance had been abandoned. Now nature had taken over where the protests left off. The highway through the Brazilian west that had the world up in arms was falling quietly, dramatically, apart. A little more of it melted away with each day of rainy season. The billboards that were plastered all over the highway—LET'S PAVE RONDÔNIA—were meant as encouragement from the gung ho, development-driven state governor. To motorists negotiating the moonscape that had become BR-364, they must have read like a desperate prayer. By the end of this punishing decade Rondônia seemed less like a new frontier than a dead end.

A small nonprofit organization in the torpid river town of Porto Velho, twelve hundred miles from the Brazilian capital, was one group trying to turn things around in Rondônia. I found Iphae, the Institute for Prehistory, Anthropology, and Ecology, tucked away on the second floor of the fading powder blue and white colonial-style edifice of the Federal University of Rondônia. A security guard, in a miniskirt that was just longer than her holstered service revolver, shrugged off the torpor of her vigil and kindly led the way upstairs to a corner room. The door opened to a high-ceilinged office and an arctic blast from a growling air conditioner. The office's tenant, like its climate, seemed sorely out of place.

His solid six-foot-nine frame sprawled casually in a reclinable office chair, which protested slightly as he swiveled. He was surrounded by a small arsenal of computer technology—fax, a PC and a laptop, and a laser printer—that patched him into the rest of the world. A small refrigerator was jammed with seedlings of assorted tropical flora. Like a slow elevator, he rose to greet his visitors—myself and a fellow reporter—and reached down a story to shake hands. A billowing white shirt only inflated his stature. But if Roland Barthes were describing the picture, he might say the most remarkable thing about Willem Groeneveld was not his size but the pipe, a deep-bowled Petersen, fixed constantly to his mouth, and the crop of blond hair, combed skyward for another inch or two. Rondônia, where features are duskier and altitudes more modest, was altogether a strange venue for this Dutch ecologist.

When he was not lecturing abroad or coaxing a Jeep through some mudhole, Groeneveld, a tropical forest ecologist, could be found tending to this budding ecological institute—nongovernmental organization (NGO, in the lexicon of the environmental movement)—in Porto Velho, the steamy state capital and an old rubber boomtown. Iphae was founded in 1989 by a handful of eminent Amazon scientists, including the noted American archaeologist Betty Meggars. Groeneveld is the executive director. A recent recruit is Kimo (né Langston James Goree VI), a onetime professional clown and now a computer cognoscente. I first saw Kimo at his old vocation in the lobby bar of a hotel in Brasília, where delegates at a tedious environmental congress had repaired to resuscitate their speech-wearied spirits. In a routine he used to enchant kids at birthday parties, he kept a dozen Ph.D.'s spellbound as he deftly inflated and twisted long colored balloons into elaborate crowns, hats, vehicles, and a veritable bestiary of creatures, from snakes to a pregnant poodle. Kimo now tends Iphae's communications and data banks. Together, Groeneveld and his collaborators have made tiny Iphae into one of the best informed, and probably the most technologically sophisticated, of NGOs in Brazil. Their beat, Rondônia State, the size of Wyoming, occupies a special place in the Amazon disaster narrative. And no wonder.

Rondônia's settlers were agents in what had to be one of the most brazen experiments in frontier history. Nowhere in the Americas had there been such a massive, deliberate attempt to transform the local biota. In a region known for tubers, tree crops, and weak soils, the settlers imposed the intensive farm practices and demanding field crops of the temperate south. In the vocabulary of ecology, this was seed culture's collision with vegeculture. Rondônia's landscape heaved and complained. When the forest cover was slashed, topsoil bled away by the ton every rainy season. The soils, stripped of the vegetation, were deprived of natural composting and gave out after two or three harvests.

Agriculture in Rondônia had been a series of waves of cure-all crops. First the rotational, seasonal crops were promoted, and rice, beans, and corn sprouted all along the BR-364, from Vilhena to Porto Velho. But when the harvest was good, there was a glut; storage was poor, where it existed at all, and tons of this perishable produce spoiled every year. After three seasons these demanding crops had sucked all the nutrients from the patina of topsoils that covered most of the state, leaving the land virtually barren and farmers high and dry. From the beginning the preferred cash crop was coffee, but it could hardly compete with the plenteous harvests from fertile southern plantations, which enjoyed far easier access to markets and ports. Then came cacao; originally from the Colombian Amazon, by the mid-eighties it had spread all over Rondônia. The state map today is appointed with towns like Cacoal, Cacaulândia, and even Theobroma, the scientific name for cacao. But in Amazonian plantations cacao went the same way as domesticated rubber, falling prey to the myriad diseases that thrive in the saunalike conditions of the humid tropics. The worst was the witches-broom, a plant fungus which swept through the *cacaual,* wiping out as much as a third or more of each crop.

Likewise, the fortunes of small landholders washed away. Even when crops didn't fail, they fetched miserable prices at distant markets. Many began to wonder if farming Rondônia was viable at all. "Sometimes," Groeneveld admitted, "I look around and see all this ruined land, pasture but no cows, poor people everywhere, and I think 'What the hell am I doing here?' "

In Rondônia, as in many other regions of the Amazon, deforestation and the lack of technical assistance to farm communities went hand in glove. The rural extension agents were few, and their agencies underfunded. The environmental agency, Ibama, came to be known in many parts not as a counselor to the small farmer but as a cop. Visits by Ibama's field agents generally brought not assistance but dread and fines to the *colonos* strewn about the state.

Irací Quirina de Oliveira, the wife of a small farmer and herder in Ouro Prêto do Oeste, had nothing good to say about the agency. She was thirty-nine but looked fifty. Four children bunched around her in the pleasant, simply arranged three-room house of roughly sawn wood planks. Paper cutout snow-flakes quivered on the windowsill. An old Singer sewing machine stood in one corner of the bare wood-floor living room. Four photo calendars, with bright pictures of rural scenes, as well as a watercolor portrait of the family, were the only wall decorations. A "diploma" for literacy earned by one of her sons, Osvaldo, was proudly displayed. The house crowned a rolling plot of a hundred hectares (250 acres), where eighty head of cattle grazed.

The previous dry season her husband had set fire to an over-grown pasture to clear it of debris and prepare for reseeding. Cutting all of it down with scythes and machetes and clearing it by hand would have been brutal work. Irací's husband, Walter Batista, was already battling malaria, which he contracted "every ten or fifteen days," she said. "He carried his malaria medicine wherever he went." Besides, she explained, the original forest had been cut and cleared away years before, and all that was left was capoeira, the gnarled and useless second-growth weed and brush that spring up where the rain forest has been disturbed. But when two inspectors from Ibama pulled up at noon on that September day, together with two police-men, she knew trouble was brewing.

"They asked for the title to the lot and asked Walter to sign a receipt. It was for the fine. Five hundred thousand cruza-dos," she said. "We had to sell a calf to pay it," she said. The visit still puzzled her, and she looked down at the worn broad floorboards. "They didn't explain anything, just that fires were not allowed." She looked down again. "I don't agree with this," she said after a moment. "We have to burn the lot to clear it. If someone needs to work, why does the government get in the way?" Such stories could be heard up and down Highway BR-364.

One particularly dismal portrait of Rondônia was Cujubim, a government settlement project, begun in the mid-1980s. It lay at the end of a dirt road, about a hundred miles north of Highway BR-364. Children with parasols and peasant women balancing baskets of produce on their heads walked along the road's shoulder, stopping to stare when the rare car or horse and wagon passed by. "You're almost there. About an hour more," said one woman, shouldering a hoe, when asked directions for the town. "About five kilometers [three miles]." Here, not an hour's drive from the asphalt highway, was a different universe. Roads were mainly footpaths, and travel was reckoned by the hours, or days, it took to walk from one place to another.

Suddenly, one day in May 1990, a helicopter lowered down out of the sky and landed imperiously in the center of Cujubim. From its innards issued half the cabinet of Brasília. Out strode the agricultural minister, the health minister, the minister of infrastructure, the secretary of the environment, and the secretary of science and technology. Then came the Brazilian president himself, young, tanned, his shirt sleeves rolled halfway up his biceps, all energy and earnestness.

Collor had flown four hours from Brasília especially to visit this suffering community of small farmers. He surveyed the town and, like a candidate still on the stump, climbed atop a pickup truck and gave an impromptu open-air speech. "Friendly people of Cujubim," he began. He admired the fruit culled from the farms of Cujubim, frowned darkly, and then declared. "Now, about this lie that the land here is no good, that the earth is not fertile, I want to say the following. I come from the northeast, and nowhere there is the land fertile like this," he said defiantly. "I've never seen starfruit or pineapples this size," the president thundered. Collor went on, talking about the future and how things—health, land disputes, slumping prices—would get better. Mark my word, Collor bellowed. Cujubim was going to be a "model project," he vowed. "Keep me honest."

Had Collor bothered to read history, he might have dropped that speech for shame of having filched a script from the Age of Discovery. Back then, five centuries ago, Columbus and a host of navigators were busy gawking at such wonders from the New World and filling their dispatches with hyperbole. Behold Cuba, Columbus exalted, with its "trees and fruits of such marvelous flavor." The forests, he reported, seemed to "touch the heavens," and wafting on the breezes came "smooth scents of flowers and trees, the sweetest thing on earth."[3] Collor stopped short of the fantasies of mermaids, Cyclopes, men with tails, and the snouts of dogs. But his speech in Cujubim was a work of pure post-Columbian ecstasy.

Had he bothered to read the reports from the World Bank, he might also have curbed his enthusiasm. In the early 1980s, when the land reform agency Incra was laying out its tidy grid of planned settlements there, the bank had concluded that colonization on the soils of Cujubim might well be a debacle. Marketable timber was scarce, the soils were acid, and the top soil was thin—a depressing picture even by Amazonian standards. Scraped of the forests, this terrain would support one or two harvests before erosion set in and fertility gave out. Cujubim lay a hundred miles from the nearest market, at the end of a dirt road to nowhere. Malarial mosquitoes would breed and provoke an epidemic. Better the whole thing be scrapped, the bank recommended. In 1987 it even argued for the evacuation of Machadinho, a nearby town that mirrored Cujubim in misery and malaria.[4] Instead, Incra bulled ahead and handed out lots to 563 families and planned to settle 1,800 more. Dozens more families came on their own, on the thin hopes of securing a deed and access to government credit. The forests were cleared, roads scraped out, and the settlement suffered for years. Malaria became epidemic. Some 70 percent of the towns farm produce spoiled before reaching market. "We had nothing before," said one Incra official, Claudio Gil. Cujubim, after all, had been beset by years of malign neglect. "We had no lunch for schoolchildren. There was no doctor, no medicine, not even any serum for snakebites." Gil, who had been promoted to director of the Cujubim project after Collor's visit, though things were getting better now. The roads had been scraped and packed. A doctor made regular calls.

A survey around town told another story. The rural extension office had received no money in weeks from the state agricultural secretariat to distribute seeds to farmers. "We are practically paralyzed," said Riodemar Vieira Maia, the local extension worker. "We had to stop visiting farmers because there was no gasoline for our motorcycle." The Incra office had to take up a collection to pay for light bulbs and other basic supplies. Six months after Collor's visit, when I dropped into Cujubim's health clinic, a doctor finally had been assigned to the town. But even then the clinic registered dozens of cases of malaria every week, and more than two for every official town resident during the past six months. Even the improvements brought headaches. The newly scraped roads sent a green light to landless peasants and drifters. Some forty new families had followed the bulldozers into Cujubim.

"That was the most foolish thing the president could have said," said José Pinto da Silva, former head of the Rondônia agricultural planning agency, Iteron, speaking of Collor's bold proposals for Cujubim. "Only by importing energy at a tremendous cost will Cujubim become a model settlement."

The main street of this town was a dirt scar flanked by boarded-up houses and shops and an occasional charred tree stump. Around the central plaza was a ring of buildings, circled, it seemed, like wagons against some imminent attack. But instead of danger, the town itself radiated tedium and quiet disillusion.

Far worse than poor soils, worse even than the epidemic of
malaria, most peasants in Cujubim suffered from a lack of
assistance and a surfeit of bureaucracy. One farmer in a small
house just outside the main town told of how he was forced to
spend an entire day away from his field, pay two thousand
cruzeiros (about twenty dollars at the time), to go to the Ibama
office in Ariquemes, the nearest town, all to acquire a two-
cent permit to clear an already deforested plot, and then take
it back to the center of Cujubim for an official stamp. By some
mystery of endurance, in the Brazilian backlands such indig-
nities became the topic of giddy bewilderment and raucous
joking. No matter what hardship or disgrace, these people,
humble people, with rubber sandals for shoes, whose only wealth
was their children, turned their plight into a source of wonder
and remarkably detached amusement. Get this! this farmer
seemed to say. "We become their slaves," now loosing a belly
laugh that came from some place deep inside him.

"Model city," grumbled the clientele at the Bahiano's bar in
the central plaza of Cujubim. The electricity had been off for
three days, and since the water pump was electrical, there had
been a drought for the same period. Cujubim was parched,
thirsty, and beginning to stink.

But after nine years in Rondônia Groeneveld had put on
some calluses. "Okay," he reasoned aloud. "Let's say all this
isn't possible. Is that going to stop farmers from slashing and
burning?" Groeneveld smiled now for emphasis. "I'm not in
favor of putting up a fence around Amazonia and throwing
away the key," he said. "I am a tropical forest ecologist. I
want to save as much of the Amazon as possible, but I want
the people living here to get a fair deal out of it."

A fair deal, Groeneveld soon concluded, meant something
more than the miserable living that the standard farm portfolio
of beans, rice, cacao, and coffee afforded. That's when he got
the idea of natural honey. Indians and mixed-blood caboclo
peasants had collected wild honey for years, but almost no one

had thought to domesticate it. So Groeneveld contacted rural union leaders in Ouro Prêto do Oeste, one of the state's oldest settlements, and set to work.

The government was no help. Officials had no bee boxes and couldn't be bothered. The other problem was the farmers. "People thought I was crazy," said Walmir de Jesus, one of Rondônia's pioneer beekeepers. "They thought the bees would attack us." Walmir had packed off to Rondônia after being blacklisted in his home state of Espirito Santo, where he led a series of strikes against a chocolate factory. Walmir and six brothers bought up some mostly forested land in Rondônia and began to farm.

Never the conformist, Walmir took the leap and cajoled a friend at the local rural extension office into scrounging up an old bee box. He made ten more himself and started an apiary. In a short while he started making money. "A small farmer now earns more from fifteen hives than from two hectares [about five acres] of cacao," calculated Groeneveld. The Ouro Prêto cooperative caught on and marketed some 1.4 tons of quality honey in 1990.

But Groeneveld knew that honey alone was not enough. "The challenge is that a small farmer needs to make money every year from his farm." So Groeneveld set out to design a long-term plan of gardening, forest extraction, and tree cropping. This is what the specialists call agroforestry, and together with careful herding of cattle, it is proving more and more to be an option for Amazonian peasants. Groeneveld's idea was to combine food crops, for subsistence, with high-value cash crops, such as honey and oil from the copaiba tree, which can be used for soaps and cosmetics. Brazil nut, rubber, or tropical fruit trees could be nurtured for returns in the medium to long term. Thinking still farther ahead, some small landholders planned to replant degraded land with prized tropical timber, such as mahogany, cedar, or cerejeira. Today Groeneveld works with two other state unions and counsels rubber tappers and Indians. Iphae keeps a computerized inventory of agricultural and forest products and, with the help of Jason Clay, an American anthropologist from the human rights advocacy group Cultural Survival, is leapfrogging price-chiseling middlemen to get to buyers abroad. This plan was ambitious but not grandiose. It was grandiosity, after all, that had leveled and burned so much of the forest cover of Rondônia in the last disastrous decade. Instead, these peasants were trying to work with their complex Amazonian ecology, not do battle with it. To be successful, agroforestry still depended on good harvests, backbreaking labor, and, most important, safe transport of these diversified products to markets in southern Brazil and across the oceans. These were daunting tasks for any community of farmers, let alone the isolated and impoverished communities in remote corners of Rondônia.

After eight years in this capital of the western Amazon, the towering Dutch ecologist had become inured to ogling Rondônians. He was somewhat less accustomed to the sudden rush of official attention that had come his way. In 1985, when I met him, one of Groeneveld's biggest frustrations was that the debate over the fate of the Amazon was too often confined to ponderous summits in luxury hotels in North America or Europe and nowhere near the source. Things were changing now. The upper hemisphere continued to agonize over Amazonia, and many of the summits, he confessed, were of little practical value, all earnestness and scientific showmanship. But Groeneveld was now a protagonist in these talks. His institute had received funding from NGOs in Holland and Sweden and got a fat grant from, of all places, the forestry service of Essen State, in Germany. More important, Groeneveld was being courted now as a resident expert and not as an isolated researcher toiling away at the equatorial margin.

CHAPTER

TEMPERING THE TROPICS

> And the desolate land shall be tilled. . . . This land that was untilled is become as a garden of pleasures.
>
> —Ezekiel 36:34–35

Takashi Shida bent down in a field of soybeans, briefly disappearing in the sea of pea green stalks that swelled off toward the flat horizon. Surfacing again, he brandished a plant better than a yard long. He grasped it firmly and, as if playing loves-me-not with a daisy, tenderly pulled off the flat soya pods, one by one. "Two, three, four," he reported precisely. It was nearly noon, and shadows had shrunk to almost nothing as the sun ambled toward the zenith. The midday heat was spelled only by the odd breath of wind that made the plantation of soya shiver slightly, like green Jell-O. "Forty-three, forty-four," Shida continued, beaming now under the bill of his baseball cap. The porcelain blue bowl of sky above him seemed to reflect back his satisfaction.

No one took the temperature, but the thermometer would easily have registered ninety, with the humidity pushing a hundred. It was wet season, and the heat drew up the moisture and held it in the air like a sauna. In a few hours the skies would blush and then bawl their daily thunderstorm. "One hundred and eleven," he announced the total, triumphant.

This pastoral portrait, of a farmer's cheer over a suppliant earth, may stir little sympathy now that the plow and bulldozer have long ago dispatched most of the world's untamed places. It is wilderness, not arcadia, that we exalt today. Yet Shida's small harvest that afternoon told part of a remarkable and unlikely story. For both he and the soybeans that engulfed him were strangers here.

Shida is a first-generation Brazilian, born of an immigrant Japanese farmer. His father made his home in São Paulo State, Brazil's green belt, with a mild climate and rich red soils. But Shida had gone a giant step farther. An engineer, he helped plan and build Itamaraty North, a vast plantation in the middle of the scrubby tablelands. It is the property of a São Paulo agrimogul, Olacyr de Moraes. He is said to be the largest soybean farmer in the world, and his farmland carpets hundreds of miles of western Brazil.

The Itamaraty North plantation lies at the heart of Mato Grosso. This is Brazil's big sky country, an inverted ocean of blue capping an eternity of plains, broken only by the occasional bunching of storm clouds or the severe rocky bluffs that hide gold, diamonds, and other semiprecious stones. It was these riches that first drew the *bandeirantes* west in the seventeenth century. They started a gold rush, then a land rush. Today a parquet floor of farms and ranches stretches from horizon to dusty horizon. In the rains, which last from November to May, the terrain is damp and green, mantled in the grain crops like soya that have been adopted from the temperate zones to the punishing conditions of the tropics. During the dry season the earth reddens from the iron and silica in the soil; clouds of orange dust veil great sowing machines as they course through the endless rows. The splendid carpet of green belies naturally nutrient-deficient soils, but the *cerrados* are today the stage for great plantation crops and machines that have revolutionized tropical agriculture in Brazil.

And everywhere you look there are the rheas, giant wingless birds related to the ostriches, which forage endlessly for insects and can suddenly burst into a lightning sprint. No one bothers the rhea. Their flesh is unpalatable to humans, so they prance supreme, picking their way through the fields. In one of the most amicable partnerships struck between feral beast and husbanded earth, they browse for a lunch of caterpillars that prey upon the budding soy seedlings.

Jungle—or, to be precise, a low-lying, twisted scrub called *cerrado* (bush)—once covered this rhea paradise. Before the rhea there were other wild beasts and dozens of Indian tribes throughout the Big Bush (Mato Grosso). But the first finds of gold and diamonds ruined their timeless isolation. For as long as there was yellow ore, the mercenaries resorted to another prize, "red gold," Indians pressed into the service of the mine magnates and colonial plantations. Three centuries ago the Paulista expeditions battled the Paiaguá and Guaikurú and the fierce, cudgel-wielding warriors called the Kayapó. The peoples of this scrubland were fearsome. Legend had it that some tribes of Mato Grosso were in the habit of eating their intruders or else pelting them with stones, spears, or arrows. Today the Kayapó have migrated hundreds of miles north to the Xingu Basin. There is no sign of the Guaikurú or Paiaguá. In fact, by the mid nineteenth century the Paiaguá's only survivors were found fifteen hundred miles to the south, in grubby tent villages on the outskirts of Asunción, living off their meager sales of firewood, fish, and knickknacks to the Paraguayan city dwellers. "The recompense from their labor," writes historian Sérgio Buarque de Holanda, "they spent entirely on getting drunk."[1]

When the *bandeirante* outposts grew into camps and then towns, herding and farming intruded even farther onto Indian land. Like a tropical Texas, cattle soon roamed over the scruffy, windblown range. What was once referred to as Brazil's Indian problem was safely relegated to a few discreet reservations. To a modern-day visitor, the Indians are hardly visible anymore. Their proud headdresses and lethal arrows are souvenirs, encased in the tinted glass cases of airport gift shops. There are still gold and diamonds to be had, but the mining camps share a landscape with boomtowns, farms, and spreading ranches. The Big Bush is smaller now. It has given way to great fields of soya, cotton, wheat, beans, and corn. Today the beasts of Mato Grosso have names like Massey-Ferguson, Caterpillar, and John Deere. They prowl a land that is Brazil's newest and perhaps most promising agricultural zone, and also one of its most unlikely.

The three-hundred-thousand-acre Itamaraty North is not so much a testament to the glory of agribusiness as it is to science. You could say that Moraes has done for grain farming what Armand Hammer did for venture capitalism. He traffics behind the iron curtain of geography and climate. At the bottom of the Amazon Basin, just twelve degrees shy of the equator, Moraes sows thousands of acres with crops that belong to another world, the temperate zone. The climate and soils there are like the savannas of Africa, a torrid habitat for human beings and no place for traditional farming. A decade ago no soya had been planted anywhere close to the tropics, and top agricultural scientists said it couldn't be done. Aristotle's pronouncements on the uninhabitability of the tropics would remain, nearly as canon law, well into the age of modern agriculture. But a foolish few researchers bulled ahead, and the result today is this buffet for rheas and an empire of green in the *cerrado,* some of the hottest and harshest lands in all the Americas.

In every frontier, the sweat of pioneers and the perusals of scientists have played vital roles in harnessing hostile environments. In Canada the obstacle was the topography of the Precambrian Shield, "a barren and rocky wilderness," writes the historian Paul F. Sharp, that for decades only fur traders and hardy mountain men could tackle. In Australia it was the Blue Mountains, "that wall of rock and scrub which for a quarter of a century hemmed in this colony of New South Wales within the coastal plains," in the words of Sharp.[2] Where in the Amazon the problem is moisture, diseases, and suffocating heat, in the frontiers of Australia, the prairies of Canada, and the western plains of the United States, the problem was the pronounced dry season and a lack of groundwater. Sharp, who has studied many of the world's frontiers, writes that "slowly and painfully, pastoralists and farmers devised systems of land use, experimented with drought resistant crops and invented new machinery to cope with their problems." In Australia it was the Ridley Stripper, the stump-jump plow, and new wheat strains engineered by William Farrer. Frontiers are not only trying for pioneers but consolidated through constantly renewed experiences of trial and error.[3]

Originally from China, soya has now conquered farmland around much of the globe's traditional grain belt, from the Middle West of the United States to the llanos of Uruguay. The fanciful idea of planting soybeans in the "short latitudes" bloomed among a small group of Brazilians who studied under the famous American agronomist Edgar Hartwig. Hartwig, who taught at Mississippi State University, schooled his pupils well— so well, in fact, he eventually drew heavy flak from the American farm lobby for aiding the competition. The adaptation of crops to alien environments is as old as agriculture. Yet outside an arcane circle of agricultural scientists, the tale of Brazilian soya is surprisingly little known. To the protagonists it has taken on the dimensions of an epic novel.

On a February morning, in an empty meeting room at the Cerrados Research Center near Brasília, one of those scientists, Plínio Itamar de Souza, began to recount that story. It was already midmorning, and an important staff summit meeting beckoned. Radical changes in agricultural research policy were looming, and the corridors were buzzing with anxiety and speculation. Now and again fellow scientists poked their heads through the door of the meeting room, their brows stitched with concern over their sequestered colleague. But after an hour and a half of sifting through charts and tables and designing maps on paper, de Souza was only just warming up to his theme. "Believe it or not," he confided, "I'd rather talk about soybeans."

Souza, today, downplays his own role in the soya story. But in fact, he worked closely with another agronomist, Romeu Kiihl, whose research has made him a household word in third world agriculture. Kiihl, a Brazilian of German descent, had earned a master's and then a doctorate under Hartwig and returned to work at the Agricultural Institute of Campinas, in São Paulo's farm country. Nearly all of southern Brazil was being overhauled then. Coffee, the traditional crop, was being torn up after successive frosts. In its place came wheat, sorghum, soya, and citrus, but especially soya. In the decade since 1969 Brazil increased its soya production tenfold, and today it has become the world's second producer, behind only the United States.

But Kiihl knew that by the 1970s the frontier spaces of southern Brazil were nearly all settled. Many smaller farmers were already being squeezed off their plots, for they could not compete with the machines and capital of the powerful agroindustries. Many of the displaced ended up in city slums. Others were lured west by the cheap land and wide open spaces at the bottom lip of the Amazon region. That was when Kiihl began to think seriously about the tropics, where Brazil had plenty of land and a dearth of planters.

About that time de Souza took a position at a farming institute in Bahia, the northeastern state where Brazil was born. There the climate was hot and arid year-round, hardly grain country. But de Souza also had a notion about the tropics and drew up a research proposal to plant soya in the Bahian *sertão,* the dusty backlands of arid northeastern Brazil. His colleagues, who hailed from Brazil's temperate regions, turned it down. "The institute was full of southerners. They thought it couldn't be done," he said. It took a job change and an appeal to the head of the new Brazilian Center for Ranching and Agriculture, Embrapa, before de Souza won over the policy bosses.

This was the early seventies, and a number of the new farmers in the west had already lost their shirts with the same idea. Like the pioneers of any land, the southerners had brought their habits and crops with them to the frontier. The soya they planted bore names like Lee, Bragg, Hampton, and Major, in honor of the saints of temperate agriculture who had made America's Middle West into a cornucopia. These were the same strains that had been imported and planted with spectacular success in southern Brazil, below the Tropic of Capricorn.

But the *cerrado* was not Illinois, or Rio Grande do Sul for that matter. The low-lying bush and scrub were easily cleared and burned off, and the soils readily turned over and sown. But the results were frustrating. The seeds germinated well, yet the soya of the Mato Grosso climbed only to about a man's knee, flowered, and stopped growing. A measly few pods sprouted on each puny stalk. It was a green desert. Though they had no idea at the time, the soya farmers of the *cerrado* had bumped up against the rude exigencies of the torrid zone. Ironically the problem was not so much the excess of heat, as Aristotle imagined, but the lack of light.

De Souza grabbed a piece of chalk and drew a long arc across the blackboard, bisecting it with a vertical line. This, he lectured, represented the normal growth cycle of soybeans, from germination to flowering and on to barren old age. Above it he designed another curve, tracking the sun over the 365 days of the year. Soya, he said, grows to its maximum height and flowers at the summer solstice, when the days are not only warm but long. De Souza put his index finger at the apex of the curve. "In southern Brazil, as in North America and much of Asia," he said, "there are up to fourteen to sixteen hours of sunlight at the height of summer. In the tropics there is sun all year round, but never more than thirteen-point-five hours a day." De Souza drew another sun curve for the tropics, its apex nosing just below that of the first curve.

Just the hour or so less of sun in the *cerrado* made all the difference. The plants did not have the time to mature, and flowering came early, halting growth. "It's sort of like a ten-year-old getting pregnant," de Souza said. "She may be able to deliver a baby, but neither she nor the baby will be well developed." Botanically the runt soya served as an interesting science lesson. Commercially it was a disaster. So de Souza and Kiihl in separate corners of Brazil went to work to find out why. De Souza had long heard about Kiihl's pioneering work, and through a colleague, the agronomist Irineu Bays, they finally met. "He was in the wrong latitude. I needed materials," de Souza said. They exchanged letters and phone calls, then literature and seeds. It was the beginning of fourteen years of correspondence that were to consecrate one of the most aggressive expansions of an agricultural frontier in this century.

By the early eighties, Kiihl had moved south to Paraná, to Embrapa's Soya Center. He and Bays developed and then sent the multiple seed strains to de Souza, who had taken a job in Brasília at Embrapa's newly inaugurated Cerrados Research Center. Their challenge was to fool the seasons by altering the genetic coding of the plant. The goal: to make soya flower later, allowing full growth even under the reduced daylight of tropics.

Kiihl, Bays, and a third scientist, Leones de Almeida, crossed thousands and thousands of varieties, trying to combine later-flowering strains with disease-resistant ones and still maintain high productivity. As soon as he got them, de Souza put the new seeds in the ground at the Cerrados Center's test plots. In Brasília de Souza worked around the clock at times, simulating longer daylight hours after dark by flashing lights over various strains germinating in the laboratory. Bays was the evangelist. Kiihl hated to fly, so Bays took to crisscrossing the country, introducing the improved varieties of soya to farmers and research stations from Brasília to Maranhão. Tragically, in 1984 Bays lost his life on one of these missions when his twin-engine Bandeirante craft crashed into the Brazilian interior.

Yet thanks to these researchers and Hartwig's counsel, a new hagiography for tropical soya was written. Lee, Hampton, Bragg, and Major became Dôko, Tropical, Teresina, Carajás, and Cariri. The best of these varieties managed to combine high yield with high resistance to the canker that routinely plagues soy fields in humid regions. Some of the new strains, like the one Takashi Shida plucked, reached nearly chest high to a grown man and produced up to four tons a hectare, double the normal. A new frontier for soya had been blazed—within Brazil and without. Following Brazil's lead, Bolivia, the Ivory Coast, and other nations imported these new strains and become part of the expanding tropical soya belt. Souza spent several months on the Cape Verde Islands, off western Africa, where yet another country was experimenting with Brazil's new soya technology.

Now the forbidding *cerrados* have become part of the agricultural frontier. Nowhere else in Brazil, and perhaps in the world, can so many crops—soya, wheat, corn, beans, and peas—be harvested twice a year. With irrigation, Itamaraty's researchers have managed three harvests in a single year. Some ten million hectares (twenty-five million acres) had already been planted by the beginning of the decade, but that represented only about 10 percent of the arable *cerrado* land. Roberto Peres, chief of the Cerrados Center, said the *cerrados* "have about everything: water, sunlight, a good soil structure, and good infrastructure." Lime and phosphorus, expensive items that are also vital for treating the acid and nutrient-poor soils of the Amazon, are also abundant in the region. By the end of 1990 the *cerrados* were already producing 30 percent of Brazil's fifty-six million tons of grain a year. There is an ecological advantage to soya as well. Instead of simply draining the soils, soya "fixes" nitrogen—absorbing it through its leafy surface area from the air and depositing it in the earth. A crop of soya can prepare the way for the next season's more nutrient-demanding crops, such as beans, rice, or corn.

Yet it is one of the cruelties of farm country that what science accomplished over a decade a sour economy can undo in a few harvests. In early 1991, when I visited Itamaraty North, most of the region's intrepid farmers had plowed over row upon row of soya. The price had collapsed as the result of oversupply on the international market. At home, freight charges, controlled by an oligopoly of transporters, had sky-rocketed. At the same time, a series of price freezes and thaws over the recent years had conspired to hold down artificially the domestic price of soya and soya oil. The farmers barely earned back what they had spent on planting soya.

In its place the farmers had begun to plant another temperate climate crop, cotton, which soared on world markets. Cotton, too, required painstaking research and adaptation to the humid tropical climate. A classical problem in plant genetics recurred. High-yielding varieties proved susceptible to diseases in the humid season, while resistant strains were less productive. The researchers at Itamaraty North scoured the world's cotton belt, from the Sea Islands to Israel, to select different varieties. The research proved to be well worth the effort. In 1990 a truck-load of cotton fetched twenty-five times the price of a load of soya. The *cerrado* farmers now were counting on cotton to bail them out of the soya slump. "The *cerrado* is the great agricultural frontier of Brazil," said the optimistic Peres.

For the administrators and agrocrats of Brasília, under increasing heat for allowing the destruction of the Amazon forest, the technology of soya in the tropics was also a political windfall. Though most of the *cerrado* lies within the area known as the Legal Amazon, it does not harbor the botanically rich rain forests for which the region is most famous. The mean, gnarled bush and its unlovely squat forests simply do not evoke the same sort of passions as the imperiled jungle primeval. No one marches in London or Berlin to save the *cerrado*. There may be good scientific reasons for such environmental favor-itism. The dense, multispecied tropical rain forest is cast today as everything from a natural pharmacy to the regulator of global weather. Though scientists may debate these ideas, to Brasília such botanical bias is a blessing. "We can expand grain production in the *cerrados* without deforesting one single acre of rain forest," exclaimed Murilo Flores, president of Embrapa.

Now that despoiling the environment has been roundly denounced as the dirty work of development, the idea of the endless farm frontier has become unthinkable. Environmentalists are drawing the line, and it stops at the edge of the world's primary forests, particularly the tropical rain forests. However, science has made possible what may be unthinkable politically. Already soya has spread through Mato Grosso and invaded southern Rondônia, the two northwestern states where farming, ranching, and road building have claimed forty-five thousand square miles of forest, larger than Scotland and Wales combined.

Of course, not even the most hidebound of technocrats advocates clear-cutting the rain forest to plant waves of wheat or soya. That would be both economical as well as ecological lunacy. Yet one hardly needs the bullish fantasies of a Roosevelt to appreciate the significance of the *cerrado* pioneers. For centuries the deadly tropics confounded the headiest of ambitions. "Can these Amazonian Selvas [jungles], which form the largest unoccupied fertile space on the earth's surface, be reclaimed for the service of man?" pondered the British historian James Bryce, as he toured the Brazilian countryside in 1912.[4] Bryce's prognosis for the natural bounty of Amazonian soils may have been exaggerated. But now, thanks to the obstinacy of researchers and the sweat of the settlers, the Amazonian frontier is at hand. "We can plant soya almost anywhere in Brazil today, even at the equator," exclaimed Plínio de Souza. "Exploring the *cerrado* will be the first step toward the rational exploration of Amazonia." Now that soya, cotton, and wheat have crossed over into the torrid zones it may be difficult to hold them back behind the ever-shifting man-made frontiers of politics.

CHAPTER 11

JAPANESE IN THE AMAZON

So, I will cast you forth out of this land, into a
land which you know not, nor your fathers: and
there you shall serve strange gods day and night,
which shall not give you any rest.

—Jeremiah 16:3

Every evening, when work was done at the farmers'
cooperative, Noburo Sakaguchi drove home to his small
plot of land a few miles out of Tomé Açú, an agricultural village in the heart of the Brazilian Amazon region. Sakaguchi, an agronomist by schooling but a woodsman at heart,
looked forward to evening when the tedious paper work was
done and the searing equatorial sun slid fat and red over the
horizon.

He sat down at the long hardwood kitchen table, took a long
belt from a can of Pitú cane liquor, climbed into a Caterpillar
bulldozer, and set out for the forest. Every night for two months
he maintained this surly ritual, punishing the jungle with his
growling machine. In the end Sakaguchi had bashed a 2-kilo-
meter (1.2-mile) road through the woods. To the innocent
observer this might seem just a reprise of the age-old story of
civilization's assault on nature, a drama that has claimed

woodlands from the Black Forest to Borneo. But Sakaguchi's road was really a path to invention.

It was to be the main access way through his farm, a patch of land where over the next thirty years he coaxed thousands of trees, bushes, crops, and creepers into bloom. You could call it a living emporium. In August 1990, when I visited him, some seventy-three species were crowded onto his estate of 150 acres. The plantation towered with tropical hardwood trees, from mahogany to Brazil nut, and was resplendent with exotic produce like the mangosteen, a lime-size fruit stuffed with a subtly sweet pulp, and cupuassú, a dusky relative of cacao. His driveway was shaded by hundred-foot andirobas, whose wedge-shaped fruit is boiled down into a bitter oil that, in 1853, served the great naturalist Wallace as an insect repellent. The same oil can be strained and used for cooking or fine cosmetics.

Sakaguchi insisted that his forest farm was merely the work of a green thumb and an incurable itch to see what could come up on a single patch of Amazonian soil. In Tomé Açu they called it, only half in jest, the Botanical Gardens. For the last three decades, in fact, it had become a veritable biological library, serving as a reference for an entire community of newcomers puzzling out a living on some of the most niggardly lands in the Americas.

Sakaguchi, who was now fifty-three, was one of the sages of this colony of Japanese immigrants. Their more than sixty-year tenure in the eastern Amazon had been, predictably, one of suffering and sacrifice. Illness and despair had frequently gutted their number. Lately inflation and a national economic slump had taken their toll. Yet despite the setbacks, the Japanese and their descendants not only survived but, in many ways, flourished here. This was no mean feat. Eastern Amazonia, after all, was perhaps the meanest region of the humid tropics and the undoing of dozens of settler colonies over the span of a century.

Today Tomé Açú is, fittingly, a hybrid of unlikely elements. There are a half dozen houses of worship, from Buddhist to Baptist, and the town's faithful may choose between Sunday services that range from high mass to Holy Roller evangelical revivals. Even after six decades in Brazil, Japanese is the common language, and negotiating Portuguese can still be a painful exercise for many residents. In restaurants, chopsticks, miso, and tofu accompany black beans, manioc, and beef steak, the staples of Brazilian cuisine. In June 1990, while every Brazilian soul was glued to the television for the soccer World Cup, Tomé Açú was preoccupied with its annual baseball tournament, held at the harvest of the spice pepper crop. The centerpiece of town night life is the karaoke, the Japanese sing-along, where patrons emboldened by whiskey or saké belt out Sinatra ballads, Brazilian pop hits, and a wealth of Japanese torch songs. The immigrant Japanese, their Japanese-Brazilian children, and Amazonian natives mingle easily here, a rare sort of amity that owes less to conscious cultural diplomacy than to the intimacy of neighbors sharing years of routines and burdens.

This town is the fruit of one of this century's most remarkable diasporas, which scattered millions of Japanese across the globe in scant decades. Fleeing overcrowding and depression at first, and then the ruins of World War II, poor Japanese poured out of the cramped islands and set out for the empty frontiers of Asia and the New World. One wave of emigrants went to Korea, Taiwan, and Manchuria. Several more hit Hawaii and the American mainland, until immigration authorities slammed the U.S. borders shut in 1924. Yet another washed up in South America, all the way to the Andean highlands and down to southern Brazil. São Paulo, with a million Japanese, now harbors the largest community outside the home country.

In September 1929 the steamer *Montevideo Maru*, jammed with Japanese immigrants, docked at Rio de Janeiro. Most of the arriving immigrants headed to São Paulo and Paraná, but forty-three families turned north, sailing all the way to Belém, near where the Amazon empties into the Atlantic. They went

130 miles inland, deep into the rain forest, and built farms, schools, houses, and hospitals.

By all rights this community ought not exist. For more than a century the eastern Amazon had been the target of ill-starred official colonization plans. The first was in 1875, not so far from Tomé Açú, in the Zona Bragantina, where fifteen "colonies" were founded. The settlers were mainly Italians and Germans, lured by land grants from Brazilian Emperor Pedro II. But the distances from farms to the markets in Belém were considerable, and the terrain was severe. Worse, the Bragantina's soils were acid when they were not sandy. Nor were the newcomers' customs suited to the Amazon environment. Their idea of working the land was closer to prospecting than farming, and their preferred implements were "the machete and the match box," the historian Roberto Santos writes. By 1901 the 70,000 settlers had dwindled to only 16,456. "Agricultural colonization by Brazilians in the Amazon left only melancholy memories."[1]

Recruited by a Tokyo colonization company, Nantaku, which beckoned colonists to a "second paradise," the Japanese found instead intractable jungle, undependable markets, and endemic disease. But a core of immigrants stuck it out. They founded a pair of villages, Tomé Açú and Quatro Bocas, and began to negotiate a covenant with the new and strange land.

Noburo Sakaguchi's romance with the Amazon began thirty years ago. The young graduate had a row with his family in Japan: They wanted him to study law; he wanted to make things grow in the tropics. His dream then was to go to Cambodia to plant rubber trees, whose milky latex was the raw stuff for the gadgets of the early industrial age: automobiles tires, hermetic seals, weatherproofed clothes, surgical gloves, and syringes. This was the time of "white gold," as rubber was called at the beginning of the century, "gold on trees." But by 1960 Southeast Asia was still engulfed in war, so Sakaguchi sailed on to Brazil.

It is one of those little jokes of biology that plants found wild in one place often fare better cultivated on alien soil. So it was with coffee, native to Ethiopia but most successfully planted in Colombia and Brazil. The puny maize of the Andes burgeoned into hardy, giant-eared Kansas corn. The English potato came from South America. Amazonian cacao is routinely ravaged by fungus when planted in its home habitat but thrives in the semiarid coastal plains of Bahia. Likewise, while Amazon rubber seedlings sprouted all over Malaysia, repeated attempts to plant rubber in its native Amazonia were consistently thwarted by plant disease. Today biological engineers tinkering with genes, fertilizers, and climate control have managed agricultural marvels. But these are long-term projects with slow results. Besides, by the time Sakaguchi got to Belém, the rubber boom had long since left the wild rubber groves of the Amazon behind.

The pioneers of Tomé Açú soon fell into the millennial farming practices of the Amazon Basin. They felled the jungle, burned off the debris, and planted subsistence crops— mostly rice, beans, and manioc—pressing on when the soils gave out. That happened often. For instead of a fecund paradise, the immigrants encountered "highly weathered acid Oxisols"—agronomic jargon for a rain-gutted, stubborn, and undernourished earth.[2] But they also innovated, introducing radishes, celery, cabbage, and green peppers. However, these strangers with their strange new foods failed to win over local palates.[3]

Then malaria and blackwater fever struck and soon became epidemic. Satoshi Sawada, one of the community's pioneers, arrived in Brazil in 1930. Six years later he buried his mother and his father. In the next decade Sawada watched 480 families pack up and leave. By 1940 only 40 families remained. "Everybody got malaria. The parents died," he said. "Only the children survived."

The Amazon looked ready to swallow one more pioneer experiment. However, even as illness raged, the seeds of renewal were germinating. Those who held on were to call this the time of black gold. In 1933 one more immigrant ship, the *Hawaii-Maru,* steamed out of Tokyo for the New World. On the way an elderly Japanese woman fell ill and died, a sad but all too common occurrence on the arduous monthlong passage. The ship detoured to Singapore for the burial. On a whim Makinosuke Ussui, the colonial recruiting agent, picked up twenty seedlings of Indian spice pepper.

Virtually unknown in the New World, pepper had long built fabulous fortunes in Europe and the Far East. It was pepper that helped turn Lisbon, with its bountiful spice colonies, into the status of a world-class trader and made Antwerp into the sixteenth century's financial center.[4] The chance acquisition in Singapore not only changed forever the fortunes of this embattled Amazon community but also wrote a new entry in the ledger of agriculture in the Americas.

Legend has misted over history now; in Tomé Açú it is said that three pepper plants survived, though some swear it was only two. However many there were, these few seedlings were enough to start an agribusiness. Once again farmers cleared their fields, sowed the black pepper, and waited. The results were startling. Every rainy season this landscape of mottled greens and browns blushed in the glorious red of ripening pepper fruit. By 1956 Tomé Açú's pepper crop satisfied the Brazilian market, and the town began to export. By the late 1970s farmers all over Amazonia had caught on, and Brazil became the Western Hemisphere's leading producer. Malaysia and India growers have since taken the lead, but in 1983, thanks largely to Tomé Açú, Brazil briefly led world pepper exports. "My rubber trees turned into pepper," Sakaguchi said, loosing a wry laugh.

Hiroshi Muroi, a quiet man in his sixties and a confessed "lover of pepper," recalled those times fondly. I found Muroi raking over a tarpaulin spread with neat squares of black and white pepper, laid out on his front yard like dismembered parts of a giant chessboard. The peppercorns drying whole in the sun saturated the air with their sweet perfume.

In the early 1960s Muroi, formerly a pear farmer in Japan, hired a peon to clear 62.5 acres and planted five thousand pepper bushes. "The first harvest I got six hundred kilos [1,326 pounds] of pepper," he told his visitors. "The second year I got six tons. The third year, twelve tons. By the fourth"—he smiled—"eighteen tons." In ten years, with his pepper wealth, Muroi built a roomy wooden farmhouse, where he lives to this day. The garden was draped in delicate mosses. Cacti of all geometries decorated the windowsill. A twelve-foot-tall pomporé bush, with startling red flowers, framed the doorway. The house rang with the calls of a dozen caged curió (rice finch) and sabiá (song thrush) birds, their songs mixing riotously against a counterpoint of tinkling Japanese mobiles.

Inside, a forest of brass trophies—awards for pepper, cacao, and dendê palm crops—had sprouted on Muroi's mantelpiece. To one side was a chocolate box, chock-full of delicate pink and mauve seashells, reminders perhaps of the now-distant island home country. In fact, Muroi had returned only once to Japan, and that was not until three years ago. He was a Brazilian now, though the pained Portuguese that emerged through a thick accent and the short, stiff bows he offered his visitors betrayed his roots. But nostalgia went no further than his decorations and the elegant living room built of tropical hardwoods by a Japanese carpenter. He had a farm to manage and thirty hired hands to administer during the pepper harvest. Even his native Japanese gave way to occasional Portuguese idioms and the words for the crops—*dendê, pimenta,* and *cacau*—that had become his life.

But the Amazon has never been kind to wonder crops. Henry Ford lost his endless rubber groves on the Tapajós River to the leaf blight. Ludwig's trees grew only grudgingly in the sandy soils on the banks of the Jari. The witches'-broom plagues cacao farmers throughout the Amazon. Likewise, fungus struck the pepper plant. But this time nature played it straight. After a few spectacular decades the black gold of the East fell prey to the ills of its new, foreign habitat.

Sakaguchi explained. In Amazonia, he said, where hundreds of species coexist in a single acre of land, this tremendous biodiversity acts as a protective shield. The myriad species, each with a different genetic makeup, form a natural barrier, isolating the fungi and microbes that abound in the hothouse of the jungle. A monocrop, by contrast, is a sitting duck for disease. "I am Sakaguchi." He thumped his chest. "If there are thousands of Sakaguchis, one right next to the other, and one gets the grippe"—he now grabbed his throat—"every Sakaguchi will get the grippe."

The grippe this time was called fusarium; it attacked the vine at the root and wouldn't let go. Plants that normally bore fruit for up to fifteen years now lived for only five, barely enough time for a farmer to earn back what he invested. The root blight first appeared in 1957, and in fifteen years it had romped all over the eastern Amazon.

Once again Tomé Açú hunkered down for a crisis. To compensate for losses, farmers planted more and more pepper. For their efforts they reaped successive bumper crops but also a price collapse caused by oversupply. The only solution for Tomé Açú was to intensify planting on existing plots and to diversify. Few families gave up on pepper completely, but now they wanted to hedge their bets. Much of the inspiration came from the Botanical Gardens.

Sakaguchi, mulling over the dilemma in Tomé Açú, came to the conclusion that Amazon farming practices had to be turned upside down. "In agricultural school we were taught to pay attention to the soil. Prepare the soil, and you will get a big harvest." He nodded. "Very modern. Very wrong."

In the Amazon "the nutrients are aboveground. The soil is very poor. The fertility is in the vegetation," he continued. "It's in the trees. They control light, humidity, and protect the soil. In Amazonia you have to take care of the trees."

So the farmers of Tomé Açú began to redesign their plots, not as unichrome carpets of single crops but as a mosaic, imitating the diversity of the rain forest around them. Soon Tomé Açú was a checkerboard of "polycultures." As many as ten to twenty-five crops are now planted in "consortium," where Brazil nut, rubber trees, or assai palms shade cacao, and food crops are sown in the alleys between passion fruit or pepper vines. To the untrained eye, a fifty-acre plot, an average farm in Tomé Açú—and modest for the Amazon—looks nearly like a patch of virgin forest.

Most important, the Japanese settlers all but dispensed with the seasonal food crops that are prey to the vagaries of local markets and hard on the poor Amazonian soils, forcing farmers to deforest ever-larger areas. Now they concentrate instead on rarer items, such as exotic fruits, with secure markets at home and abroad, and handsomer prices. "Everywhere we went we noticed people were interested in tropical fruits," said Toshitsugu Kuhayakawa, Tomé Açú's botanist. Kuhayakawa was seventy-five, a fragile white-haired man with large horn-rim glasses and an easy laugh that splintered his face into a million lines. Kuhayakawa spent years in Taiwan experimenting with endless varieties of sweet potato, but he longed to try out his sciences on the complexities of the Amazon. He arrived in Tomé Açú in 1970 and, together with Sakaguchi, began selecting seeds of the best varieties of tropical fruits.

Now the co-op runs a juicing plant, which processes up to seven thousand tons of passion fruit pulp for a juice maker in São Paulo. Lately the co-op has begun cultivating more select items, such as acerola, the Caribbean fruit that Divino Araujo brought to Alta Floresta. Another is cupuassú, with a rich, creamy pulp ideal for juice, jam, and ice cream and a seed that makes a fine chocolate.

Jorge Ito, a young Japanese-Brazilian farmer, was Tomé Açú's champion of cupuassú and of this newest phase of diversified agroforestry. One summer morning, when most Amazon farmers were sweating over stubborn fields, I found Jorge Ito ambling about his tidy green lawn, driving golf balls. The workday had only just begun in Tomé Açú, but already the sun was punishingly high. Ito, by contrast, looked almost cool and elegantly at ease in a white polo shirt, pressed jeans, and rubber sandals. As our car turned into his drive, we caught Ito in mid-swing. He grinned slightly, collected a fistful of golf balls, and waved his visitors—myself and Saito, a Japanese agricultural extension worker—into his home.

It was a new structure of red brick and freshly painted plaster, a home that suggested a life of simple comfort. Ito poured some bright red juice squeezed fresh from the acerola, one of the dozens of exotic fruits culled from his tree farm, and told about his life in the Amazon. Ito was a nisei, the Brazilian-born son of a Japanese immigrant farmer. Trained as an electrical engineer, Ito gave up the trade early to dedicate himself to his father's farm. You could say the Itos had done all right. If it weren't for the relentless sun and the unruly flora, this might have been scene from the Napa Valley or the affluent south of Brazil, where the soils are generous, labor is decently remunerated, and leisure an ordinary part of everyday life.

Like his town, Ito is a hybrid of elements, with the dedication and conscientiousness of a Japanese factory laborer and the suavity of a native Brazilian. He inherited his father's passion for work and tidiness and his host country's proclivity for enjoying life, the sort of mixture that allows him a morning bout of golf before a tough stint in the fields. It is a combination that seemed to agree with Ito. He had caught on to the new ways of working the land in Tomé Açú and in the last couple of years had been producing half of the community's total harvest of 150 tons of cupuassú.

In a country where lumbermen almost never bother to replace the forests they've logged, a handful of Tomé Açú farmers also began to look ahead. Over the last ten years Tomio Sasahara replanted much of his 100-hectare (250-acre) spread with tropical hardwoods. "This is for my children," he said, tramping around his own man-made forest, pointing to the stand of strapping mahogany, rosewood, cedar, Brazil nut, and jacaranda—some of the most precious timber in the world market.

Daunting obstacles still lay ahead for Tomé Açú. All over Brazil, in fact, another tropical blight, perhaps the worst—endemic inflation—had set in and, like the fusarium, refused to go away. Despite President Collor's "life and death battle" with the beast, inflation rose a startling 1,800 percent in 1990. The next year it was tamped down but hardly vanquished. The result in farm country had been soaring fertilizer costs, a steady erosion in the value of produce, and a drought of subsidized credit. Worse, in a sort of shotgun wedding of economy and ecology, the debit-strapped government in Brasília simply canceled credits for farming above the twelfth parallel, the southern edge of Amazonia. The measure may have been meant to brake the advance of agriculture in the already threatened rain forest, but it also abandoned half a million poor farmer families to their own meager devices.

As a result, Tomé Açú began to suffer the same syndrome that assails rural communities the world over: an exodus of young people and an inexorably aging population. The farmers' co-op, which once had 350 members, was down to 150 in 1990. The young adults of Tomé Açú had mostly drifted to Belém or Rio de Janeiro or São Paulo. Some 300 families had sent sons and daughters back to Japan in search of cash and jobs, thus reversing the historic journey their grandparents had made sixty years ago. Too often this was a one-way trip.

"None of my children want to come back to Tomé Açú," said Ryoji Funaki, director of the co-op. Between strenuous drags on a cigarette, he recited a catalog of problems in the countryside: "No electricity, no schools, poor health, no security, no nothing." His nervous gestures left a web of smoke trails. Funaki spoke as we waited on the banks of the Guamá River, halfway between Belém and Tomé Açú. We had just missed the ferryboat, a steel-hulled barge that slowly traversed the mile and a half girth of the Guamá. There was no bridge across the Guamá, and if you were unlucky enough to miss the boat, you could wait an hour or, if there was a long line of cars, many hours, for the next ferry. Funaki ground out the dwindling butt and automatically reached for another cigarette. "No one wants to come back here."

Chris Uhl smiled when asked about Tomé Açú. "I sometimes think it's the final proof that agriculture is impossible in the Amazon," he told me on a hot, dry August afternoon. Uhl, an American biologist who is based in Belém, had spent much of the last decade searching for the chimera of "sustainable agriculture." Put oversimply, that meant farmers who do not farm their lands to death. Too often he had seen the Amazonian small landholder, locked, like some backlands Sisyphus, into an endless cycle of slash-and-burn farming trying to spirit crops out of ever more impoverished fields.

Indeed, for all their ingenuity, the farmers of Tomé Açú may not be so much an example for Amazonia as an anomaly. Unlike their Brazilian neighbors, they have been blessed at times with aid and credit from abroad. They have also relied in the past on high doses of fertilizers, both chemical and organic, costly inputs that are unthinkable for the average Brazilian small landholder. "If the Japanese, with all their talent and resources, are still barely getting along, what hope is there for the far poorer and scattered farmers of the Amazon?"

Uhl's question required no answer, of course, but his own research betrayed a clandestine optimism. In the Amazon, he has commented, virtually all colonists are aliens and there are no privileged castes. Nor, one might add, is there any deus ex machina poised to pluck foundering settlers from disaster. It is rather the glue of a common culture that has helped bind this community together through countless crises. What is more, while many farmers' associations in the Amazon have folded, Tomé Açú has fought to maintain a cooperative, which has been running continuously, in various incarnations, since 1931.

The co-op provided members a vital network of financing, markets, and, most important, information. The successes here owed less to beneficence from abroad than to solidarity and sheer doggedness. "The only way is to try, and try, and try and make mistakes and try again," said Kuhayakawa, hunched over a microscope and a chaotic assortment of test tubes and petri dishes. "Mostly we have been on our own."

The example of Tomé Açú, Uhl and his colleague Scott Subler believe, "provides the hope that perhaps someday man [in the Amazon] can reside in harmony with nature." That may seem pale encouragement for immigrants who crossed the oceans to make a new life half a century ago. But if the farmers of Tomé Açú were to fold up and decamp tomorrow, that legacy alone would be nothing less than monumental.

It may not be any one crop or technique, finally, by which they help solve the riddle of this land, for the Amazon has played havoc with virtually everything these farmers have tried. Rather, it is in their ability to read and adapt to the land, feeling out the changing soils and flora and weather. Just as their forebears withstood war, famine, overpopulation and a shattered economy, at each crisis, so the people of Tomé Açú—immigrants, nisei, and sansei alike—have reached deep into the well of cultural experience and, again and again, come up with a response.

My last evening in the village Sakaguchi took me on a lengthy tour of the Botanical Gardens. Later, over a savory dinner of roasted fish and spiced eggplant, irrigated by generous doses of Pitú *cachaça,* he spoke at length about the rules of tropical agriculture. Farmers everywhere like to jawbone about the weather or prices or prospects for the next harvest. Sakaguchi talked about the future. "Am I rich?" He shrugged. "No. Right now I don't earn anything from this." He gestured into the night toward his gardens. "Fifty years from now I won't be here, but these trees will." Suddenly he went silent and sat now nearly motionless, puffing on a cigarette fixed onto a long metal pipestem, lost in private thoughts and a veil of white smoke.

I ran into Sakaguchi a last time on the bus back to Belém the next day. He was dressed in pressed shirt and trousers; on top of his head was a natty plaid sports cap. He smiled broadly and said he was headed to the Dominican Republic for a two-month consulting job. There, too, it seemed, a wave of the Japanese exodus had rolled ashore years ago, and now another colony of immigrants was in need of counsel. Sakaguchi smiled again, contented, I supposed, with his new mission. Then he pulled the lid of his cap over his eyes and, in the sort of miracle managed only by those inured to the punishing landscapes of the third world, slept through the entire bone-jarring five-hour journey to Belém.

As the bus heaved and pounded its way over the dirt top, I couldn't help feeling that the fate of this Amazonian community turned largely on a special formula: uncanny endurance, the judicious use of a bulldozer, and the forehead that rested under the brim of that plaid sports cap . . . and maybe, Sakaguchi might add, a dollop or two of Pitú.

OF CATTLE
AND KUDZU

> He looketh about the mountains of his pasture and
> seeketh for every green thing.
>
> —Job 39:7

Judson Ferreira Valentim stooped down into a shin-high field of weed and tore out a wad of tangled greenness. "Kudzu," he said, and smiled. The word alone would have been enough to strike terror in the heart of suburban America. God-fearing gardeners and lawnkeepers across the United States do daily battle with this legume, which, left untended, sweeps across backyards like Hannibal with roots. Before this botanical intruder practically everything that grows— grass, mosses, begonias, and bonsai—is choked into surrender. More alarming still, the scourge of Northern Hemisphere summers thrives year-round in the balmy equatorial climate.

But lately the vine that makes American suburbia tremble was helping retrieve ranchers in this corner of the Brazilian Amazon from waste and possible ruin. In fact, some of this weed's most ornery attributes—aggressiveness, alarming growth rates, the bullying of other plants—were precisely its appeal for the Amazonian rancher. It spread fast and thickly, forming a vast green carpet that protected the soil from the punishing

Amazonian sun, halted erosion, warded away pests, and returned life-giving nitrogen to the soil. That was why Valentim, a Brazilian agronomist, son of a frustrated Amazon farmer, and witness to a good deal of devastation wrought in the name of development, was smiling as he clutched his evil bouquet.

You have only to drive along Highway BR-317 to Senador Guiomard, a cow town in the westernmost Amazonian state of Acre, to take in one of the most brutal ecological transformations in the New World. Senador Guiomard lies about thirty miles south of Rio Branco, the regional capital. The trip there, along BR-317, cut through a leveled landscape. On each side of the road pasture stretched as far as the eye could see. The 150-foot canopy of the forest that once stood here had been toppled, burned, and scraped away. Replacing it now was a deep-pile carpet of mottled grass. There was nothing startling in this, of course. Since man learned to husband wild animals and work the earth with seeds and plows, wilderness has given way to farms and grazing lands the world over. But there was something wrong with this picture. Where were the gleaming herds? The bleached Nelore and dappled Girolando? You drove for miles to find only a lonely scrum of cows foraging on odd tufts of grass.

A very few of these ranches were lush and green, clearly well tended. But they were oases in a living desert. In dry season, from May to October, the majority of the farms of Amazonia were a sorry sight. The tropical sun, unencumbered by trees, pounded down on the pasture, baking the barely covered soil to brick and leaving the surviving vegetation prey to pests and blight. The fields went yellow and dry, the brittle grass rattling in the breeze like so much loose straw. Cicadas sawed the torrid air with their angry symphony as thinning cows scrounged for a precious bit of green.

Judson Valentim's assignment, to arrest the ruin and revive this barren terrain, was as controversial as it was formidable. Acre was the land Chico Mendes tried to save from precisely those Valentim wanted to abet: the cattlemen. If Rondônia was center stage in the Amazonian disaster drama, then the cattlemen—especially the cattlemen of Acre—were cast as the black hats of the piece. Ranchers, after all, had been fingered as the chief culprits in the destruction of rain forests in Brazil and just about everywhere else, in fact. In Central America they were the dons of the notorious "hamburger connection," razing the primary rain forests to make the second-grade beef patties of U.S. fast-food cuisine. Amazonia had never been a part of that connection (actually, it is a net beef importer), but thanks largely to the ranchers and their charges, Brazil had lost a swath of rain forest the size of Portugal in thirty years.

Critics might protest that he was consorting with the enemy, but Judson's reasoning was as simple as it was compelling. If the stockmen could mend their ways and begin to ranch sensibly, that was already going a long way toward retrieving the rain forests of Brazil from near certain pillage. Judson's work was as important as it was unsung. No plaques of bronze or keys to western capitals adorned his mantel. His calendar was not crowded with conference dates in London, Geneva, or Toronto. In fact, these days he was lucky to get out of the mud-sotted capital of Acre.

There are more prominent guardians of Amazonia, whose chronicles ring with eminently quotable prophecies on how the forest is being irrevocably destroyed. One of the most dedicated of them is Philip Fearnside, of the Institute for Amazonian Studies, in Manaus, who has continuously challenged the ruinous Amazon policies for two decades, often on his own. But the Jeremiahs have said their piece. The Judson Valentims of Amazonia keep a quieter sort of mission. They roam the Brazilian backlands, knee-deep in muck and weeds at times, groping for a way to make things work. They work the uncharted territory beyond the twelve-alarm headlines, trying daily to work out a modus vivendi with this strange and confounding frontier.

Fifteen hundred miles to the east of Acre, at the other extreme of the Amazon Basin, lies the town of Paragominas. This was one of the early boomtowns of the old Amazon frontier, and easily one of the roughest. Founded when the government opened up the Belém–Brasília highway, Paragominas is really an acronymn, in homage to the three states and the rude ways that contributed to its making. Pará gave the land, Minas Gerais the money, and Goiás the gunmen, so legend has it. This was also where Judson cut his teeth in the countryside and where his father, José Ferreira, lost his shirt. "If you were still a farmer in the Amazon," Judson liked to remind his dad, "you'd probably be dead by now."

In 1969, when the government finished paving the Highway of the Jaguar, the military men in Brasília cast about for patriots to fill the demographic void they saw as the Amazon region. "Settle so as not to surrender" was their slogan. So a farmer from the central state of Minas Gerais, and father of thirteen, answered the call and bought three thousand acres of bottomland near Paragominas. The only problem was that the property didn't exist. When José got to the place his deed described, other claimants were already there, with their own overlapping land titles. It was no surveyor's error, just part of a venerated frontier custom, land chiseling, that had swept along the Belém–Brasília highway like brush fire. "There were so many deeds floating around Paragominas, they used to say it was the first two-story county in Brazil," José recalled.

Judson talked to me in his father's rented apartment in Governador Valadares, a small town known for farming and minerals in Minas Gerais State. It was a cramped but comfortable home and sometimes served as a landing pad for the baker's dozen of Ferreira children (all of whom, in one of the curious habits of families of the Brazilian interior, had first names that began with the same letter—*J*). José had a pleasant loquaciousness and gently competed for airspace with Judson. Though his easy manner belied it, he was the scarred survivor of a land war that has been going on in the Amazon for as long as settlers had been going there.

In rural Brazil, where deeds are plentiful and land is scarce, a property title is a pretty thing. Ferreira pulled out the documents that he had saved from Paragominas—partly out of nostalgia, partly out of some faint hope of someday petitioning for his rightful purchase. It was a big thing, made on a fine, thick parchment, covered with filigreed script, looping official signatures, and blue-inked rubber stamps of all sizes. He had two separate documents for the original "property," each of them running two to three pages. He held them up for a snapshot, bending over the orante pieces of paper, as if to locate the plot he had bought somewhere in the calligraphy.

It was not that Ferreira had failed to check things out beforehand. "I walked all over the forest," he said, recalling his visit with the realtor. "I went down by the river; it had a huge pond, full of fish, that stretched around a bend. I loved it, adored it." Ferreira paused, as if to let the reverie linger. "My land is still there . . . somewhere," With this he let out a laugh and said, "We had a friend in a neighboring city. He had bought many lots in the city to sell to arriving settlers. He would say, 'Hmm, I have so much land without documents and so many documents without land. Let's see what we can do.' "

After three years of battling the bureaucratic wall, Ferreira gave up on his purchase and bought another property, only to find it totally invaded by squatters. But José had no stomach for land wars and ended up giving away three-quarters of the property. Only then did he set down to work. He hired workers, cleared 100 hectares (250 acres), and planted upland rice. The harvest was good. Ferreira brought his produce to the roadside to sell and went bust. "Everybody was selling rice," he said. "The price was terrible."

So he sold out again, bought yet another, smaller plot of 500 hectares (1,250 acres), put down pasture, and fetched the family in Minas. This was 1973, and he packed everybody into a big Ford station wagon and drove three days straight up to Belém. With the proceeds from the sale of the second plot of land, he bought a cattle truck and settled down, finally, to be a rancher. He began a farm and a ranch with forty head of cattle. In the end, he had put all thirteen children through high school and managed to send Judson off to the University of Florida at Gainesville for a master's degree and a Ph.D. José paid with a bleeding ulcer and the beginnings of emphysema. In 1982, his children safely parceled out among spouses, jobs, and schools, he left the Amazon for good and headed back down south.

Now Ferreira convalesced in his small apartment in Minas. He was lucid and lively, if a bit thin, with a full head of wiry hair and an angular face, cut like the precious stones found in the subsoil of that mining territory. José had no more land left in the Amazon, or anywhere else, in fact. "The only thing I miss is having a place in the country, a farm, like where I grew up in Minas. Everybody needs a little green," he said. His apartment, a comfortable, if smallish, second-floor walk-up, was a stone's throw from the Vale do Rio Doce mining company railway. Thirty times a day the train went by, hauling iron ore from the mines to the coast down south and bringing farm produce back north. The house rattled and the conversation was drowned out for several minutes each time the long line of cars lumbered by. Adventurer that he is, José said he would face the Amazon all over again if he had to. But for now the closest he got to nature was the jutting flattop mountain looming beyond the tracks and the placid acrylic paysage, of a pond and woods, hanging on the living-room wall.

"It was partly from seeing my dad suffer that I wanted to help cattle farmers in the Amazon," Judson said. There was a lot of rescuing to be done. Only a brief visit to the countryside was enough to demonstrate just how stranded are the small landholders, the herders, and the farmers trying to squeeze a living out of the Amazon. Judson, like so many Amazon researchers, could have cloistered himself happily in some university or the climate-controlled headquarters of a research institute, tinkering with petri dishes and test plots and publishing weighty papers for scientific tomes. But Judson, who was now thirty-four, had spent a boyhood milking cows and making things grow before he went off to get his Ph.D. Now he rattled off a compendium of farm esoterica—stocking rates, soil chemistry, agronomic stability—in the twangy accent of the Minas backcountry and at the clip of an evangelical preacher. A small, strong-framed man of medium height, he would seem equally at home behind a plow or a lectern.

One of his college professors in Belém was from Acre, and he sowed in the young ag student a seed of interest for that state in the far western Amazon that germinated over the next several years. Back from Florida with his new diplomas, Judson made up his mind when an opening appeared at the Acre branch of the Brazilian Center for Ranching and Agriculture, Embrapa. This was in the late 1980s, and things were changing rapidly in that state. In 1991, 94 percent of Acre's magnificent dense rain forest was still intact, but the percentage that had fallen fell fast, within the last twenty years, when stockmen stormed north for one of this century's biggest land grabs.

Before the cattlemen paved the land with pasture, rubber had been the Amazon's glory crop, and Acre the glory of the Amazon rubber boom. But by early this century rubber tree plantations in Asia were flourishing. Now and again Brazilians pumped money and men into the Amazonian rubber groves, but by the 1970s the latex-gathering economy was moribund. In a reverse alchemy, Acre's white gold turned eventually into red ink. By the last decade the ranchers moved in, buying up dollar-an-acre land from failing rubber estates. In a few years the groves of the stately rubber trees became acres of flat forage.

All over the Amazon cattlemen were blessed with lines of easy credit and subsidized loans from Brasília. At finance they did well, irrigating the money markets and reaping far more than they sowed. At ranching they mostly failed. They cleared the forest, with chain saw armies, bulldozers, and skidders, then torched the debris, turning each dry season into a conflagration.

Not much of this easy money ever made it as far west as

Acre; the ranchers in the eastern Amazon were given preference under Sudam, the Amazon development agency, based
in the eastern Amazonian port of Belém. Nevertheless, the
Acre herders faced the same problems as their counterparts in
other parts of the Amazon. Their fields, turned lush and green
from all the potassium and carbon compost left by the fires,
were robust in the first year or two. Shortly afterward the fields
began to go brown and bald. In five years pastures that had
supported twenty cows on twenty-five acres, par for the Amazon, barely fed five cows. The thinning grass allowed the sun
to bake the soil hard as rock in the dry season. In the rains,
erosion ate away tons of precious humus. The patches of grass
that remained were often attacked by spittlebugs, which sucked
the grass dry, leaving only a field of foamy insect phlegm and
nutritionless straw. Just to stay in business, cattle ranchers,
like the small farmers (except on a far larger scale), were forced
to press on, slashing and burning more and more woodlands
to make new pasture.

Fury followed soon after failure. This was the eighties, when
budgets were tight and the world environmentalists on patrol.
Turning green biomass into red didn't seem much of an alternative for this storied tropical ecosystem. Credits and subsidies for ranching in upland forest areas were suspended in 1989
and were still on ice two years later. (Throughout 1990 and
well into 1991 the Collor government maintained credits for
those herdsmen who already had pastures, though not for those
proposing to deforest new areas to form grazing lands.)

Judson had no qualms then about bailing out the foundering
cowmen. In fact, he had a different idea. Most polemics on
the Amazon universally cast blame on the ranchers while saying relatively little about why they went north in the first place.
Financial incentives were an important perk, of course, but
other economic factors also beckoned. Even more than most
frontiers, the Amazon has suffered from chronic shortages of
hired labor as well as precarious roads and distant markets.

Most farm products demanded hard labor, fetched meager prices, and often rotted before they got to market.

By contrast, a cattle ranch required only a handful of cowboys and farmhands. The rancher's commodity, cattle for dairy and beef, had been in constant demand and retained its value even in times of high inflation. Better still, cows walked to market. Even small landholders in the Amazon, struggling today to wring their livings out of plots of coffee, cacao, and kidney beans, saw the advantages of keeping a few head of cattle. "The rural savings account, I call them," Judson said. As a result, the Amazon herd grew from a mere 4.5 million in 1960 to 20 million in 1990.[1] "Ranchers are in the Amazon to stay," he said. "Ignoring them won't help. We have to work to make them viable."

In every frontier pioneers brought old habits to new lands. The farmers who left the eastern United States took (albeit unintentionally at times) wheat, white clover, and bluegrass with them across the Appalachians. White clover and purslane, likewise, romped through the Australian settlements. The Portuguese navigators took sugar and grapes to the Madeira Islands. Many of these old crops took vigorously to their new habitats. But most frontiers have been in regions whose weather and temperatures were not unlike those of the home country. More, the imported flora was almost always far more aggressive than the native vegetation in the "neo-Europes" of the New World, which rolled over before the invaders.[2] The Amazon, by contrast, is at the heart of Aristotle's torrid zone, where the heat and humidity played havoc with the health and habits of the newcomers.

Likewise, the herdsmen from the temperate and subtropical south imported their know-how, tools, and pasture grasses to equatorial Brazil. They tried myriad exotic forage species— colonião, jaragua, and brachiaria—but almost all of these fell prey either to pests, blight, or the withering sun. A few years ago Judson began reading up on pastures when he came across kudzu. A tropical version, pueraria, was brought to northern Brazil in the 1970s to cover the soil between rows of planted rubber trees, but soon it began cropping up wild all over the western Amazon. Judson began to experiment with this rogue weed.

Acre farmers were a stubborn lot. Only a handful of mavericks, less sanguine than desperate, joined in Judson's experiment. The results were startling. The kudzu did indeed grow voraciously, but instead of a menace it proved a blessing. The thicker vegetation produced three times as much forage as other grasses, allowing more intensive grazing. Planted in "consortium" with other species, kudzu helped keep pastures in balance. In the dry season, when everything else in the Amazon withered and died, kudzu thrived. During the rains of winter it grew more slowly, allowing other grasses room to expand. It needed virtually no maintenance, meaning savings of up to 30 percent for ranchers forming, or re-forming, pastures. Dense and mean, it also shunned pests like the spittlebug and expelled other weeds, eliminating the need for herbicides and pesticides.

From a miserable average of 70 head on a hundred hectares, the "stocking rate" rose almost fourfold, to 250 head. That may be low for Texas or the Argentine pampa, but it was superb for the Amazon, where naturally weak soils supported feeble pastures. What is more, the cows that starved on thinning pastures thrived on kudzu, gaining 220 kilograms (486.2 pounds) a year instead of a standard 90 kilos (198.9 pounds). Milk production increased.[3] The reluctant farmers soon came on board. "If there's one thing a farmer can't stand," Judson said. "it's seeing another farmer make money."

Suddenly Judson, then a young researcher at an underfunded and understaffed government research center, found his services in growing demand. He opened a consulting business and soon was spending much of his days tramping through ailing fields, clucking his tongue at the damage, photographing the sins of bad farming, and teaching the ways of kudzu.

By 1989 everyone wanted kudzu seeds. "The price of seeds went through the roof," he said, rising from next to nothing to fifteen dollars a kilo. In fact, in mid-1991 it was a far better deal for farmers to pull up beans and plant kudzu, just to produce seeds for the seller's market of Acre cattle country.

Kudzu soon drew praise from cattlemen *and* ecologists. Use of Judson's grass became canon law in Acre. In order to brake new deforestation, the state environmental authority, Imac, began issuing permits for pasture clearing only if the rancher agreed to work already disturbed forest areas and plant kudzu in his new fields.

But a nagging question remained. If this new technique could make ranching viable, would not this provoke another rush to the Amazon and so even more deforestation? Judson did not think so. Pastures with kudzu, he argued, could actually help contain expansion of ranches by allowing more intensive grazing. He believed that with kudzu fields, Acre's herds could be more than doubled, from 600,000 to 1.5 million head, without felling a single acre of virgin rain forest. A successful rancher, he noted, is a far less reckless creature than a failing one.[4]

For all its marvels, kudzu was still no miracle crop. The Amazon has long had a way of turning most miracles into dust. In an ecosystem famous for its mosaic of species, a monocrop is a sitting duck for blight or pests. What is more, no one technique or crop can be prescribed for all the Amazon Basin. Something like thirty-five "microecological" zones have been identified in this region, and the land ranges from barren sand to rich volcanic *terra roxa* soils.[5]

In recent years the chapters on ranching in the Amazon disaster narrative have begun to be reedited. Indeed, most of the studies on ecologically damaging herding practices were based on research from the 1970s, when the first calamitous wave of cattlemen pushed north, to the eastern Amazonian region of Pará. A good deal of improvement has been made since then, and the Amazonian herds have continued to grow, despite the problems and the end of massive subsidies.

Throughout the Amazon, Judson and a handful of scientists like him have been working in partnership with second and third generations of cattle ranchers. Already the techniques of pasture management were changing radically. By the late 1980s cattlemen were regularly using fertilizers to restore soil fertility and frequent rotation of cattle to avoid overgrazing. Instead of the grasses from the temperate zones, they had turned not only to tropical kudzu but to a dozen varieties of forage species, more suited to the punishing humid tropics. Many ranchers, pressed to the wall by environmental inspectors and tight budgets, were now reviving spent pastures, rather than chewing up more rain forest.[6]

As much as any one kind of grass or gimmick, prudent pasture management appeared to be vital for the continued tenure of cattlemen in the Amazon. Armed with kudzu and wiser counsel, a group of Acre ranchers now had a fighting chance, where before they simply presided over wasting pastures, razing ever-larger areas of forest, even as their herds thinned out and died.

In late December 1990 reporters, politicians, ecologists, and scriptwriters from a handful of continents descended on the tiny Acre town of Xapuri, to see justice done in the Chico Mendes murder trial. After the four days of testimony, a landowner and his son were found guilty in the murder of the union leader and ecologist, who was shot down as he stepped out his door in 1988. The verdict set a precedent for this surly territory, long known for a nearly untouchable class of land barons.

Judson didn't go to Xapuri. He couldn't even go to work. The problem was that the paltry eight miles that separate the capital from Embrapa headquarters were still unpaved. The "highway," the continuation of Rondônia's BR-364, melted away during the torrents of rainy season, severing this state from the rest of civilization. The paving ought to have been done five years ago. But work was waylaid first by constant construction contract squabbles and then by a barrage of protests, led by Chico Mendes himself, over the government's failure to protect the Indians and forest communities along the highway's route.[7]

Thanks to Mendes, environmental safeguards were finally written into the highway plan, and now even the rubber tappers agreed that BR-364 must be paved. If not, their goods, like everyone else's in Acre, were doomed to languish and rot in the rains every wet winter. During the trial Judson had gone, hat in hand and solo, to the state governor's palace, one more beggar for funds and asphalt. That mission, I learned later, did not succeed. The governor's coffers were already bare; so were the feds' in Brasília. It wasn't the end of the world, of course, just another day's battle in the Thousand Years' War.

Though the verdict in Mendes's trial was widely hailed, the rubber tappers were still digesting a bitter political defeat. A month before the trial their candidate, Jorge Viana of the Workers party, had won an unprecedented balloting in the first round of the governor's election, only to lose a tight contest in a runoff vote held just before the trial. The defeat at the ballot box dampened slightly the cheer over the courtroom victory. The man who assumed office, Edmundo Pinto, was no easy ally; he belonged to the Democratic Social party, which was nearly synonymous with the military regime that had run Brazil for twenty-one years, and he was also a member of old-guard Acre politics. True, he was young and perceived as a political moderate, but Pinto inspired little enthusiasm among the rank and file of the highly politicized rubber tappers and union men of Acre.

In a surprise move, however, Pinto named Judson to head the Acre technological foundation, Funtac. This was a highly respected institution, staffed by dedicated young professionals with a fat budget, foreign credit, and a tradition of aiding the rubber tappers. Judson's expertise was in cattle, of course, but his boyhood in the Amazon and his studies abroad had cemented in him a solid commitment not only to the new age of ecological awareness but also to the people of the Amazon whose everyday lives were consumed by the epic struggle of trying to get by. Soon he was sitting down not only with ranchers but also with rubber tapper representatives, agronomists, and rural extension agents. It was tough going at first. But Judson's appointment seemed at once a spark of innovation and ray of compromise in a state that had seen too little of either in recent times.

CHAPTER

THE DEATH AND LIFE OF CHICO MENDES

Let us honor the rubber tappers,
Honor this nation great and brave.
For it is with the labor of this people
that the tires of cars and planes are made.

So many things about rubber that
to explain I just cannot.
I even found a piece of it
in my pressure cooker pot.

—Rubber tapper's song[1]

It doesn't look much like a battlefield. A huddle of wooden huts raised on stilts crowns a grassy knoll. Tidy dirt paths stitch the way between the houses. Lush orange trees dot the hill, throwing deep shadows, and at the crest, a pair of goalposts marks a makeshift soccer field. Children gambol among grazing cows. Now and again a pair of macaws takes wing, a startling flash of primary red, blue, and yellow against the mottled sky. A hundred yards away the jungle begins, a mat green wall rising to a splendid ten-story canopy. A visit to the Cachoeira Extractive Reserve is like walking into a canvas by the younger Breughel, as Lévi-Strauss once described the Amazon, where "Paradise is portrayed as a place in which plants, animals, and human beings live together in tender intimacy."

Yet it was here, in the westernmost Brazilian state of Acre, near the Bolivian border, that the Amazonian labor leader Francisco Alves ("Chico") Mendes Filho and the rubber tappers made their stand. Early in 1988 a local rancher, Darly Alves da Silva, bought out one rubber tapper's lot, pressured others to sell out as well, and proceeded to deforest. Mendes organized an *empate,* a standoff, mustering *seringueiros,* or rubber tappers, to stand in the way of the ranchers' forest-clearing crews.

For a decade *seringueiros* had increasingly resorted to *empates* to halt deforestation, for each forest that encumbered potential pastureland was also a *seringal,* a grove of rubber trees, and home to dozens, often hundreds, of the fifty thousand Acre families that lived off the "weeping wood" of the Amazon. Ranchers and small landholders had already slashed and burned their way through 160,000 square miles of Amazon rain forest and were steadily advancing on Acre. This was the extreme western corner of Brazilian territory long known for its magnificent rain forest and, more recently, for murder by hire. Up close, Mendes's territory seemed as far from paradise as Jerusalem's Aceldama, that land "purchased with the reward of iniquity" and rendered a "field of blood." The standoff at Cachoeira was Mendes's last. That same year, three nights before Christmas, he was gunned down as he stepped out his back door.

In rural Brazil, where the law and police have generally been the tools of the comfortable classes, such crimes have almost always gone "unsolved." But after international outcry had turned Mendes into an ecological martyr, Brasília sprang into action. Silva and his son, Darci Alves Pereira, were promptly arrested and charged in the murder. Finally, in December 1990, father and son were tried and found guilty of murder. The jury ruled that Darly, less out of rage than icy calculation, had ordered his son to lie in the tall grass behind

Mendes's wooden house and gun down the union leader who dared stand in his way. The old man was sentenced to the maximum penalty of nineteen and one-half years, Darci to nineteen years.[2] The conviction of a rancher and, more significantly, the mastermind of a murder crime was nearly without precedent for the porous justice system of the Amazon, where the murders of peasants, union leaders, and rubber men have been a grisly rule and the punishment of the murderers has been the rare exception. Though human rights watchers complained about the delay, the case was, in fact, tried with lightning speed for the overtaxed Brazilian courts.[3]

With the sudden whiff of justice, the rubber tappers revived their mostly peaceable existence, for the brutal murder had at once eliminated one of Brazil's most eloquent union leaders and alerted the world to the peril facing a largely untouched part of the Amazon and a disinherited community of forest dwellers. It also set off a chain of events that reached around the world and profoundly changed the politics and economy of this country's troubled frontier.

Ever since Mendes's death, the *seringueiros* he championed had become something of an international cause célèbre. No sooner had Mendes been buried than eleven Hollywood movie producers, and five Brazilian companies, rushed to place bids for film rights to the Chico Mendes story. Ecologists decorated *seringueiro* leaders with awards and escorted them to the halls of Congress, Parliament, and the Bundestag. Osmarino Amâncio Rodrigues, Mendes's most eloquent successor, traversed the globe on speaking tours. Almost monthly Europeans and Americans called on tiny Xapuri, the sleepy river town where Mendes lived. Mendes was compared with Gandhi, and his name adorned T-shirts, parks, plazas, and foundations. Now help from abroad—loans, outright grants, trucks, technology, and consultants—was overflowing.

In homage to Mendes, and under heat from the world environmental movement, the Brazilian government proceeded to set aside more than five million acres of "extractive reserves," vast, protected areas like Cachoeira, dedicated to the collection of natural forest products, such as rubber, nuts, and fruit. Just one of them, the Chico Mendes Extractive Reserve, sprawls over 2,400,000 acres, three times the size of Rhode Island. In June 1990 Brasília announced plans to demarcate another 63,550,000 acres of reserves, an area larger than West Germany.

In a trip to Acre, in 1905, Euclydes da Cunha, stupefied by the *seringueiros'* medieval existence, called for "urgent measures" on behalf of "this obscure and abandoned society." It took almost a century, but today these "fellahin" have won legal tenancy to the land they have occupied for generations. Rubber tappers now have exclusive claim to these extractive reserves, which enjoy a legal status similar to that of Indian reservations. They do not own the land but have guaranteed usufruct rights for renewable thirty-year periods. In a country where land reform has never gotten off the ground, this was hardly a modest achievement. For the *seringueiros,* who had next to nothing, it was remarkable.

There is arguably nothing especially new in this sort of arrangement. Back in Eden, when life was easy, the earth's first tenants were assigned to a bountiful natural garden. No tilling was necessary. Sustenance hung from every bough, just an arm's length away. That was paradise. In the parlance of today's environmental movement, it might be called the first extractive reserve.

Since the Fall, however, things have not been so simple. Life in the wilderness forced civilizations to evolve from the simple economies of subsistence to those of cultivation and industry. That mandate produced fabulous harvests, inventions, and eventual empires. "Then Isaac sowed in that land, and received in the same year an hundredfold. . . . And the man waxed great" (Genesis 26:12–13). But that was the end of environmental innocence as well. "Increase and multiply and replenish the earth. And the fear and dread of you shall be upon every beast of the earth, and upon every fowl of the air, upon all that moveth *upon* the earth . . . into your hand they are delivered. Everything that moveth and liveth shall be meat for you . . ." (Genesis 9:1–3).

For millennia, civilizations have increased and multiplied and subdued the earth, just as the Scriptures ordered. Now, as we approach the eleventh millennium of agriculture, extractivism has been revived. Nowhere is this more evident than in the Brazilian Amazon, especially in Mendes's state of Acre. Society, choking on the by-products of progress, seems to have soured on the miracles of industry and turned instead to a gentler, more ecological past.

On the ground, life in the extractive reserve is not so enchanting. Cachoeira may no longer be Acre's Aceldama, yet harvesting the seringal is a labor soaked in sweat and sacrifice, in which nature is as much adversary as ally. The *seringueiros* have captured the world's imagination and sympathies. But their worst enemies—bitter poverty and a dead-end economy—still loom large. These were formidable obstacles a century ago, when rubber was king and Amazonia the unrivaled kingdom. They are brick walls today as the superharvests of the rubber-planting nations have all but buried the intrepid extractors of the native forests. Mendes's successors are paradoxically bathed in limelight at the same time they battle simply to make ends meet. Now that the *seringueiros* are in charge they must discover how to make their hard-won swaths of Amazonia prosper. A recent trip to the Seringal Cachoeira, where Mendes spent part of his boyhood and which is now an extractive reserve, illustrated just how hard a task it is to reinvent Eden.

The "highway" to Cachoeira is a thin ribbon of clay running south from the sleepy river town of Xapuri, through a gauntlet of cattle ranches, all the way to Bolivia. The fifteen-mile stretch is passable only in the dry season, and then only at the cost of a bruising two-hour ride along a crater-pocked track. Along the way passengers piled atop a flatbed truck are shrouded in a man-made sirocco of red dust kicked up as truck wheels pound the bone-dry road. For miles the only trace of the lush forests that once clothed this territory are the occasional towering Brazil nut trees. The *castanheiras* are protected under the environmental code, but in a travesty of that code, ranchers clear-cut and burn everything else, scorching the roots of the Brazil nut and stripping the surrounding vegetation that harbors the bee that pollinates the flowers of its towering canopy. So the *castanheiras* eventually die standing up, their desiccating trunks posted like sentinels in a senseless vigil over a stolen landscape. The seringal, which is now part of the larger Chico Mendes Extractive Reserve, lies at the end of this leveled landscape, like a final trench of green against the advancing fazendas.

I arrived there on a May Sunday, the day of a community assembly. About thirty men gathered in a three-room schoolhouse, built by the community, to discuss the problems and prospects at the seringal. Francisco de Assis Monteiro, the co-op president, presided. A small man with a trim mustache, Monteiro had the manner of someone acquainted with exacting work and few rewards. His calm might have been an inheritance from his father, a man from Ceará, a land of dust and drought and early graves. His frame was slight but strong. He was outwardly calm, but his eyes were nervous and penetrating. Monteiro took a seat on the windowsill as men in straw hats and rubber sandals slipped into school desk seats. The items on the assembly agenda were hardly new: accounts receivable, depressed prices, short credit, and the trials of getting goods to distant markets.

Yet before, during the days of the rubber bosses, this scene would have been impossible. *Seringueiros* were contracted by the *seringalista* or *patrão,* the rubber boss, and obliged to sell him all their nuts and crude rubber at the price he named. They were equally obliged to buy back coffee, sugar, kerosene, and medicine at fabulous markups. The *seringueiros'* incomes rarely caught up with their debits, of course, and most fell into per-

manent debt peonage. Liberty meant, at most, moving downriver and transferring one's debit from one boss to another.

"The *seringueiro* realizes a tremendous anomaly," wrote
Euclydes da Cunha. "He is the man who works to enslave
himself." Nearly a century later the rubber bosses were gone,
but the burdens remained. As the assembly began, each co-op
member's name and the amount he owed the central store were
read out loud. The indigents' roll call loosed a series of pent-
up frustrations, and for the next two hours the co-op members
boiled with anger. Where were the oxen and mules to haul the
nuts from the forest stashes? Who would pay for the nuts perishing in the rain or eaten by rodents? Everyone at Cachoeira,
of course, had pitched in to build the co-op and drive away the
patrão and the *marreteiros,* the price-chiseling itinerant merchants who roamed the rubber groves. But now many seemed
at a loss. They asked for money up front to pay for transport
and credit at the store. Someone, they demanded, should come
fetch their produce.

But Monteiro was unflinching. The days of easy credit at
Cachoeira were over, he announced. "Everyone," he said, "is
going to have to pay for what he gets, on the spot." He raised
a hand, quelling the murmurs, and began to talk about what a
co-op means. "I'm not anyone's *patrão,*" Monteiro said, his
voice tightening with emotion. "There are no more bosses.
You all"—he panned an index finger around the room—"are
the bosses now. You have to understand, our finances are your
finances. For all that we've complained about the *patrão* in the
past, we are not about to become one ourselves." Some heads
nodded in mute consent. One man quit the meeting in a huff.
The grumbling lasted all morning.

For a brief time the milky latex of the rubber groves generated fabulous wealth for Brazil. It was white gold that built
the magnificent Opera House of Manaus and the Teatro da Paz
in Belém, the Amazon's contributions to the *belle époque,* and

made these once-torpid river towns into regular ports of call
for European ocean liners. While the streets of Rio de Janeiro
and São Paulo flickered with gas lamps, Manaus's boulevards
blazed with electric lights. Dollars were abundant. So were
pchillingas, as locals in Pará State called the British currency.
"Never has Pará seen so much gold in circulation," gasped the
historian Manoel Barata.[4] In no small way Amazonia was then
another country, closer by ship to London than to Rio de Janeiro
and beholden more to the demands of the industrial world than
to the whims of the Brazilian monarch. "Unimaginable for the
rest of Brazil," sang Cunha, "is the city of Belém, with its
giant buildings, incomparable plazas and people with the habits of Europe, gentle and generous."[5]

But by 1912 Malaysian plantations, nurtured from Amazon
rubber seedlings, came on stream and soon eclipsed the Amazonian groves. Hopes of a revival in Amazonia were raised in
the 1920s, when Henry Ford launched Fordlândia, his grandiose scheme to plant rubber on an industrial scale, but those
hopes moldered with the deadly leaf blight that ravaged his
Connecticut-size plantation. Washington's effort to stimulate
rubber production during World War II, "the battle for rubber," again briefly revived the moribund rubber sector. It also
created a well-financed Banco da Borracha (bank of rubber),
meant as a "new motor" to revive the sputtering system of
latex extraction. But the decline was irreversible. "To tell the
truth," the noted agronomist Felisberto Camargo told the Higher
War College in Rio in 1951, "the new motor has done everything it could to move an old, archaic machine of production."

That same year, when the Brazilian economy was beginning
to stir to the rhythms of a new industrial age, the former
monopolist of the world rubber market was forced to import
just to meet manufacturers' demand. Today Brazil, like most
other countries, uses three times more synthetic elastics than
natural rubber. But the scandalous fact is that the nation that
once sent its rubber bounty to manufacturers around the world
must today import 75 percent of the natural latex it consumes.

By 1990 almost half of what it still produced came from plantations, located far away from the rubber-rich Amazon forest. Slowly the *seringalistas* began to disappear, and the last of them cashed out in the 1980s, when the rich ranchers arrived. They left behind a typical extractivist's legacy: virtually no investments in technology, a few personal fortunes, and a handful of crumbling monuments.

One of those monuments is the town of Xapuri itself. Since the zenith of the rubber age, this rubber-trading post earned a special place in Brazil's frontier pantheon. It was in Xapuri and other Acre towns that a ragged army of Brazilian rubber tappers united under a charismatic southerner, Plácido de Castro, and rose against the Bolivian occupation of Acre. Thanks largely to that revolt and the able diplomacy of the Baron do Rio Branco, Acre was ceded to Brazil in 1903. During World War II, when Brazil recruited thousands of northeasterners to march into the rubber groves to lend a hand to the Allies, it was in Xapuri that many of these "soldiers of rubber" mustered. Thanks to Chico Mendes and the age of ecology, that fame lingers. But the once-proud and wealthy town is today just another sluggish river port, with a potholed main street, a couple of no-star hotels, and a gutted economy. Many merchants made it rich off the rubber wealth that poured through Xapuri, and most of them packed up and moved on. One who stayed was Guilherme Zaire.

One midafternoon in late December 1990, while everyone was gathered at the courthouse, hanging on every moment of the Chico Mendes murder trial proceedings, Zaire sat in the shade of the veranda of a riverside *botequim,* playing dominoes. I had reluctantly sought him out, for Zaire was not all that fond of the press. And no wonder. It was the press, particularly we of the foreign press, who had brought so much tumult to Xapuri, by making Chico's death into an international spectacle.

Zaire, of Lebanese descent, was one of the last great *serin-*

galistas of the region, who had plied Acre rivers for decades, buying up rubber and selling food and supplies. Dressed in a colorful cotton shirt, stamped with a brilliant tropical design, Zaire had black hair streaked with silver and a rectangular face framed by square horn-rims with thick lenses. I begged his pardon and hovered, awaiting his acknowledgment for what seemed like an eternity as he studied his chips in silence. Finally he raised his chin slightly and, still studying his dominoes, said he wasn't interested in talking. Another long pause. "Maybe later," he finished.

Later I caught him on the stoop of his supply house, on Major Salinas Street. Smiling now, his guard slightly down, he still balked at the presence of a reporter. Zaire was one of the rare *seringalistas* who got on well with the rubber tappers and had been both a friend and an employer of the young Chico Mendes, who worked for a time in his store. Since Chico's death, however, tensions had grown several notches tighter in Xapuri. The trial, after all, had brought on the biggest foreign invasion since the Bolivian intendency, and foul humor seemed to smolder downtown. But cordiality is part of the Brazilian gene pool, and though foreigners may often mistake it for a genuine welcome, natives often find it hard to resist working their charms on a low-risk first encounter such as this one. As we wavered there for a long moment, I gently imploring, Zaire gently waffling, a man in nothing but nylon shorts and rubber thongs with a two-foot-thick block of pressed rubber on his back puffed up the riverbank and disappeared into the back of Zaire's shop. So I asked Zaire about the rubber business.

His laugh was more a honk, and merrily now, he waved me inside. "Come see this crap." We walked back into the warehouse where the man had set down his burden. Like the pressed *pranchas* (slabs) of rubber he hauled, this man was a deep oily brown. His block, which weighed perhaps sixty pounds, fell with a dull thud against the stained cement floor, where similar bricks of rubber were untidily piled. The smell from this deposit was almost unbearable, a heady mix of drying latex and rotting vegetable matter, stewing in the tropical heat. Handling this stuff leaves for days an odor on the skin that no soap or solvent can hasten away. "No good for anything anymore." Zaire nudged the block with the point of his shoe, as he might a dog turd.

Indeed, a few doors down, at the Xapuri rural workers' cooperative, where the rubber tappers ran a general store and bought rubber and Brazil nuts from Cachoeira and other rubber groves, the bad news was already posted. A notice from the rubber-processing factories in Rio Branco advised that precisely these pressed rubber blocks would no longer be acceptable. Orders from industrial buyers in São Paulo, the notice said. There was, it seemed, a total lack of quality control in the making of these rubber blocks. They contained too much water and discolored latex. Too much junk.

The romantic photos of the rubber tapper's glory days show a different picture: a man in a straw hat slowly ladling creamy white latex onto a wooden shaft that he rotates slowly over a wood fire. The latex hardens slowly and evenly, as a pleasant, hickorylike odor swathes the forest camp. Rubber cured in this way emerged already semivulcanized from the woodsmoke and so was serviceable as a raw ingredient for most industrial purposes. Though today virtually all tires of passenger cars are made entirely of synthetic rubber, industry has found no suitable substitute for natural latex for many products. The tires of trucks and airplanes require natural rubber, which is more resilient and heat-resistant. The best surgical gloves and condoms are made from liquid natural latex.

But those days died with the rubber boom. The sort of practice that fills the yellowing pages of Amazon photo albums required speed and care, both of which the rubber tappers had shirked. In order to produce the smoked ball of latex, the rubber tapper had to tap his trees in the morning, walking a forest path weaving over seven hundred to a thousand acres, and return to collect the latex in the afternoon, while it was still liquid. Then he proceeded to smoke it all in the same day.

Latex begins to coagulate as soon as it makes contact with the air, and the *seringueiros* have only a few hours' leeway. Once hardened, rubber will not return to its liquid form.[6]

The tedious routine and the negligible difference in price for the semicured rubber eventually discouraged this picturesque craft. Now *seringueiros* tap the trees in the morning and return only a day or two later to collect the latex that has hardened in the little plastic cups. By then all matter of impurity—water, leaves, twigs, and insects—will have fallen into the mixture. All this, rubber and junk, is then compacted under a wooden press, to form the *pranchas,* which are piled into canoes, and the fetid lot is paddled for hours or days into Xapuri.

This rubber may still be used for watchbands, the soles of shoes, and some auto parts. But it is employed less and less for the purpose Henry Ford dreamed of sixty years ago. "We cannot use the native Amazonian rubber without putting our customers at risk," said Marco Lo Russo, an executive with Michelin of Brazil. Michelin, in fact, once sent a representative to Acre to work with the *seringueiros,* in an effort to improve the quality of their rubber. But he gave up in despair after a few months. Now Michelin and other tire companies fulfill their national rubber quotas by buying from their own plantations.

Many visitors to the pristine forests of Acre have marveled at the harmony between the rubber tappers and their forests. The *seringueiros* slip through the woods with a grace and ease that no city man could imitate. They call out not only the names of every tree but also the uses of their bark, leaves, and roots. This one for an upset stomach, that one for a toothache, and this other for impotence. They stalk the pacas and the coatis with the stealth of a jungle cat and go about the simple ritual of their work with a serenity and contentment that belie the misery of their vocation. Their intimacy with the forest, their skill in working the veins of the rubber tree with deft strokes of the knife have been the topics of much poetry. From their simple hands and knotted forearms, after all, sprang the wealth that white gold gave Brazil for a few glorious decades.

But poetry pales before the crushing grammar of the modern economy, and rubber tapping in these times is less a matter of verse than engineering applied to soil and botany. Fifteen hundred miles southeast of the rubber groves of Acre, a few hours' drive from the regional capital of Cuiabá, lies the Michelin tire company's largest Brazilian rubber plantation. It rises suddenly like a green forested island in a monotonous sea of soybeans. This 10,000-hectare (25,000-acre) spread is an industrial-scale rubber farm. Here a multinational company, the largest in the tire business, is busy turning soil, trees, and tappers into the cogs of a giant botanical factory.

What this landscape lacks in raw, natural beauty it makes up doubly in precision. Some 8,600 hectares (21,500 acres) are spread out in meticulous order, divided into 100-hectare (250-acre) blocks and again into 25-hectare (62.5-acre) squares, where maturing rubber trees stand in obedient rows. Eucalypti are planted as a windbreak, enclosing each of these minirubber stands with a taller green fringe. The distances and weights are calculated exactly at the Michelin farm; the company found that a single man could comfortably haul 16 kilos (35.2 pounds), of rubber, for up to 250 meters (272.5 yards). The rubber is then deposited into a box at each miniforest, each of which is tagged with the initials of its gene type: ROG3 from Rondônia, RBM from Malaysia, and so on.

The cutting of the rubber tree is, likewise, a calibrated affair. The worker holds his knife at a thirty-three-degree angle to the trunk and makes an incision no more or less than 1.2 centimeters (slightly less than ½ inch), deep enough to get to the veins under the bark but shallow enough to avoid the tender core. There is even a science to the way the tappers step around the tree—wheeling counterclockwise, a slow-motion dance with a stationary partner—while the right hand bears down on the trunk for a single, clean incision. After each cutting, the tapper pauses to clean the path of debris and to peel the loose bark from the wound. This peeling is then deposited into a sack, attached to his waist; nothing is squandered here, and the peelings will be the source of as much as 2 percent of the total latex harvest.

No cutter may be issued his knife and assigned to a rubber stand until he has gone through the training course, a twenty-five-day class that begins with a simple walk in the groves, proceeds to "tapping" paraffin mannequins of seringa trees, and then moves to cutting on living but damaged or aged trees. No more than four days go by between the bleeding of the rubber trees and the stocking of semifinished rubber in the storehouse. (In Acre, where just the trip between the rubber tapper's home and the trading post can be a week's journey by boat, the whole cycle could take a month or more.) The *seringueiros* of Acre would be as lost here as a peasant in an automobile factory, and Michelin says no Amazonian tappers have ever shown up for jobs, nor, if they did, would they be readily accepted. They would have to unlearn their poetic craft to master the assembly-line lexicon of plantation rubber.

Though Michelin's rubber groves were only just coming of age in 1991, prospects were bright. In ten years this one plantation's expected harvest—sixteen thousand tons—would match the latex currently produced in all of Amazonia's wild rubber forests.

Many companies are still trying to plant rubber in the Amazon region, pursuing a stubborn vision that has haunted Brazil since Malaysia's first rubber plantations began to produce. But no one has been able to beat the deadly leaf blight, *mycrocyclus ulei,* which thrives in the humid jungle climate and sweeps through planted groves of rubber, rendering them next to useless. Trees attacked by the fungus drop their leaves, and all the latex is spent in regenerating foliage, leaving little for milking. In Mato Grosso, however, as in São Paulo and Bahia, the rubber groves have found a niche, what agronomists call an escape zone. There enough rain falls to nurture the rubber trees but not enough to create the saunalike conditions that are perfect for nurturing the fungus that ruined Henry Ford. If the blight can still be staved off from the Brazilian plantations outside the Amazon, by the year 2000 rubber farms will meet virtually the entire domestic demand for natural rubber. If that comes to pass, the folkloric practice of gathering white gold from the wild rubber groves of Acre will probably be destined to exhibits in dusty museums.

Guilherme Zaire was one of the Amazonian *seringalistas* who saw the handwriting on the forest wall. As Xapuri began to crumble, he started thinking ahead, and his busy store on Major Salinas Street is today a tribute to that foresight. Zaire walked back from the deposit into the lighter, and more fragrant, storefront salon. There he pointed to a more recent line of goods: a stack of aluminum buckets, farming tools, hoses, and other implements of plastic and tin. These modern factory-made consumer wares are the items he buys and sells today. Another corner was dominated by a mountain of granulated sugar—"Zaire Sugar," the label said. It was bought in São Paulo, packaged in Rio Branco, and hauled back down the sometimes mud, sometimes hardtop highway to Xapuri, to sell to the rubber tappers. More and more of their putrid rubber would be needed to pay for modest amounts of this pristine white Zaire sugar—as long, that is, as anyone still needed the rubber.

Reinventing Eden

But romance still mists the portrait of the Amazonian *seringueiro*. Their decades of battles—from the Acre revolution to their efforts for the Allies during World War II—made this starving class of workers into international heroes. Now, thanks to Chico Mendes, they are heroes again. Yet another battlefront, ecology, has hoist them into the international spotlight. The soldiers of rubber have turned into sentries of the forest, the cherubim at the gates of this last patch of Eden.

Such notions may be a tonic to our times of overdevelopment, but they are not new. The rubber tappers are exalted, like Rousseau's savages, and Cunha's *sertanejos,* by a civilization that no longer shares their world. The wild outdoors and its rough tenants are not only admirable but also judged uncorrupt and vessels of authenticity. "Wild wool is finer than tame," exclaimed John Muir. He saw the sheep multiplying over the western United States much the way the *seringueiros* saw the growing bovine herds: nothing but "hoofed locusts."

But behind these paeans is also a series of firm beliefs about Amazonia's proper "vocation." The promoters have stated basically that it is the rubber tappers, Indians, and other gatherers who will show the way toward "sustainable development." The arguments are simple but persuasive: In the extractive reserves, economy and ecology are happily wed. The forest people will preserve their habitat because it is the forest that sustains them. And this sylvan synergy will at once retrieve Amazonia from the jaws of environmental disaster and nurture a bountiful tropical arcadia.

Scientists have published lengthy papers showing that the standing forest is more valuable than the ranch or plantations created by removing it. A much-cited article in *Nature* magazine tallied the bounty of the Peruvian Amazon, reporting that a single hectare harbored seventy-two different marketable fruits, fibers, and medicinals, worth $6,820 in "Net Present Value."[7] Stephen Schwartzman, an anthropologist with the important Washington-based NGO Environmental Defense Fund, has written extensively on how the economy of petty extractors is far superior to that of Amazon ranchers. "The extractive reserves are the most promising alternative to land clearing and colonization schemes," the World Bank concluded in 1982. Seminars on extractive reserves have been held from London to Panama City.

Some have taken their convictions to the field. Jason Clay of Cultural Survival, has trekked all through the Amazon, collecting samples of potentially valuable forest products. Through his initiative, Ben Cohen and Jerry Greenfield of the Vermont-based ice-cream chain Ben & Jerry's Homemade, got into the rain forest support business. Clay met Ben Cohen at a Grateful Dead rain forest benefit concert in September 1988, and the two hit it off from the start. Clay had tired of all the talk about the perishing Amazon and set out to try to help the people who lived there. Cohen was a businessman tugged by a social conscience and the desire to do good while doing well. In January 1989 they met for dinner at an Italian restaurant in Boston's North End and over pasta and red wine discussed just how an ice-cream salesman could help halt deforestation. Clay talked about using forest fruits, such as cupuassu, assaí, and Brazil nuts, in food products. Cohen outlined the manufacturing side of the business, explaining about the volume and quality of products required. The next month Clay headed for the Amazon and rounded up half a ton of fruits, dyes, crafts, and honey. After he got back, Clay piled the Amazon produce into his car and drove up to Ben's place in Jericho, Vermont. When he arrived, Ben and his fiancée were already trying out an idea that had been hatched during the Grateful Dead benefit concert: a rain forest nut brittle and ice cream. Clay headed to the kitchen and threw in some Brazil nuts. He also whipped up a batch of cupuassu ice cream.

Ben had invited a number of dinner guests that night, including several of Ben and Jerry's board members. They tasted the concoction. "They loved it," said Clay. The first year, 1990, Ben and Jerry's placed an initial order for no less than two hundred thousand pounds of nuts.

In February, while he was on his search mission for Ben and Jerry's, Clay met Anita Roddick, the owner of the Body Shop and a soft touch for the cause of salvaging Amazonia. She invited Clay to Scotland to meet her husband, Gordon, and to talk about doing business in the rain forest. After skiing and snooker and downing whiskey late into the night, they decided they could do business. The Roddicks had already raised more than four hundred thousand dollars to help save the rain forest and wanted to know how to spend it. Clay suggested

that they put the money toward helping local Amazonian organizations and to raising more rain forest funds. Clay promised
that Cultural Survival would match any funds from the Body
Shop. He then shuttled back to the Amazon to contact rubber
tappers, Indians, and other local communities. Soon the London-based beauty products chain was testing a whole line of
rain forest cosmetics.

Then the press caught on to this new partnership between
profits and peoples of the forest, and all of a sudden a whole
new market blossomed. In a matter of months the small human
and ethnic rights center founded by the Harvard anthropologist
David Maybury-Lewis and run by a small band of young scientists dedicated to defending the world's endangered minorities had turned into a broker (nonprofit, of course) for rain
forest wares. Clay and Co. left behind a dusty attic office in
Harvard's Peabody Museum, rented a two-story house in busy
Harvard Square, and started a marketing program. The handful of ethnologists turned into a staff of thirty, with skills ranging from business administration to environmental consulting.
In the span of two years, and through their initiatives, thirty-
five companies in Europe, Canada, and the United States were
cashing in on the Amazon, selling Brazil nut cookies, copaiba
soap, babassu and Brazil nut oil bath beads, nut and dried fruit
breakfast cereal, ice cream, frozen yogurt, and snacks.

There is a slight deception involved in the corporate sales
pitch. The majority of these products are not rain forest products at all. Banana, oats, papaya, coconut, cupuassu, cacao,
honey, and guava are not culled from the wild woods but husbanded from land where forests have been removed. (Some,
such as cashews, don't even come from the Amazon.) Nevertheless, the marketing of these products has helped an equally
deserving and castigated class, the small farmers of the Amazon. Most important, a part of the profits from the sale of the
cookies, candies, cosmetics, and such goes back to the people
of the Amazon. The products are *for* the rain forest even if
they are not all *from* it. "When we started," noted Clay, "none

of the forest residents were processing anything for sale internationally." Now the *seringueiros* have all they can handle just filling the orders.

Environmentalists have long decried the current model of development in Amazonia, concentrating on land grabs by small landholders and cattle ranches, not only as highly destructive but also as uneconomic. The rubber tapper, by contrast, milks latex and collects nuts without harming the forest. He generally lives far better than the *seringueiro* who has quit the forest for the teeming *favelas* of Rio Branco.

There are many kinds of extraction, of course. Brazil owes its name and early commercial history to one of the most predatory kinds, the felling of the resinous timber known as brazilwood, from which a colorful dye was extracted. Lately what scientists have been concentrating on is something else: the extraction of oils, essences, medicinals, and fruits on a continual, "sustainable" basis. Despite the flush inventories of the forest emporium, however, the economics of gathering is a complicated affair. The doubters have weighed in with their own studies.

One is Alfredo Homma, a researcher at the Humid Tropics Research Center (Cpatu), a branch in Belém of the Brazilian Center for Ranching and Agriculture, Embrapa. He has devoted fifteen years to the subject of extractivism. "Down through history, one by one, the extractive plants were replaced by cultivated ones," Homma explained. "Cultivation proved cheaper, more reliable, and the only way to feed a growing population." Some natural products, such as the anesthesic curare, cannot be easily or cheaply synthesized. "Right-handed molecules sometimes come out left-handed molecules in the laboratory," in the words of Marc Plotkin, a pharmacologist with the environmental advocacy group Conservation International. However, Homma has found that in the vast majority of cases the very success of natural products in the marketplace can also "destabilize" the extractive system or even destroy it. The inability of simple gatherers significantly to increase supply makes buyers chary and encourages farmers and businesses to plant. Eventually the forest products are muscled out by cheap synthetic substitutes or farm-grown goods.

For years forest dwellers collected guaraná, a caffeine-laced Amazonian fruit, to make a soft drink of the same name. Along came the Juice Law in the 1970s, requiring that all fruit-derived beverages contain a fixed minimum percentage of the natural product. Demand for guaraná skyrocketed, from 250 to 1,600 tons a year, far outstripping the capacity of the petty extractors. "Now," notes Homma, "all guaraná is planted." Likewise, since the eighteenth century, when sipping "chocolate" became the rage in Europe, wild cacao gathering gave way to plantations and agribusiness. Coffee, mint, and quinine are other wild plants that have gone domestic. There is perhaps no better example than coca, the alkaloid-containing plant that grows wild in the subtropical rain forests of the Andes and in parts of the Amazon. Since cocainetrafficking became a multibillion-dollar business, coca has been planted with spectacular success. In the Huallaga Valley of Peru and the Bolivian Chaparé and Yungas regions, peasants manage three to four harvests of coca leaf per year.

In these times of save the rain forest crusades, Homma's thesis is not a popular one. But he has delivered this message in forums the world over—and generally drawn bitter denunciations. It is his misfortune that many of the detractors are more eloquent and at ease with their audiences than he is. They always have a bon mot for reporters and, more important, the blood right to invoke Chico Mendes's legacy. Once, at a debate on extractive reserves, in Manaus, the president of the Conselho Nacional dos Seringueiros, the rubber tappers' national council, Júlio Barbosa, squared off with Homma. An astute politician and normally a gentle-spoken man, Barbosa listened to Homma's exposé, then scorchingly lit into the *técnicos* (technicians), who fiddled away with graphs and spreadsheets and befuddled listeners with theory. Applause thundered through the auditorium. Inured to the storm of hostility, a patience born, it seemed, of Asian roots and plenty of experience in the wind chambers of environmental congresses, Homma sat placidly through all this.

But Homma is no Amazonian interloper. His grandfather Rioto Oyama was one of the region's early entrepreneurs. This Japanese immigrant had the idea of importing to the Amazon region a few seedlings of jute, the fibrous plant used for making sacks for grain and coffee. Brazil at the time imported burlap and jute sacks from India, at a tremendous cost. But Oyama, then the president of a farmers' cooperative in Oka-yama, Japan, bet that jute would take well to the *várzea,* or floodplains, of the Amazon and its tributaries. He gathered his wife and four children and boarded the *Montevideo-Maru,* the same ship that brought the founding families of Tomé Açú. He was fifty-one then but had fixed on the idea of planting jute in Brazil. He sowed two hundred seedlings along the Rio Amazonas and watched a national sacking industry sprout. For his innovation Oyama got the glory, but not much else. While the jute boom lasted, the industrial sackers secured the patents and the middlemen got the lion's share of the profits. Then along came synthetic bags, overtaking the jute of Amazonia. Oyama died a poor man in a plain clapboard house in the Amazonian river town of Parintins.

Alfredo Kingo Oyama Homma, like so many nisei and san-sei, embodies in striking ways the two cultures he represents. His language is punctuated with the informality of Brazil; his manner is correct, somewhat stiff at times, and as precise as his grandfather's Japan. He speaks with a certain breathiness, born, it seems, of timidity and the intensity of his commitment to his scholarship.

The criticism leveled by the *seringueiro* leaders is well taken: Amazon investigators often dwell in a reified world of labora-tories and conference halls, whose science never seems to trickle down to sod level, where the people are crying for solutions. But these ills are not Homma's doing. Actually Homma has tramped all over the Amazon, from Acre to Altamira, visiting

extractive reserves and settlers' farms, ranches, and plantations. Embrapa, the agency he works for, is better than many
in getting technology and know-how to the countryside.

In fact, Homma's analyses have served as an alert to the
people who are supporting extractive reserves. The emotion
that thickens his voice and shortens his breath at the podium is
in part charged with indignation at those who would fool their
constituents with magic and panaceas. He talks less like a
technician, in fact, than like an evangelist, warning against a
kind of glib formula that he believes will hurt not only the
rubber tappers but all Brazilians. He is indignant that in the
rush to exalt and aid the *seringueiro,* the *colono,* the Amazon
small landholder, who outnumbers the tappers two- or three-
fold, is totally ignored. They are not peoples of the forest but
peoples of the frontier, jettisoned there under grandiose government settlement schemes and then left to fend for themselves.

Messengers like Homma may not be much liked, but willy-
nilly, they are being heeded. Lately, in fact, the terms of the
debate on extractivism have changed entirely. Instead of
breathless apologies for the *seringueiro* and impressive inventories of the forests' bounty, ecologists and activists are paying
close attention to the hard numbers. Though many may rail at
the cattlemen and extol the economy of extraction, the statistics tell a more troubling story.

In their defense, the rubber tappers and their backers have
pointed to a 1990 report by the technological institute in Acre,
Funtac, which showed that in 1988 extractivism (nuts and rubber) accounted for 87.4 percent of value added taxes in the
primary sector, while cattle ranching supplied only 6.7 percent.[8] However, more recent studies demonstrate that even
though cattle ranching was notoriously unproductive in the past,
its contribution to the local economy has only risen while that
of rubber and nuts has declined dramatically.[9]

More discouraging still, some 90 percent of Acre's revenues
traditionally derive not from any economic activity but trans-

fers from the federal coffers.[10] This state, Brazil's centerpiece of extractivism, is constantly operating in the red. In the stuffy language of agronomy, the extractivism of Acre is supported "exogenously." Put simply, this means that the Acre economy does not stand on its own but depends instead on protectionism and other external life supports.

It is not the rain forest that nurtures the *seringueiro*. What buoys him, and the entire rubber economy of the Amazon, is a fabulous system of subsidies. This is the Tormb, the Tax for the Regulation and Organization of the Rubber Market, a duty on imported rubber, imposed to give preference to the costly Amazonian product. As if the 100 to 200 percent duties weren't protection enough, Goodyear, Michelin, and Firestone are also barred from importing rubber until they have bought up the local produce.

In mid-1990 the Tormb generated about $2 million a month. That money once funded programs for planting rubber. But as historian Warren Dean vividly details in *Brazil and the Struggle for Rubber,* the leaf fungus and an even worse blight, corruption and bureaucratic incompetence, buried most of those programs by late in the last decade.[11] Now the Tormb money goes to Brasília's environmental institute, Ibama. Tire factories still pay the Tormb up front but then mark up tire prices. It is finally the largess of the Brazilian consumer, not the rain forest, that sustains the *seringueiro.*

What happens, Homma has asked, when someone pulls the plug on the *seringueiros'* iron lung? Few rubber tappers can read or write, and virtually none have had formal schooling. Yet every one of them understands the intricacies of the Tormb. "If the Tormb were eliminated, the extractive sector would end overnight," said Paulo Sérgio Coelho, a rubber expert at Ibama. Coelho favored the Tormb, but only as a support to the embattled *seringueiros.* "We don't have a single economic reason for maintaining the extractive sector."

When Alfred Russel Wallace plunged into the Amazon jungle in the mid-nineteenth century, he was so impressed by the savory brew the locals concocted from this "vegetable milk" that he mixed fresh latex into his morning tea.[12] Now that the rubber economy has curdled, the friends of the *seringueiros* are trying to wean them from rubber and develop alternative forest products. In contrast with rubber, Brazil nuts fetch attractive prices in the world market today. After years of selling cheap, unprocessed nuts to the local merchants, the rubber tappers are now running Xapuri's first nut-processing factory.

In 1990 the nut factory's entire output was presold at a guaranteed price of $1.15 per pound. This would have raked in a handsome $180,000 in gross revenues. With the travails at Cachoeira, however, production was only about half the expected seventy tons, and because of shipping delays, the first shipment of fourteen tons of Brazil nuts arrived in New York totally rancid. A second load of fourteen tons was safely delivered, and *seringueiros* were confident that the future production and shipment would go much more smoothly. The factory now employs fifty shellers, and the rubber tappers have lined up buyers for all the nuts they can produce.

But while *seringueiros* enhanced their incomes with a nut factory, the relics of an old effort cluttered the way. Piled in one corner of the Xapuri nut factory were the rusting parts of dismembered miniprocessing plants for rubber. Ibama, in a bold campaign, set up some hundred such *miniusinas* in Acre and planned another two hundred. The rationale was simple: Processed rubber fetches at least three times the price of the crude slabs the rubber tappers traditionally sell. By 1990 there were only about fifteen such *miniusinas* left in all Acre. Worse, many industrial-scale rubber plants had shut down in Rio Branco as the result of the collapsing market.

Some blame the rubber tappers for their lack of organization. Others say that the program was "too centralized." Still others argue the plan was rejected as a plot to co-opt the recently formed rural unions. Officials at Ibama counter that it was none other than Chico Mendes, ever-suspicious of government stewardship, who sabotaged the plan. Whatever the reason, this failure suggests that as well as deforestation, the vagaries and hardships of the gathering economies are at least partly behind flight from the rubber groves.

"Only an elementary life can be maintained by digging up roots and tubers and trapping wild animals in these vast and hostile spaces," the historian Fernard Braudel once wrote about communities of gatherers.[13] The *seringueiros'* life is a cut above the elementary, but not by much. They all plant gardens for subsistence, but virtually their entire cash income still depends on just two products, rubber and nuts. Between the two, rubber tappers say they pocket about two-thirds of the Brazilian minimum wage, or a meager forty dollars a month. (Even at the artificially buoyed official rubber prices, which are two to three times the international price, *seringueiros* must collect fifteen kilos [33.1 pounds] of rubber just to buy a can of powdered milk.)

Academics may extol the forest's treasures, but the rubber tappers have few illusions about their fragile vocation. "What we need is to get out from under the tutelage of rubber. We want to exploit other products," said Osmarino Amâncio. In fact, the extractive reserves may have solved the *seringueiros'* land tenancy problems and charmed an ecologically sensitive world, but the question of balancing survival and conservation was left begging. Again, Braudel is lucid on this point:

Some historians thinking primarily of the New World, have said that those who burned forests and set up cultivated zones in their place were much misled, since they were destroying one kind of wealth which already existed, in favour of another, yet to be created and not necessarily worth more. There is a clear fallacy in this argument: forest wealth only existed when incorporated into the economy through intermediaries—shepherds tending their flocks, (not only the pigs at acorn time), woodcutters, charcoal burners, carters: a whole community whose profession it was to exploit, to utilize and to destroy. The forest was worth nothing unless it was used.[14]

Had he seen them, the flames and charred stumps of the Amazon burning season might have tempered the French scholar's opinion some, for wealth, both private and public, went up in smoke even as the forests were being "used." However, the quandary Braudel points out lingers. Expectations of preserving the forests and at the same time adequately providing for those who live in the Amazon are tantalizing but illusory. Anthony Anderson, an ecologist and a program director at the Ford Foundation in Rio de Janeiro, has studied Amazon extraction for more than a decade. He is unromantic on this matter. "This is not a haven for the birds and the bees," he said. "The extractive reserve is a model for development, not preservation."

Perhaps the *seringueiros* will never have to clear-cut their lands, but in order to prosper and support a growing population, the extractive reserve is unlikely to remain, as some of their defenders have imagined it, a pristine ecological sanctuary. Now tappers and their friends talk not so much about the forest emporium, as about how not to be simple gatherers anymore. Mary Helena Allegretti, a Brazilian anthropologist who heads the important Institute for Amazonian Studies and has devoted years of her life to the betterment of the lot of rubber tappers, even suggested a change in the vocabulary. "Instead of extractive reserves, we should refer to reserves for ecodevelopment," she said, after an exhaustive tour of the Amazon in 1990. To that end many have suggested "densifying" the rubber groves, planting more rubber trees within the seringal. Others suggest planting a range of other cash crops, such as cocoa, coffee, and cupuassu, under the shade of taller hardwood or rubber trees. Agronomists call these agroforestry systems, and promising experiments are being conducted throughout the tropics. In much of the Amazon, in fact, the careful combination of all these systems—silviculture, crop farming, tree farming, herding, and extraction—may be the key to working the land without mauling it.

In Acre, however, no one seems to be holding his breath.

Years of neglect and ossified rural customs also still block the way. *Seringueiros* may be at one with their forests, but they are notoriously mediocre farmers. "Sometimes they reap fewer beans than they sow," said one exasperated researcher at Funtac. From dirt level, the *seringueiros* are, in fact, not so different from settlers, ranchers, and city people—interested in, desperate, in fact, for, some strategy to rise out of the poverty that engulfs them. "We are looking for help. We're talking to every kind of 'ologist' there is," said the rubber tapper spokesman Amâncio one hot evening in Rio Branco, at the national council of rubber tappers headquarters. Gomercindo Rodrigues, Amâncio's closest adviser and an agronomist who has lived for years with the rubber tappers, agreed. "These are mid- to long-term projects. We need alternatives *now*."

Rubber Politics

While these alternatives are budding in test plots, the rubber tappers have lately been thrown back to an old, familiar routine: lobbying for higher rubber prices. Fortified by NGOs, like the Washington-based Environmental Defense Fund, they have launched vociferous protests by phone, fax, and letter against what they see as Brasilia's draconian rubber price policy. Like gasoline, galvanized steel, and beer, rubber prices have long been under government control in Brazil. Too often Brasília has tamped down such prices in fleeting attempts to stanch inflation. Yet floating the rubber price—an idea that has tempted the government at times—would send local rubber prices crashing to the international market rate and create havoc throughout Acre.

Now, to hold on to their miserly subsidy, the *seringueiros* launch all manner of argument, invoking everything from national security to prudent urban planning. Cutting the rubber subsidy or further depressing the controlled prices, they say, would empty the "vulnerable" forested borderlands and send rubber tappers streaming into the slums by the miserable thousands. However, their most powerful argument now is ecology. The onetime soldiers of rubber and gatherers of white gold, are, after all, the disciples of Chico Mendes, who first woke the world to the threat to the Amazon rain forest. Their tenancy, the argument now goes, is a cordon sanitaire to the ranchers and agrocrats who want to tear down the forests and replace it with grass and rice and corn.

These impassioned protests have an eerie echo. "The routine prevails in the production of rubber," said Felisberto Camargo, back in 1951, of the shameless rubber bosses of the old Amazon. "Its defenders resort to the most astute arguments and devices, now appealing to sociology, now to the defense of national integrity, in order to sustain the most irrational exploitation of the jungle and of men."[15] Now the rubber barons have all sold out and, like Guilherme Zaire, moved on to more attractive ventures. The rubber tappers are finally out from under their thumbs, but in a real way they remain trapped in the glory of a fading past. "One of the first things that struck me about the *seringueiros*," said Allegretti, "is that they still believe that what they do is important for the economy." That makes the rubber tappers' plight all the more poignant. Today the *seringueiros* have inherited none of the splendid wealth or privileges of the Amazon rubber bosses, only their arguments.

The fate of Brazil's extractive reserves will finally rest on the skills and politics of those who occupy them. In the wake of Chico Mendes's death, this uphill battle sometimes proved disheartening for the rubber tappers and their backers. "All we can manage to do," said Ronald Polanco, an economist who manages the Xapuri co-op and nut factory, "is administer the misery."

In fact, they had managed much more than that. Mendes's genius was his ability to parlay world anxieties over global warming and the tear in the ozone into vital aid for a castaway class of rural laborers. His death sowed doubts and some bitter divisions among *seringueiros*, but his successors have astutely grasped their special position. Now this "obscure and abandoned society," which Euclydes da Cunha reported a century ago, has forged solid unions. Their co-op, for all its trials, operates every day in Xapuri and has succeeded in raising the local price of nuts and rubber. *Seringueiros* today traverse the globe, raising funds and consciences. Entrepreneurs scour the Amazon for ecologically friendly products.

Finance has followed fame. The Canadian Embassy has donated boats and a flatbed truck. Cultural Survival raised thirty thousand dollars for the Brazil nut processing factory and now peddles its goods to corporations in New York, London, and Toronto, while the Brazilian Bank for Economic and Social Development pitched in with a low-interest loan. Japan's Sasakawa Foundation gave the *seringueiros* two hundred thousand dollars as a posthumous prize for Mendes's environmental work. Consultants from Canada, the United States, Holland, and all over South America drop in and out of Acre on a regular basis. The Ford Foundation, in 1991, was paying the salary of the tappers' co-op manager, who had lost his state job when a new governor was elected. The Inter-American Development Bank (IDB) made a grant-in-aid to the rubber tappers' council. You might even call these the new financial incentives for Amazonia. (The official ones, awarded to cattlemen and industrialists from the south, were frozen in 1989, after the fires in the Amazon and environmental inspection had got out of control.) This gushing of extraterritorial support is hardly a solid foundation on which to build a "sustainable" rain forest economy. But it has gotten the *seringueiros* on their feet and fighting again.

Though sometimes bitterly divided, the *seringueiros* have also become protagonists in the Brazilian frontier. Mendes discovered that in 1987 when hand in hand with the world's environmental lobby, he managed to block an Inter-American Development Bank loan for the paving of a highway into Acre. When funds were finally released, the strict damage controls he demanded were written into the contract. It is hardly an exaggeration to say that today almost any development loan to the region from abroad and virtually any Amazon policy from Brasília will have to bear the imprimatur of the *seringueiros* or else turn into the target of shrill public controversy.

One hundred and twenty miles north of Cachoeira, in the busy Acre capital of Rio Branco, dusk gave way to a hot jet night. Amâncio, the sharp-witted and quick-tempered *seringueiro* leader of the post-Mendes days, was still telling stories at the council headquarters, a squat house with a steel gate not far from downtown. As shadows melted into solid darkness, talk shifted from ranchers and *pistoleiros* to sustainable development and a greening planet. "A few years ago we didn't know what ecology was. We thought it was some kind of dessert," Amâncio said. A knot of aides and reporters hung on his every word that busy evening. The Brazilian press had been ringing all day, another leaflet needed drafting, and Amnesty International was on the phone again. "But we understood that it pleased people abroad. So we began to talk about ecology." The world seemed to be listening now.

Amâncio stood up and began to pace the council floor, working his argument as he walked. "After all, the ranchers had twenty years and millions of dollars in financial incentives, and what did they produce?" No one answered, but the question hung in the air, like an echo. Now the *seringueiros* had the land, funds, technical aid, and the world's blessings to try things their way. For all the fanfare over the Amazon's bounty, they knew finally that it was up to them—and not green parties, government grants, or goodwill from abroad— to make things work.

CHAPTER

THE JUNGLE OF POLICY

Such are the disgraces of Brazil:
A soft patriotism,
Loquacious laws,
Sloth,
Rust, Ants,
and Mold.

—Paulo Prado, *Retrato do Brasil*[1]

In the crowded calendar of the Amazon frontier the recent chronology goes something like this: The turning point was 1988, when Chico Mendes was murdered and a New Jersey-size piece of rain forest was cleared and burned. The year of collision was 1989, when international environmentalists and foreign governments went to war with a defensive and unloved government in Brasília over its Amazon policies. The next year, 1990, and much of 1991 as well were the time of reckoning. The proud policies of the past decade that had drawn so much flak were put on ice. The Amazon region, desperately poor, unruly, and manhandled, more than ever required urgent attention and repair.

Suddenly that old and occasional genre of discourse the Amazon conference took on new mass and meaning. Nearly every week, sometimes two or three times a week, there was another worried summit convened somewhere on the globe to fret over the fate of the South American rain forest. Conference members dealt with violations of Indian rights or how to make a living from the standing forest. Still others focused on the yearly burnings that turned forests into smoke and ash and smoke and ash into greenhouse gas. Some of the venues—New York, San Francisco, Rome, London, and Geneva—were familiar. But some less likely addresses began to compete for attention. Manaus, Belém, Quito, San José (Costa Rica), Brasília, Porto Velho, and Rio Branco climbed onto the conference map.

A half dozen of these summits were convened in Rio Branco, the sleepy capital of Acre. The town's three modest hotels at times filled up to near capacity with anthropologists, union leaders, government officials, agronomists, and even foreign lenders and diplomats. In the Amazon, hotels can be dubious places, assembled in haste and entirely, it seems, out of mildew, rust, and hosts of alarming insects. In most regional capitals there is usually one shrine of modern lodging, with the appropriate totems of contemporary hostelry, like tinkling chandeliers and waiters in bow ties. These spots become magnets for the local elite of bankers, ranchers, and merchants, who flock almost nightly for a little upmarket social bonding. Lately, though, the natives have had to rub shoulders with strangers with odd accents and traveler's checks.

This tremendous ferment of congresses rounded up Amazonophiles from across two oceans and three continents. The protagonists of world tropical research and policy—allies and adversaries alike—had a chance to sit down, roll up their sleeves, and thrash out their views and their differences on the fate of the Amazon and its inhabitants. Some of them had never even met face-to-face before they booked into one of these Amazon hotels.

And a lot was at stake. Past policy in the Amazon was based on a massive mobilization of money, machines, and men in one of the world's most aggressive campaigns of expansion into a frontier territory. Now the Collor government, which had made a rhetorical crusade of tending to the environment, especially the Amazon, was thrown into reflection. The major move, suspending fiscal incentives to agribusiness and large ranching projects, had been taken under the previous administration.[2] What was next? The question loomed like a cumulus cloud over Brasília. Collor's government began sending out feelers to leading scientists, a community whose voices had never really been heard over the din of the military's own frontier music. The barrage of Amazon meetings was called not only to deepen the archives of isolated research institutions but presumably to ground future policy. However, a good many of the participants in these conferences ended up believing that many, if not most, of the gatherings were a tremendous waste of breath and effort.

One of the most heavily flogged, and the most disappointing, took place in October 1990 in Manaus, the mistreated old rubber boomtown that sits at the confluence of the Amazon and the Rio Negro. The town, now with 1,130,000 people, had grown by unruly proportions. An urban sprawl of cheap cement chockablock apartments, skyscrapers, and a few crumbling reliquaries from the age of the rubber barons spreads out like a sore from each bank of the river. One of the more elegant edifices is the governor's palace. Roosting black vultures form a raggedy line, like a bushy eyebrow over the white marble pediment. The stately structure overlooks a plugged-up swamp, where the poor have squatted, building a whole neighborhood atop stilts that are sunk into the stink and sewage. Euclydes da Cunha, redoubtable creature of the outback, never liked cities much, not even Amazonian cities. "Noisy, sprawling, badly arranged, monotonous, opulent capital of the *seringueiros,*" he sneered at Manaus. "Brazil, someday, will get here." That was in 1904. It's hard to imagine his verdict if he'd stuck around another nine decades.

But the participants in the Forest '90 conference were spared all that unpleasantness. They were installed comfortably, if unauthentically, in the Hotel Tropical, twenty miles out of town. It looked like some Miami Beach architect's rendition of Xanadu. The building was an imposing edifice that recalled more a bunker than the *fazendeiro*'s estate house it was meant to resemble. The outside was dressed in suitably white stucco; inside, piped Muzak floated through endless corridors. The smell of mold, sometimes faint, sometimes overwhelming, clung to the upholstery of each room. Everything about this place—the scale, which was Olympian; the twin pools, replete with waterfall and wave maker; the zoo, where a fat, rheumy-eyed jaguar lolled, too old and ill even to turn around in the tiny cage to which he had been condemned; the armies of gardeners, tidying the grounds where tropical jungle had bowed to manicured hedgerows—seemed tacky and entirely out of place. In fact, you could roam the grounds of this much-touted Amazonian hotel and never get a sense of the exuberant jungle or much more than a glimpse of the river that made this town famous.

There were, however, some important issues on the conference docket. Here someone was speaking about ways to harvest timber without ruining the native forest. There a German researcher lectured on Brazilian charcoal and forestry, although the chief delegates of the national charcoal and pig iron industries had not show up. There was a raucous exchange on the viability of extracting fruits, nuts, and oils from the standing rain forest. The believers and the naysayers did battle for the better part of three hours.

Mostly, though, this was elegant wheel spinning. Many key speakers (such as Anthony Anderson, the ecologist who oversees the important environmental programs at the Ford Foundation, and the Smithsonian Institution's Thomas Lovejoy, an ecologist and one of the world's ranking Amazonian experts) did not show, while the ones who did seemed to be preaching to either the converted or the bored. Debate, when it appeared, was tepid. Overall the sessions themselves seemed less dialogue than performance, with the same weary researchers launching the same pithless attacks against venal authorities and foreign powers, but producing no concrete strategies for retrieving the suffering communities and ruined landscapes of the Amazon. Conference delegates seemed to wander the endless corridors, lost in a fog of Muzak and mildew, searching for the appropriate salons and their designated workshops. In a central area there were booths set up by the corporate sponsors, each hawking its wares while touting ecological awareness. It seemed more an Amazon trade fair than a conference meant to focus on the problems and get something done.

Paulo Alvim, perhaps Brazil's seniormost tropical agronomist, aptly registered the conference fatigue by falling sound asleep in the middle of a colleague's diatribe against the designs on the Amazon by world capitalists. He snorted suddenly awake and scribbled a question on a piece of paper and passed it on to the moderator. "With the experience you eminent scientists have accumulated over your years of research at the various institutions where you serve," the moderator solemnly intoned Alvim's query, "surely you gentlemen have come up with some answers to the problems you so eloquently raise." Some of the panelists were nonplussed. Others groped for an answer. The debate staggered on for another hour or so.

It was at about that point that a colleague, Bill Long, from the *Los Angeles Times,* suggested getting out. So we left the fogged double glass and squawking microphones of the conference rooms and stepped out into the unfettered tropical outdoors. We hired a cab and took the ferryboat across the Rio Negro and hit the highway south of Manaus. Farm country and forest spread out invitingly from each side of the newly retouched asphalt.

After a brief visit to a community of small farmers, we stopped by a ranch at the side of the road. A large, rugged-looking man with sandy hair and light eyes answered the door. He wore shorts and a denim work shirt unbuttoned over an ample torso. His right hand was missing its index finger, the mark of an old accident. He gave us a solemn-faced welcome and asked us to sit and wait while he finished lunch in the adjacent room.

Conversation was awkward at first. We explained that we had seen his farm on the drive by and were curious about life in the countryside of Amazonas, the largest and least settled of the Amazonian states. He seemed to relax visibly when we explained we were journalists, and then he told us why. "If you had said you were from Ibama or Emater [the rural extension office], I would have said, 'Sorry, but I don't have the time.' Those people never come around unless it's to hassle you."

The farmer, Leonir Neumann, then loosened up and talked about his spread on the Highway Colônia Bela Vista, forty miles from Manaus. The name rang a bell, and suddenly I remembered why. In the 1930s, when the rubber boom was already a whimper, the energetic dictator Getúlio Vargas sent thousands of *colonos* to the Amazon in a renewed push into the hinterlands. The scheme was announced with grand rhetoric. "Nothing," Vargas declared in 1940, "will hold us back in this drive, which is, in the twentieth century, the highest task of civilized man: the conquest and domination of the equatorial valleys and [its] great waters," These colonies had stirring names like Bela Vista and were to be the outposts of Vargas's "March to the West." In the rough decades that followed, Vargas's marchers had come and gone, and this Brazilian west remained mostly unconquered and only sparsely settled territory. Newcomers, like Neumann, had come on their own to pick up the pieces.

Like Vargas, he was a gaucho, as the rugged people from the grassland prairies of Rio Grande do Sul are called. He had settled in this region nine years before, buying twenty-eight hundred acres from a failed Amazonian settler. "He planted what he could, and when that didn't work anymore, he went away." The problem, Neumann said, is that these colonists had come to depend on the government—for materials, technical assistance, and credit. "That is the quickest road to hell," he said.

In 1981 Neumann left Selbach, a town settled by descendants of German immigrants like his father, and went to the Amazon. Neumann saw no opportunities for farm work in the crowded south, so he ventured to the state of Amazonas on his own. He set up a tarpaulin on sticks and went to work laying down a farm along the highway. Most of it was still untouched forest, less a result of ecological consciousness than a response to bureaucratic frustration. "It doesn't do to deforest in the Amazon without correcting the acidity of the soils for planting. There is plenty of lime in the Amazon to do this, but it's not being mined. And anyway, Ibama requires a kilo of paper work before they approve forest clearing."

About a quarter of the land, 750 acres, was already deforested, and another 125 acres had been cleared to plant rubber trees. He had also laid out a series of sixteen pastures and grazed cattle on each of them for thirty-three days at a time, then rotated them to the next patch. But it was not cattle, nor even the rubber grove, that really piqued Neumann's interests. "Watch this," he said, stooping down to scoop up a dried chip of cow dung. He threw it into a nearby pond. The water broke with a heavy splash and the ripples fanned out like radar over the smooth screen of the pond's surface. "Tucanaré," he said. "There are also pirarucú and tambaquí." These were the large river fish of the Amazon Basin and a delicacy in restaurants throughout Brazil.

Then Neumann did some applied rural math for us. "On one hectare [2.50 acres] of pasture, I can raise one steer, which will weigh maybe two hundred eighty kilos [618.8 pounds] in three years. On a one-hectare fishpond, I can raise ten thousand tambaquí. Each tambaquí reaches about seven kilos [15.4 pounds] in three years." He smiled now and, in case we hadn't grasped the point, did the sums. "That's seventy thousand kilos [about 69 tons] of fish." Ravaged by predatory fishermen, the local stock of Amazon river fish had become so depleted that this staple item on Manaus menus topped even the price of beef. The only expense, he said, was creating the fishpond— a simple affair involving the damming of a stream and taking care to create an outflow to keep oxygen circulating. Soon, he said, he would purchase a refrigerated truck and haul his chilled tambaquí, pirarucú, and tucunaré into Manaus. The only obstacles, he said, were the rutted road, part of which washed out in the wet season, and the sluggish ferry over the Rio Negro, which could hold up traffic for as much as a day.

All told, he said, his farm had become a nearly self-sustaining system. The twenty-three cows grazed under the shade of rubber trees, which also provided fresh latex and helped protect the soil from pounding sun and rain. The rotational grazing procedure was a way to sustain a few cattle without depleting the pasture, the problem that has beset most Amazon ranches. The cows produced 220 pounds of cheese and milk every week and also plenty of manure for fish feed. Most of all, Neumann seemed proud of the fact that no *técnico* from the government had dropped in to teach him this. "I was on my own," he said.

Though pioneer lore has painted us a picture of lonesome settlers battling out the elements family by family, not all the world's frontier folk were totally on their own. In Canada law and order arrived well before the bulk of the prairie settlers. The provincial government had built a railway, surveyed the land, parceled out 160-acre lots, carefully stewarded their settlement, and even sent the Royal Mounted Police in to keep the peace on the prairies. Newspapers and trade fairs also carried national news and, more important, key information to the struggling pioneers.[3] Similarly, Siberia's migrants were eventually attended by colonial settlement agents and relied heavily on the monthly agricultural magazine *Khutor* and the newspaper *Peasant of the Altai* for vital tips on farming.[4] The agricultural press in the United States was also a blessing to the settlers who ventured west.

In the Amazon peasants have not been so lucky. Not many Amazonian small landholders were so able, or so well off, as this self-made southern rancher. But many shared Neumann's disdain for the government's feeble presence in the countryside. There are some five hundred thousand families of small farmers scattered along the highways and their feeder roads throughout Amazonia. They were often handed out lots and promised assistance and credit, and of those who survived, many were still waiting.

Rural extension, the key link between research and farmers in the field, is most conspicuous by its absence in Brazil. In 1990 Brasília, in a spasm of administrative streamlining, closed down the central agency, Embrater, that coordinated rural extension throughout Brazil. The agency had become too cozy a harbor for rural agents who went to work in suits and ties and climatized rooms. Suddenly, though, each state had been thrown back on its own resources to run its extension offices, known as Emater. Everywhere these agencies were barely scraping by, mired by lack of funds, lack of enthusiasm, and a surfeit of work for thinning staffs.

In Acre, in the wake of Chico Mendes's death, the *seringueiros* have been courted by Canadian embassy people, American NGOs, and labor leaders from distant São Paulo. But they were never once paid a visit by the Emater officers who worked in the building across the town square from the Xapuri rubber tappers' union. "We've never even talked to them," said Francisco de Assis Monteiro, president of the *seringueiro* cooperative in Xapuri. (The ice was broken only in 1991, at the initiative of Funtac's president, Judson Ferreira Valentim, who assigned a rural extensionist to work exclusively with the struggling rubber tappers.)

In Mato Grosso State one senior extension officer was eager to take me to the countryside to visit a small rubber-growing community a few hours' drive from the state capital. But what might have been a routine call on this extensionist's beat proved a major financial hurdle. The matter was handily solved when I agreed to pay the gasoline and hotel bill, which came to a grand total of about forty dollars. The agent, Antônio Rocha, was apologetic about his tight budget and spent much of the drive lamenting how difficult it was to get qualified extensionists to serve in the countryside. "We lost one fellow to a snakebite," he said. "But most of the time it's boredom that gets to them. You can usually tell right from the start who's going to be able to hack it and who isn't. We lose a lot of people out in those godforsaken towns." Later, back in Cuiabá, I dropped Rocha off at the Emater offices and suddenly appreciated the budget crunch. The palatial building rose on a bluff like a modern fortress, made of tier after tier of steel, tinted glass, and reinforced concrete. It could have been an IBM or Sony office tower. The money that was meant to help laborers in the Mato Grosso countryside appeared to have contributed instead to urban extension.

Such extravagance testified mostly to the wanton spending of the past. But at least part of Brazil's rural problem could be traced to a vacuum in policy making in Brasília. Collor had a soft spot for the environment but was distracted by his tooth-and-nail fight against inflation. Ibama, the superagency for the environment that had been cobbled together from three separate entities, seemed as vague as it was large. There were three presidents in the institute's first year and a half, and the coming of each new regime sent shivers of staff changes throughout the whole structure. Its main achievements, in fact, were disciplinary. Former Ibama President Tânia Munhoz, a longtime administrator with a respected record at the forestry institute, told me proudly of how fines for environmental code violations had increased—from four million in 1989 to nine million dollars in 1990—as the result of stiffer penalties and inspections in the Brazilian interior. Indeed, as a quick ride up and down the BR-364 revealed, Ibama inspectors had become the terror of the interior. Yet Munhoz saw the police work as essential to restoring the government's tarnished reputation. "This year, Ibama had to lay down the law," she said in 1990. "If we didn't, we might as well have given up."

Indeed, in recent years the government had all but raised a

white flag. Impunity was the byword in the backlands, where loggers blithely raided parks or national forests and induced Indians and peasants to sell their timber reserves for a pittance. Though burnings were allowed only with permits, the smoke clouds from illegal fires forced small craft airports in the Amazon to shut down for days. Even at night, and from the height of a passing jet, the blazes were visible—red and orange tongues of flame licking at the inky jungle twenty thousand feet below. Poachers, bootleg lumberers, and predatory fishermen plied the Amazon like backlands lords, unfettered and often feared by the local authorities. Many forestry inspectors found lucrative second incomes in taking bribes from outlaws loggers.

Often Ibama's assignments meant hazard. Braz Sarube was wounded by a gunshot in an ambush after ordering poachers to vacate a biological reserve on the Trombetas River. In 1989 three other Ibama inspectors happened upon a band illegally trapping baby tortoises on the Tapajós River, in the eastern Amazon, and were forced to hide out for three days while the outlaws threatened revenge. Paulo Benníncá, of Acre's Ibama branch, received half a dozen death threats before he was finally surrounded and beaten up, presumably by thugs of ranchers who took umbrage at Ibama's crackdown on burnings and deforestation. Not even the World Bank consultant traveling with Benníncá was spared the manhandling.

Despite the booty from fines and the rubber import tax, Ibama also faced money problems. The agency's official budget was virtually hamstrung for all of 1990, as part of the economy minister's flagging attempts to slash government spending. In mid-1991, just as the Amazon was drying out and the new burning season approached, Ibama workers went on strike over gutted wages. The agency's work was paralyzed for nearly two months.

Even though Ibama had stepped up its patrols, it was like combing the seas. Speaking a few months before she was fired, Munhoz reeled off some dizzying numbers. "There are at least three hundred fifty thousand sawmills in Brazil, but only forty thousand are registered," she said. "It is impossible to patrol this country, even if we had an inspector for each tree." Most important, however, she readily admitted how Ibama had failed to go beyond the role of environmental cop. "The small property owners want information on how to tend to their land and how to burn properly, without damaging the forest or soil. We don't have alternatives to offer for this sort of land clearing." By September 1991, shortly after a particularly incendiary burning season, Munhoz, too, had lost her job, and Eduardo de Souza Martins became the fourth Ibama president in less than two years.

Everyone—lumbermen, the Carajás steelmakers who use charcoal in their smelters, farmers and ranchers who need to clear forestland—was confused over the government's forestry policy. In Rondônia projects for forest management (or the idea of sustained harvesting of native forests) were required of all sawmills and lumber operations. Yet Ibama offered no guidelines for such forest management plans. There was also a lack of coordination between the federal government and the state environmental authorities, which had veto power but rarely the staff competent to judge environmental impact reports by industry.[5]

The word at Ibama is now to work with, not against, private citizens in fashioning new environmental policy. Yet dialogue is testy, when it exists at all. One of the reasons may be traced to Brazil's top environmental authority. Perhaps no nation could have chosen a more prestigious or passionate defender of the environment. José Antônio Lutzenberger is an agronomist who first came to the public's attention by denouncing abusive application of pesticides and herbicides in the plantations of his native Rio Grande do Sul, wheat and soya and cattle country.

A gaunt, bespectacled man with a chiseled jaw and a brow permanently sewn with worry lines, Lutzenberger was an unlikely and risky choice for the new Brazilian government. Collor, a young, style-conscious scion of a moneyed northeastern family, was known for his stand (rhetorically, at least) in favor of the wave of neoliberal notions that had lately swept Latin America: unshackling business from government regulations, slashing the bureaucracy, and encouraging private investment as the best way to induce growth and progress. His religion was market economics. Lutzenberger seemed to represent a different planet.

I met Lutzenberger just once, nearly by accident. He was part of a government delegation that had helicoptered into the Rondônia countryside to inspect a tin mine. The army helicopter broke down, briefly stranding the official coterie, and the dozen or so ministers, secretaries, local pols, and reporters had to be redistributed among a fleet of small prop planes. By luck, I got on the eight-seater that Lutzenberger had also boarded. The plane, a Brazilian-made Bandeirante, was built for midair conferences, with two seats turned forward and two backward. I grabbed the place next to Lutz, as he is known, and surveyed the guests. It was a strange combination. In front of him, knees nearly touching, was Rondônia Governor Jerônimo Santana, rotund and jocular, but ferocious in his defense of frontier development. To his left sat Ozires Silva, the minister of infrastructure. Despite his weighty title, he was a diminutive, soft-spoken man, but not long for his job. A frown was engraved on Lutz's face.

All of them had come to Rondônia to announce a plan to restore degraded land and the creation of a new cooperative for a giant wildcat tin mine, Bom Futuro, in northern Rondônia. Some thirty thousand men had flocked there and scarred the terrain with their tunnels, pits, and water jets. The tin wealth was melting away like the mine's denuded stream embankments, as *contrabandistas* spirited away the ore, over the border to Bolivia. There the exchange rate was free, and each kilo of tin fetched almost twice as many dollars as in price-controlled Brazil. The big government mining company, Vale do Rio Doce, which operated the Carajás iron mine, had legal claim to the mineral rights but had been fought to a stalemate by free-lance miners and small-time entrepreneurs, who had discovered the tin find. The deal was for Vale to relinquish its prospecting claim to a cooperative representing all the miners, who in turn would agree to stop illegal sales, repair the despoiled environment, and organize the chaotic digging.

As it turned out, the pact fell through. Ozires Silva, who signed off on the deal, was out of office in a few months. He fell asleep for the flight back to Porto Velho. Santana, too, was at the end of his term, and none too soon, it seemed. That afternoon he had received a thunderous boo at the town hall in Ariquemes, the second-largest city (population 180,000) in the state, chronically short of energy, infested by malarial mosquitoes, and rotten with drug traffickers running Bolivian cocaine through Rondônia's leaky borders. But Santana was anything but the lame duck type and stumped for a bigger, better Rondônia right up until touchdown. "Come back when you have more time." He leaned forward, imposingly, with a smile as generous as his middle. "There's great things happening in this state."

As Santana narrated the flight, Lutzenberger parried with polite but unenthusiastic observations. Most of the time he chose to answer my questions in his accentless English, one of the several tongues he had mastered. Suddenly Lutz screwed up his brow and lunged forward to take in the strange spectacle spreading out below us: A giant mirror of water stretched out as far as the eye could see, with a forest of defoliated trees protruding like so many toothpicks. "Samuel," Santana said. This was the reservoir for the Samuel hydroelectric dam that supplied energy to Porto Velho. Lutzenberger began to shake his head back and forth slowly at first, then faster as indignation took hold, and then he yanked out a calculator. "How big is the reservoir?" he barked. Santana told him the surface area. "How many kilowatts?" Santana told him the figure. He punched in the numbers and wagged his head again. "One kilowatt for each flooded hectare," he gasped.[6] "Might as well plant sugarcane here," he said, hissing air like a punctured tire. "What a waste!"

Indeed, Samuel—at eighty-six thousand kilowatts for eight hundred million dollars—had fallen way short of the planners' goals. Rondônia's stunning growth rate had quickly rendered obsolete the energy curves the engineers designed ten years ago, when they dreamed it up. Not only had the dam flooded a considerable area, 224 square miles, and displaced hundreds of settlers (including, I supposed, the Pcheks' farm), but the power station supplied barely enough energy to light up Porto Velho, the overgrown capital. Ariquemes, just down the road, received steady current from Samuel for no more than three hours daily. The rest of Rondônia depended entirely on thermal generators run on diesel gas, imported from the Campos Bay of Rio de Janeiro or from the Middle East and trucked north two thousand miles overland to the Amazon.

Lutz scanned the denuded and eroded hills around the surrounding farm country and again hissed indignantly. "These people need different farming techniques," he said. "They need to be taught organic gardening." He explained about putting pigs on the land and how their manure and meat would support the farms and gardens of a new, gentler Amazonia. As Lutzenberger spoke, Santana was suddenly quiet, and the minister was asleep. There, against the hum of the Bandeirante's twin engines, three thousand feet above the mottled, broccolilike treetops of the Amazon forest, in a state where 1.2 million people had arrived to stay in the last two decades, Professor Lutzenberger made it all look so fetchingly simple.

Lutzenberger had a name for his philosophy. He called it the way of Gaia, the living planet. In Brasília, once again as the keynote speaker at an international environmental conference, he explained his vision at length to a rapt audience. The Gaia way, he schooled, celebrates family farming over plantations and agribusiness, frugality over consumerism, self-sufficiency over surplus. It seemed an appeal not so much to a communitarian or socialistic world (indeed, he has been every bit as condemning of the Communists' environmental record) as to some precapitalist utopia. "The citizen who is self-sufficient, who produces only what he consumes, is considered backward," he said scathingly at a gathering of ecologists, diplomats, and NGOs in a packed auditorium of the Brazilian Central Bank. We've got it all backward, he said.

To him, we of the consumer society and our temple, the market, were symbols of waste and devastation, egocentrically commanding a planet that doesn't belong to us. "Man is one in tens of billions of species, each with its specific function. Today," he intoned, "we are a cancerous tumor."

Applause rocked the room. There was always this applause whenever Lutzenberger left the speakers' dais. Yet he also left a wake of consternation. No one in that audience knew exactly what his message meant. Once he met with a group of businessmen, who had summoned him to discuss an agenda for business and the environment and left them paralyzed. It was not shame but astonishment that followed this diatribe against the evil market. Why had he taken this speaking engagement? *"O maluco,"* they began to refer to him around the halls of Ibama. The crazy man. His broadsides against the market system took on a religious cast. These businessmen were, like the president Lutzenberger served, the apostles of the market, the money changers at the temple.

And it was not only business that complained. The rubber tappers of Acre had been trying to get his attention for months, appealing desperately for a higher price for rubber. (Ibama, the agency he commands, is directly responsible for rubber prices.) But Lutzenberger seemed distracted. Osmarino Amâncio, the charismatic and hotheaded rubber tapper leader, was exasperated but also uncommonly diplomatic. "Secretary Lutzenberger just doesn't understand the Amazonian situation." Many of Lutzenberger's bombastic declarations also deflated over time. He had thrown down the gauntlet over

Carajás, threatening to quit office if the charcoal-burning steel-makers along the Carajás railway were not deactivated. The steelmakers remained. So did Lutzenberger.

In time Lutzenberger gradually lost ground in shaping environmental policy to other departments of government, which were more politically agile and aggressive. All the while that Lutz railed prophetically at the forest-gobbling pig iron factories of Carajás, the Secretariat of Regional Development worked quietly behind scenes, drawing up its own guidelines to discipline the steelmakers and define forestry policy for that sensitive area. Likewise, the new rules and credit for the Manaus Free Zone—the Amazon's most important industrial pole—came, again, not from Lutz's office but from Egberto Baptista, the secretary of regional development. While Lutzenberger philosophized dreamily about solar energy, José Goldemberg, the politically skillful science and technology secretary, rolled up his sleeves and actually negotiated the purchase and design of new energy technology.[7]

Lutz was caught napping again while Congress debated at length the new rules for the Amazon development agency Sudam. It was this agency, after all, that had lavished a billion dollars in credits and incentives in the past fifteen years on destructive and unproductive cattle ranches. In 1991 a new board of advisers was named for Sudam and for the Manaus Free Zone; the thirty-seven-member board included business-men, bureaucrats, and politicians, but not one ecologist. "It wasn't a slipup on Lutzenberger's part," Fábio Feldman, a federal congressman with a strong environmental record, told the press. "It was pure lack of interest."

These were not the only lapses. The former president José Sarney, in office from 1985 to 1990, was universally cast as the ecological villain of Brazil's most destructive period. It was on Sarney's watch, after all, that the Amazon's worst burnings occured and Chico Mendes was murdered. But Sarney spent thirty-three times more on the environmental budget than ecology-minded Collor. As Lutzenberger stumped the globe on behalf of Gaia and a new world ecological order, the budget for Ibama was being gutted by the bean counters in the Brazilian economy ministry. (Brasília's purse strings were loosened only in mid-1991, when authorities woke up to the then-pending world ecology parley, the United Nations Conference on Environment and Development, for which some seventy heads of state were expected to head for Rio de Janeiro in June 1992.)

Worse still, the vacuum at the top deprived fund-strapped Ibama of precious money that had already been set aside for the environment. In 1990 the World Bank had approved a $156 million loan for Brazil's National Environmental Plan. But it took seven more months before this precious hard currency was finally released. The problem was that the government had balked at coughing up its counterpart, of 25 percent of the loan. The Economy Ministry and its tightfisted fiscal policy were chiefly to blame. (Collor's budget police simply didn't want to risk printing the extra cruzeiros and restoking the fires of inflation.) The delay not only cost Brasília a monthly fine, for failing to use the bank loan, but also tarnished the country's ballyhooed new commitment to environmental caretaking. Had he used it, Lutzenberger's celebrated international prestige might have come in handy as important leverage to free up such a vital source of funding for the country's pauperized environmental programs.

The drought of money made a crucial difference. In a show of muscle the Brazilian government had in recent years created some 122 conservation areas, including parks, national forests, extractive reserves, biological reserves, ecological experimentation stations. However, Brasília had neglected to lay out the money to map and demarcate the protected areas properly, much less patrol them. These were paper parks, routinely pillaged by loggers, ranchers, miners, and small farmers. One Ibama official estimated the cost of "regularizing" the land situation in these conservation zones—mapping, surveying, and paying for expropriations—at nothing less than $1.8 billion, a sum Brasília had not even dreamed of laying out.

Though Brazil's badly administered Indian agency, Funai, did not fall under his aegis, Lutzenberger spread his flowing mantle anyway and boldly declared himself dedicated to the cause of saving the Yanomami. Ever since gold had turned up on their lands in 1987, this Stone Age tribe of Indians along the Venezuelan border had been threatened by waves of nomadic prospectors. In early 1990 Lutzenberger appeared, alongside Collor, in camouflage army uniform, for the telegenic explosion of clandestine airstrips in the Yanomami reservation. Everyone expected that sort of gesture from Collor—a showman since his campaign, he loved playing to the crowd and the cameras—but Lutzenberger's cameo was puzzling.

For he knew better than anyone that the explosion of airstrips was window dressing. The real policy question was over the Yanomami tribal lands, a huge and mineral-rich tract, covering 9.4 million hectares (37,000 square miles). The gold miners pushed for the reduction of those lands and for the creation of *"garimpeiro* reserves," alongside the Indian reservation. The Sarney government backed the deal as a "compromise" and then proceeded to break up the Yanomami reserve into nineteen discontiguous islands within a national forest. The Catholic Church, backing the Indians, protested that the compromise was nothing but frontier gerrymandering and a caving in to pressure from gold moguls and Amazonian politicians.

There might have been something to the argument that the reserve, the size of Portugal, could be more equitably divided among settlers, miners, and Indians. But more than real estate was at stake. Though the *garimpeiros* were more pawns than kings in this high-stakes game, their mere presence among the Yanomami was indelible. The culture of guns, gold, gonorrhea, and *cachaça* (rum) would make short work of the forest tribe, which lacked the immune systems, the firepower, and the social institutions to combat the invading white tribes. By 1990 missionaries estimated that some two thousand had already died, victims of the *garimpeiro*-induced maladies from malaria to malnutrition.

Just a few months after the police had detonated the landing strips with plastic explosives, the *garimpeiros* had quickly repaired them. The federal police, for a second and then a third time, scurried back to Roraima to blow up the same airstrips, while Funai helicoptered in doctors to treat dying Yanomami. The land question dragged on without a solution through the first eighteen months of Lutzenberger's tenure.

The matter exploded into the press in June 1991, when the Funai director was fired, allegedly for failing to move on the demarcation. The next month a respected career Indianist, Sidney Possuelo, was named the new president of Funai, promising—once again—to make protection and demarcation of Yanomami lands a priority. Then, in late November, Collor went a surprising step farther. Bucking pressures by the military and recalcitrant Amazon politicians, Collor signed a decree recognizing the entire thirty-seven-thousand-square mile areas as exclusive Yanomami territory and set a date for demarcation of the reserve. Finally, it seemed, after a year and a half of posturing—and hundreds of Yanomami deaths—the government Lutzenberger served was going to make good on its word.[8]

"We need decisions, immediate decisions, and these can only come from our governors, our technocrats," wrote José Lutzenberger, the impassioned ecologist, in his book Gaia, *O Planeta Vivo* (the living planet). The text was taken from an interview he gave in 1989, the year before he took Collor's invitation as secretary of the environment. The book was published about the time he was sworn into office and six months later was already into its second printing. While the book sold, the decisions stalled. But the applause never stopped.

After demolishing the cancerous culture of consumer capitalism, Lutzenberger stepped down from the podium at the plush Central Bank auditorium in Brasília and into the jungle of reporters who awaited him. Not so many months before, when he was a denim- and flannel-clad agronomist railing from the fringe at the powers that were, Lutzenberger was a journalist's dream. Devastatingly eloquent phrases tumbled out, one after the other, in impeccable English, German, Portuguese, French, and Spanish. As secretary of the environment Lutzenberger lately seemed less precise, less eloquent. He had moved to Brasília but avoided his office, preferring to retreat instead to his house, a bungalow in the city park, leaving his staff strict instructions that he not be bothered. He didn't return journalists' phone calls anymore. Now he seemed to regard reporters as a nuisance or, worse, as the enemy.

Trapped into another impromptu press conference, Lutzenberger was assailed by the journalists. The provocative declarations from the dais turned into evasive one-liners and laconic impatience. He reeled before the thicket of microphones and eager faces. He tore at his hair and tugged at his tie-bound collar, as though it were a noose. His eyes burned hard and furious, like those of an animal at bay.

Louise Byrne of the *London Observer*, out of sympathy perhaps, asked Lutz if he was comfortable in his role as environment chief. "I'm not comfortable in a situation like this." He jerked a hand at the ring of inquirers. "I'm not a professional politician," he managed. "I'm doing what I can." A pause. "It's a personal sacrifice." Another pause. "But it's worth it." It seemed more a getaway line than a declaration of conviction.[9]

For all its trials and missteps, Brazil's environmental super-agency had some good news to report by the close of the Amazon's hottest decade. Each year since 1978 some twenty-two thousand square kilometers (eighty-eight hundred square miles) of virgin forest had been cleared and burned. It was as if every two years a Denmark of tropical woodlands had gone down and then up in smoke. The flash point was 1987, when strange weather and stranger politics turned the region into a tinderbox. A peculiar dry snap had assailed northern Brazil, leaving the savannas, pastures, and disturbed forest areas parched and fire-prone. What is more, the Brazilian Constituent Assembly was debating a new constitution; ranchers and small farmers, fearing a move to expropriate their lands, took up their chain saws and axes with unprecedented fury, to demonstrate their properties were not idle. The result was a conflagration that shocked the world. In 1987, the peak burning season, 350,000 separate fires were detected. They created black smoke clouds that spread a pall over millions of square miles and spewed out an estimated 1.15 gigatons of carbon matter into the atmosphere.[10] Though automobile exhaust pipes in the richer hemisphere were chiefly to blame, that year the burnings in the Brazilian Amazon alone accounted for fully 5 percent of the atmosphere's greenhouse gases.[11]

But by the next dry season the satellites had already detected a slight decline in the felling: Seventy-six hundred square miles of forest were cleared and burned. In 1989 and 1990 a total of fifty-five hundred square miles of Amazonia was cut down. That represented an area larger than Connecticut, but also a dramatic decrease from previous years. Lutzenberger and Ibama were predicting an even steeper fall for the following year, of no more than thirty-two hundred square miles.

Ibama immediately celebrated its get-tough policies of blitzes and fines, but there were many factors involved in the cooling of the Amazon. For one, the drought had ceased and the rains were back to their normal cycle in the north country. The constitution had been drafted, and the specter of massive land expropriations put to rest. The end of Brasília's policy of fiscal incentives to ranching in upland forest areas also dampened the blazes. Most important, though, was a deepening national recession. Collor's draconian monetary policy during his first year and a recession the next dried up liquidity and fairly stanched agricultural credits. Also, the cutting off of agricultural credits above the twelfth parallel, the bottom edge of the Amazon, left farmers fairly pennyless. Amazonian ranchers and farmers had precious little capital to clear new lands for planting and grazing. (What is more, another furious bout of

Amazon fires in July, August, and September 1991 seemed to sour Brasília's earlier optimism.)

Many in Brazil have rightly pointed out the connection between poverty and pollution; a poor country is an environmentally dangerous country, according to this view. This argument has been the foundation for appeals by third world nations for strategies to relieve foreign debt and to garner finance for pollution control technology. Again, there is much sense in these arguments. Emissions controls, energy savings, and the cleansing of industrially fouled water and landscapes all require not only the best technologies but also the money to purchase them. But the fall in the burnings seemed to turn these arguments upside down. Suddenly recession was an ally, not an enemy to the environment. It was, after all, the Brazil of the seventies and early eighties, flush with foreign credits, its economy steaming along at spectacular growth rates, that tackled the Amazon with grand and destructive projects. Suddenly the drought in cash had given the forest a break and Brasília time to rethink policy in the Amazon. By the dawn of the nineties, and the end of the Amazon's decade of destruction, the rethinking already seemed to be under way.

On a whim, and back in Rio de Janeiro, I decided to look up an old Amazon hand, Arthur César Ferreira Reis. He was a lawyer, historian, and former governor of Amazonas, the largest Amazonian state, where Manuas is located and so much of the Amazon's glorious past was made. Ferreira also wrote the nationalist classic *Amazônia e a Cobiça Internacional* (Amazonia and international greed). This was the opus of a genre that fired passions, on the right and the left, for decades. With Ferreira's alert—that the resource-addicted world powers were ever poised to invade and annex the mineral-rich South American jungle—Brazil's ideological squabbles were momentarily cast aside and the barricades sandbagged to defend this prize of national patrimony. Now, with pressures mounting on Brasília from first world environmental groups, I imagined Ferreira would be fuming again.

It was a surprising encounter. A thin man of medium height with steel gray hair, he was well into his eighties when I spoke to him. He wore thick-lensed horn-rims that hid clouded eyes, and he looked a little lost in his roomy gray suit. However, he had a quick mind and an even quicker step. He marched me into the reading room of the Brazilian Historical and Geographic Institute, in downtown Rio de Janeiro, and quickly removed a handful of volumes from a shelfful of works on Amazonia, by his father and himself.

"I'm very interested in ecology," he said in a placid, almost eager way. "It will be very hard to destroy the Amazon forest." He frowned. "But I am in favor of a slow and careful occupation of the region." There was no trace of apoplexy in his voice, no invectives loosed against green imperialism. More surprising still, he did not call for an all-out development assault on the forest, the way that the policy makers of his younger days had done for decades. Who would have imagined that this man, who had mounted a tropical soapbox to scream, "Hands off Amazonia," was now a closet ecologist?

"And the international interests in Amazonia," I probed. "Do you still see a threat?"

"No," he answered right away dismissing the idea with a wave of a hand. "That subject is closed." Ferreira smiled politely and raised his full eyebrows, a sign I took to mean that the interview was also done. With that, the erstwhile apostle of Amazonian nationalism got up, straightened his bulky suit jacket, shook hands briskly, and strode off again into the institute. The tone and times had certainly changed.

CHAPTER 15

CALL OF THE WILD

But ask now the beasts, and they shall teach thee;
and the fowls of the air, and they shall tell thee:
or speak to the earth, and it shall teach thee. . . .

—Job 12:7–8

There is a chicken-sized bird in the Amazon called the jacú that squeals, the locals say, just like a pig. Another is the biscateiro, Portuguese slang for a masher, so named for its wolf whistle. A tree with a green velvety trunk and slippery as nylons is dubbed, fittingly, the lady's leg. Then there is the fel de paca, whose wood is hard as steel and sends off sparks when struck with a honed machete blade. Still another, the formigueiro, the ant tree, is a sort of botanical condominium: Sever one of its hollow branches, and it foams with the ants that are its habitual tenants.

A walk in the dark woods along the Cristalino River, in the west-central Amazon, where the dense forests of Mato Grosso meet the tall rain forests of Amazonas, is a trip through a frustrating and wondrous landscape: wondrous because of the wealth of plant and animal life harbored in this "rich realm of nature," as the Portuguese reveled when they first set eyes upon the Brazilian hinterlands; frustrating because for those uninitiated in the mysteries of the tropical woodlands, such a walk can be nothing but a passage through a damp green chaos.

Fortunately there was Sebastião, the lithe and agile woodsman, and his father-in-law, Luiz, who had trekked Brazil from the arid northeast to the dripping rain forest, to help us grope our way through the braille of the Cristalino River's forest. In fact, their knowledge and delight in imparting that knowledge were the best assets any traveler in search of an ecology tour could have wanted. The hotel, the Floresta Amazônica, had indeed provided a proper biologist, a young graduate imported from the best university of São Paulo, fluent in English and French, as well as the more arcane languages of botany, ornithology, and primatology. But a thirty-minute walk along a Brazil nut gathering path was a painful demonstration of the shortcomings of classroom diplomas when their bearers are transported suddenly to the rough outdoors. Luiz, with maybe a grade-school education and the nasal, twangy northeastern accent that is said in Brazil to be the emblem of ignorance, relished every moment of the tour.

He was there officially merely to steer the motorboat and walk us along the forest trail, while the biologist performed. But he soon started a prolonged game. Stopping by a tree with rough bark, as indistinguishable to me as any other in the sour light of the forest, Luiz would ask: What is this tree called?

The eager biologist's brow would crease, a forefinger would adjust his horn-rims, and after a moment's silence, he would blurt out a name. Wrong Luiz would laugh.

And this tree?

Silence. A guess.

You sure?

The biologist began to sweat.

The quiz went on relentlessly for the entire thirty-minute walk. The biologist clambered back into the boat and spoke quietly about how his assignment at the forest camp was drawing, mercifully, to a close. Luiz wore a large and self-satisfied smile, and later that evening, over barbecued beef and beer, he started up with woodsmen's tales. There was the one about the anaconda, longer than a stretch limousine, its middle as thick as a man's torso, that Luiz had wrestled into submission. The trick, he said, is to get your thumbs behind his eyes, and then he goes all limp. For a visual aid, he then unrolled an enormous, dried snakeskin, presumably the victim's. Then there was the jaú, a giant-jawed fish that lurks in the bottom of Amazon rivers and had swallowed more than one of his *companheiros*. He had similar stories of jaguars and probably a few about alligators, too, though we didn't get that far. This was the delightful hyperbole of the woods that many chagrined classroom biologists probably have had to swallow in silence at the day's end around the evening campfire.

Indeed, without a Luiz or a Sebastião to guide, narrate, and perhaps fib a bit, the initial encounter with the Amazon can be a fairly disillusioning experience. "Nevertheless, on the whole, I was disappointed," confesses Alfred Russel Wallace, the renowned naturalist, as he is about to start the fabulous journey that produced his classic *A Narrative of Travels on the Amazon and Rio Negro.* "The weather was not so hot, the people were not so peculiar, the vegetation was not so striking, as the glowing picture I had conjured up in my imagination. . . ."[1] Though he was eventually seduced by the subtler enchantments of this landscape, Wallace humbugged the magnificent Amazon even miles into his epic passage. "The depths of the virgin forest are solemn and grand, but there is nothing to surpass the beauty of our rivers and woodland scenery," he declared.[2]

Though most film and adventure writing has, in the name of economy and entertainment, edited out the tedium of tropical wilderness, it is finally time and patience that are required to appreciate fully and then revel in the hidden marvels of the Amazon. "Indians and forests and palms cannot be compelled. They come in their turn. They are mixed with litter and dead stuff, like prizes in a bran tub," writes H. M. Tomlinson, in his classic traveler's tale *The Sea and the Jungle,* remarking on the forests of Pará.[3] Teddy Roosevelt, the great white hunter, had his most disappointing safari in the Amazon, taking precious few jaguars and alligator and a host of less noble beasts, like monkeys and parrots. It was not the splendid mammals but the ants, "who burn the skin like red-hot cinders," that really impressed the ambassador of the strenuous life.

"It is only in time that the various peculiarities, the costume of the people, the strange forms of vegetation, and the novelty of the animal world will present themselves," Wallace finally allowed. The anthropologist Lévi-Strauss, who walked through much of the Brazilian backlands, spoke about the necessity of calibrating one's expectations in the Amazon. "One universe gives place to another," he writes, "less agreeable to look at, but rich in rewards for senses nearer to the spirit: hearing, I mean, and smell. Good things one had thought never to experience again are restored to one: silence, coolness, peace. In our intimacy with the vegetable world, we enjoy those things which the sea can no longer give us and for which the mountains exact too high a price."[4]

From the temples of Shinto to the easels of the Hudson River school, the earth's wild land- and waterscapes have always inspired the most stirring of acclaims. John Muir, the aesthetic conservationist, surrendered his life to the cause of pure preservation, arguing that wild country ought to be saved from "all sorts of commercialism and the marks of man's work." From Thoreau's famous dictum "In wildness is the preservation of the world" came an environmentalist manifesto for a century to follow. Listen again to Tomlinson, steaming up the Rio Madeira, one morning in 1910:

> There were no fences or private bounds. I saw for the first time an horizon as an arc, suggesting how wide is our ambit. That bare shoulder of the world effaced regions and constellations in the sky. Our earth had celestial magnitude. It was a warm, a living body. The abundant rain was vital, and the forest I saw nobler in stature and with an aspect of intensity. . . . You see what the tropical wilderness did for me and with but a single glance. Whatever comes after I shall never be the same.

There is something compelling, and contradictory, in these odes. On canvas, in stone and bronze, on the written page, artists have sought, paradoxically, to capture this wildness and render it, somehow contained yet still powerful, to a sedentary society. It is probably only from the safety of totally subdued environments that we can comfortably appreciate the untamed parts of the world. That is the delightful paradox of ecological or adventure tourism. Thoreau's cult of the wild, René Dubos has noted, was nurtured at placid Walden Pond, which was an easy stroll from dinner at a Concord restaurant and where the wildest beast was a woodchuck. It was likely only the cozy familiarity with "fences and private bounds" that produced Tomlinson's paean to the rogue magic of the tropical wilderness. Muir's crusade for rescuing the West from development was sponsored in part by frontier developer E. H. Harriman, the owner of the Union Pacific and Southern Pacific railways, who paid for Muir's rail tickets.[5]

Worship of wilderness is, of course, an antifrontier impulse. Pioneers could not afford such sentiments. They were too busily engaged in mortal combat with the elements we revere. The myriad marches to all the frontiers—in Russia, America, Australia, and Brazil—entailed hacking settlements out of niggardly landscapes of oak, pine, dry sod, or rain forest. These were journeys of devastation hastened by dread. Frederick Jackson Turner was chillingly clear about the pioneer's endeavor. "The destroying pioneer fought his way across the continent, masterful and wasteful," he sang in his pioneer hymn. "It was his task to fight with nature for the chance to exist," he wrote. "Vast forests blocked the way; mountainous ramparts interposed; desolate green-clad prairies, barren oceans of rolling plains, arid deserts, and a fierce race of savages, all had to be met and defeated."[6]

The forest was both a source of life and a wellspring of fear. It stood in the way not only of progress but also of deeper notions of "order and light."[7] A flat horizon was an ancient allure. "Would Logic have flourished if Greece had remained covered with an opaque tangle of trees?" asks Dubos.[8] In a sense, then, the forest line *was* the frontier, and the pioneers were hell-bent upon beating it back to make a way for camps, farms, and towns—human topographies.

Now, thanks to their murderous and ingenious ways, a good part of the world lives in comfort. And it is that comfort which allows us the vantage of remorse, repudiation, and, more recently, ecological tourism. It could be argued that Turner's industrious pioneers were hewing all that timber only to build modern civilization's own pyre. But by the same token we eat from the produce of lands they denuded; our moral high ground is, however precarious, an edifice they erected. "To us who live beneath a temperate sky and in the age of Henry Ford," wrote Aldous Huxley in a much-quoted essay on Wordsworth and the tropics, "the worship of Nature comes almost naturally. It is easy to love a feeble and already conquered enemy."[9]

As the world's wilderness has dwindled, its destruction has grown from a lament to a political concern and more recently into a casus belli. The fashioning of each frontier has sparked this crescendo of emotions, and protests, for better than a century. Roderick Nash, in his brilliant book *Wilderness and the American Mind,* points out that the impulse for conservation and adulation of nature has generally followed close on the heels of the completion of frontier quests. Europeans, having consumed their own forestlands, turned to America for the surly country beyond the Appalachians. As late as the 1870s "nature tourists" in the United States were in the majority Europeans. Americans went west for gold, land, and opportunity; the Europeans, "for fun."[10] In the eighteenth century Tocqueville marveled at the Americans' indifference to the exuberant nature he sought out. "They may be said not to perceive the mighty forests that surround them till they fall by hatchet," he reported.[11]

Likewise, the world movement for parks and national forests gained critical mass only at the beginning of this century, when pioneers were already blanketing the country, from East Coast to West and from Canada to Mexico. Wilderness had, in Nash's analysis, become relegated to the status of a consumer item, to be gobbled up domestically for as long as it lasted and then "imported" by those nations with a nostalgia for what they had only just demolished. So the hunters of moose, wolf, and buffalo of the American forests and plains committed their historic carnage and crossed the oceans to Africa for more, inventing the big-game safari. Curiously, some of the most impassioned advocates of wrestling the wilderness into submission, such as James Fenimore Cooper and Teddy Roosevelt, had become the most sentimental boosters of nature conservation. Distressed that each of his hunting expeditions in Africa bagged ever-fewer trophies, Prince Bernhard of the Netherlands created the World Wildlife Fund in 1961.

From Turner's time, after all, it was America's intimate relationship with the wilderness, this glorious combat of the frontier, that made the new country not only different from Europe but also better. To lose the wilderness, then, was to see that specialness vanish. "Out of his wilderness experience, out of the freedom of his opportunities, he fashioned a formula for social regeneration—the freedom of the individual to seek his own," Turner crowed.

America, in these descriptions, was losing not only its woods but also its soul. When the bison and Indians were all gone, Bill Cody took his leather and buffalo gun to the stage, recreating in a road show what he'd helped liquidate on the wild plains. For years, says historian Earl Pomeroy, "tourists had to be reassured, and westerners felt that they had to assure them, that the West was no longer wild and woolly—until fashions changed and it was time to convince them that it was as wild as it ever had been."[12]

So strong had this movement become that by the middle of this century national parks were now part of a global agenda. One of the prime movers, Julian Huxley, director general of UNESCO, urged the world heads of state at Fontainebleau, in 1948, to take measures for preservation all over the planet. "In the modern world," Huxley declared, ". . . a country without a national park can hardly be recognized as civilized."[13]

And there it was. A little more than a half century after the "closing" of the American frontier, and not more than a few decades after the dust had settled on most others, the legendary pioneer imperative had been totally overhauled. It was no longer expansion and domination of wild space and wild men but containment and conservation that defined nationhood. Before, conquest was the priority of an emerging nation-state, a mission for "the efficient races," in the words of Woodrow Wilson. Now superior society coddled instead of conquered, and yesterday's glorious heroes became today's brutes and villains.

Now that virtually all of the world's wests have been won, we in the Northern Hemisphere have segued smoothly to our cult of tropical wilderness. Environmentalism blossomed, matured, and now its pollen has crossed the equator. So did ecological tourism. Now the former has become a crusade, a new utopia; the latter, a booming business. Both seek to salvage and re-create the wilderness experiences that are fast disappearing from our frontier-free nations. Today, though, we overcivilized souls may still import rain forest adventures. A package tour can whisk us down the Cristalino River for a walk along a vine-draped Brazil nut gathering path or put us in a treetop hotel on an Amazonian river.

The bitter irony for Brazil is that the Amazon frontier is far from closed; indeed, in many ways, it has only just opened. Yet the wilderness impulse has already caught up and taken hold. Brazilians have been highly ambivalent about such a condition. In one breath, political leaders, especially those in the Amazon, resentful of the winds of conservation that blow most strongly from the Northern Hemisphere, point out that unlike the frontiers of the rich nations, the Amazon is still largely intact. In the next, they defend tooth and nail the right to dispose of their national territory the way they see fit—the way, in short, that the rest of the globe has done. (After all, it was this fierce notion of sovereignty that has long underscored diplomacy on the environment. It was written in Article 21 of the Declaration of the United Nations Conference on the Human Environment in Stockholm, in 1972, and was slated for the agenda again at the second go-round of that conference in Rio de Janeiro, in June 1992.) The second argument cancels the first, of course. The forest that still stands in the Amazon is less a badge of national virtue than a monument to tardiness. In reality it is not ecological consciousness but financial restraints that have detained the sacrifice of the rain forests. A richer Brazil might have long ago developed its frontier out of existence. Yet there is also an opportunity for Brazil buried in this quandary.

For years the frontier quest has stimulated a running battle among the camps of environmental thought. On the one side were the pioneers and their champions, to whom nature was an enemy, terrible and hostile, an impediment to the business and serenity of settlement. On the ground, this meant hurling down the forest, battling the Indian, and transforming the threatening wilderness into something predictable, controllable, and tame. In art, this took the form of sublime painting: twisted and gargantuan land and waterscapes, where man, when he appeared at all, was dwarfed and intimidated by an overwhelming nature. This was much the way the Europeans saw the New World when they stumbled ashore.[14]

There would seem to be nothing so radically opposed as the pioneer impulse and that of the militant environmentalists. Yet there are curious parallels. Both the pioneer and the radical or "deep" ecologist share a sublime view: of nature as supreme, awesome, and the source of both worship and fear. The difference is, the pioneer seeks to turn the tables and vanquish the beast at all costs. To the ecologist, it is man who needs disciplining. The real wilderness is made of asphalt. Earth First!, with its militant stand in favor of untouched wilderness, is the current manifestation of the sublime view of nature. The modern pioneers are like Gilberto Mestrinho, the governor of

Amazonas, to whom alligators and dense forests are encumbrances. (Brazil's environmental agency, he protested, "teaches the caboclo he shouldn't kill the alligator, but no one teaches the alligator he shouldn't kill the caboclo.") Yet both camps are united by a single, driving idea: Man and nature are mortal adversaries, inexorably and tragically opposed.

The current debate over the fate of the Amazon forest sometimes seems to careen between these two extremes, now a cry of "Hands off the Amazon," now a summons to the latter-day pioneers to subdue and prevail. The antagonists do battle still in the press, in halls of government, and in countless environmental conferences. Yet the combatants of the sublime—the Gilberto Mestrinhos, the Earth First!s, and the Rain Forest Action Networks—have been relegated largely to the radical fringe of the environmental debate. They are perhaps the noisiest parties in this debate, but hardly the most influential. Leaving the rain forest untouched sounds to most of the Amazon protagonists as unrealistic as flattening it for pasture and parking lots.

The search today is for another kind of land aesthetic, a sort of middle way. Call it a humbler sort of pastoralism. The range of possibilities is wide, from a mechanical arcadia, with a giant iron mines, colossal dams, blacktop highways, and jerry-built cities to Breughel's paradise, where small peasants and forest dwellers and their uncomplicated tools tread softly while culling the rain forest's resources for their own livelihoods.

Whatever the choice, there appears to be no escaping a strategy for the Amazon that weds the people there and their requirements for survival to the exigencies of the intricate tropical biosystem, for though much of the Amazon is still unexploited, it is no longer virgin. In the last two tumultuous decades the population of the Brazilian Legal Amazon has swelled from six million to sixteen million. Perhaps another eight million are scattered throughout the rural towns and forests of Brazil's neighboring Amazon nations. Fully half these people live in cities, and the other half is barely holding on in the countryside. The urban demand for food and consumer wares is growing. For most of these pioneers, there is no return to the south or the northeast. The hollow frontier of the days of the rubber boom is filling in, rapidly.

Yet most of these people eke out desperate livings from subsistence farming or extractivism, activities that also leave the land scorched and barren. Today most of the settlers are poor, and many are desperate. Harnessing their environment for tomorrow's meal is not only a policy dilemma but a commandment. Likewise, declaring a cordon sanitaire and leaving nature to repair itself seems even less plausible. Some sort of development is required just to sustain the communities that have rooted themselves in the Amazon and to wean them from the manufactures that must be hauled over two thousand miles of rutted highways, from as far away as São Paulo, the source of everything from tomatoes to toilet paper.

Though the burnings have slowed and the Brazilians' ecological sensibilities greened, the Amazon's wilderness is likely condemned to retreat even farther. The question is: To what will it give way? And there is Brazil's opportunity: first to identify the zones of the Amazon to be preserved, and then to protect them; second, to find the key to developing the rest of the region without completely demolishing it. The historian, novelist, and conservationist Wallace Stegner, in an impassioned article in the *Smithsonian* magazine, points out that this concept dates way back, to 1916 and the National Park Act, which destined such areas for the public's "use without impairment." Today ecologists have retrieved that old notion, buffed it, and given it a new name. Sustainable development we call it now.

To many in the environmental field, that is nothing but a glittering oxymoron. Throughout history, of course, virtually any sort of development has involved the consumption, if not exhaustion, of natural resources and the spoilation of their original harbors. The vast majority of humans live in environments they, or their ancestors, have transformed, Dubos reminds us. Harvesting the forest and at the same time preserving it, the notion that has galvanized the defenders of the rain forest, make for a difficult marriage. Even the most benign activities, such as extraction of forest products, means altering the natural forest, especially if the peoples of these forest are to rise above the misery level. Or to turn that notion around, the less altered the environment, the more rudimentary and impoverished are the lives of those who dwell there.

The search, now, is for some sort of balance, some milder kind of garden; if not, our tenancy on earth will be abruptly ended. In this, those who propose prospering from an unfettered wilderness appear destined for disappointment. To paraphrase Roderick Nash on the American landscape, in the Amazonian garden "wilderness is just as dead as in the concrete wasteland." The question for Brazil in the Amazon is not whether to build a containing wall around wilderness or to open the floodgates and allow humans to pour in. The argument over the Amazon is not so much a stale clash between preservation versus inundation, reverence versus invasion. The dilemma is not one of culture versus nature. There need not be such a sublime opposition. The preservation of wilderness is desirable not only aesthetically or religiously but also as a tool for human survival. The setting aside of portions of the rain forest, as reserves for genetic materials, is one of the best reasons for pure preservation. But again, this is no antisocial tract; the gene pool is a tool for human survival. The Amazonian riddle is more one of how to conciliate all the interacting elements of the human environment—man, beast, and elements—as they mingle and collide. If it is man and his methods that have been the agent of so much environmental destruction, then we have no one else to turn to to set things right. The way into our mess—technology, industry, and science— is also the only way out. The most reckless of fauna will have to come up with some answers.

In occupying the Amazon, the Brazilian pioneers, who are only the tardy heirs to our turbulent global legacy of conquest, managed once again to impose their will and ways on other cultures and other lands. In Acre, in Grande Carajás, in Rondônia, and southern Pará, the charred and leveled landscape is a mirror that pioneer society itself has fashioned. Now we are staring point-blank at the consequences of human folly, and they stare accusingly back at us.

"For those of us who are earth-bound Europeans," writes Lévi-Strauss, "our adventurings into the New World have a lesson to teach us: that the New World was not ours to destroy, and yet we destroyed it; and that no other will be vouchsafed to us." As it was in the American West, or the Russian east, or the Australian outback, it may also be too late to save much more than remnants of the dwindling indigenous societies of the Amazon that the outsiders overran. Anthropologists have reported that in the crush of the twentieth century, the century of Brazil's frontier, one tribe a year disappeared from the Brazilian backcountry. Yet there is still some reckoning to be done. "In grasping these truths we come face to face with ourselves. For our own society," finishes Lévi-Strauss, "is the only one which we can transform and yet not destroy."[15]

Though a pioneerless Amazon still has its apostles, the wise harnessing of this region may hold some lessons for the rest of us. Euclydes da Cunha, the explorer, naturalist, and frontiersman, struck a sensible and impassioned balance nearly a century ago. He bowed before the majesty of the Amazon, "this immensity of water under an immensity of sky," and then got up off his knees and called for its conscription to the requirements of humankind. Cunha wanted a road, the Transacreana, to traverse the western Amazon, pushing all the way to the Pacific. He wanted to help the *seringueiro,* the "fellah," by importing to his forsaken backlands proper justice, the rule of law, and the institutions that the Brazilian republic promised but never delivered. This wilderness worshiper was a pastoralist at heart.

"Man there," he said of the Amazon, "is an intruder. He arrived without being invited, when Nature was still straightening up its vast and luxurious salon. And he encountered an opulent disorder." In Cunha's view, man, the intruder, was also the arranger. The salon was incomplete without guests. And if the Amazon forest is still today, as once he eloquently wrote, the "last page of Genesis, yet to be written" then it is up to man, by intrusion, by obstinacy, by intelligence, to draft that page. Over and over again, if necessary, until he gets it right.

NOTES

1. THE CONQUEST OF THE AMAZON FRONTIER

1. *The Journal of Christopher Columbus,* trans. Cecil Jane (New York: Bonanza Books, 1987), p. 29.

2. Martin Green, *The Great American Adventure* (Boston: Beacon Press, 1984), p. 278.

3. Martin Green, *Dreams of Adventure, Deeds of Empire* (New York: Basic Books, 1979), p. 3.

4. Joseph Conrad, *Heart of Darkness,* 7th ed. (New York: Bantam Books, 1971), p. 9.

5. Charles Darwin, *The Descent of Man* (Princeton: Princeton University Press, 1981), p. 238.

6. Fernand Braudel, *Civilization and Capitalism: 15th–18th Century,* vol. III, *The Perspective of the World* (New York: Harper & Row, 1979), p. 98.

7. Alfred W. Crosby, *Ecological Imperialism: The Biological Expansion of Europe, 900–1900* (Cambridge, England: Cambridge University Press, 1987), pp. 1–7.

8. Aristotle, *Meteorologica* (Cambridge, Mass.: Harvard University Press, 1952), book II, ch. V, p. 183.

9. Darwin, op. cit., p. 152.

10. Ibid., p. 139.

11. *Columbus,* loc. cit., p. 36.

12. For more on the debate over the torrid zone, see the Brazilian historian Sérgio Buarque de Holanda's intriguing study *Visões do Paraíso* (visions of paradise) (Rio de Janeiro: Editora Bisondi, 1977).

13. Frei Vicente do Salvador, *A História do Brasil, 1500–1627,* 1627 (São Paulo: Edições Melhoramentos, 1965), p. 63.

14. James Bryce, *South America: Observations and Impressions* (New York: Macmillan, 1912), p. 562.

15. Theodore Roosevelt, *Through the Brazilian Wilderness* (New York: Charles Scribner's Sons, 1914), p. 147.

16. Press conference with Antônio Delfim Netto, *Revista das Finanças Publicas*, vol. XXX, no. 300 (October 1970). See also Thomas Skidmore, *The Politics of Military Rule, 1964–1985* (New York and Oxford: Oxford University Press, 1988).

17. Claude Lévi-Strauss, *Tristes Tropiques* (New York: Atheneum, 1973), p. 78.

18. René Dubos, *The Wooing of Earth* (New York: Charles Scribner's Sons, 1980), p. 152.

2. Crabs on the Sea Line

1. John Hemming, *Red Gold: The Conquest of the Brazilian Indians, 1500–1760* (Cambridge, Mass.: Harvard University Press, 1979), p. 378.

2. Braudel, op. cit., vol. III, *The Perspective of the World*, p. 388.

3. João Capistrano de Abreu, *Caminhos Antigos e o Povoamento do Brasil, 1889* (Rio de Janeiro: Editora Civilização Brasileira, 1975), p. 6.

4. E. Bradford Burns, *A History of Brazil* (New York: Columbia University Press, 1970), p. 50.

5. Donald W. Treadgold, *The Great Siberian Migration* (Westport, Conn.: Greenwood Press, 1955), p. 20. Copyright Princeton University Press.

6. Richard Slotkin, *Regeneration through Violence: The Mythology of the American Frontier, 1600–1860* (Middletown, Conn.: Wesleyan University Press, 1973), p. 4.

7. Treadgold, op. cit., p. 88.

8. George Brown, cited in Paul F. Sharp, "Three Frontiers: Some Comparative Studies of Canadian, American, and Australian Settlement," *Pacific Historical Review*, vol. XXIV, no. 4 (November 1955), p. 375.

9. W. K. Hancock, cited ibid., p. 375.

10. Sharp, ibid.

11. This message was made in Goiânia, in 1938, and repeated a number of times all over Brazil.

12. *Síntese Cronólogica da Presidência da Republica*, 1960, vol. II, pp. 103–4.

13. Octávio Rodrigo Ramos Jordão, "As Forcas Armadas e a Integração da Amazonia," *Revista Brasileira de Política Internacional*, vol. XI, no. 41/42 (1968), pp. 101–15.

14. General Emílio Garrastazu Médici, in a state of the union address on

the third anniversary of his presidency. Published in *Revista de Financas Publicas,* vol. XXXII, no. 312 (November/December 1972), p. 5.

15. Do Salvador, op. cit., pp. 58–59.

16. Robin Hallet, *Africa to 1875, a Modern History* (Ann Arbor: University of Michigan Press, 1970), p. 327.

17. Sérgio Buarque de Holanda, *Moncoes* (São Paulo: Editora Brasiliense, 1990), p. 164.

18. "In the agrarian economy," Buarque de Holanda comments in his *Raizes do Brasil,* "the bad methods . . . oriented merely towards immoderate and immediate advantage by those who applied them, tended constantly to expel the good methods," p. 21. Sérgio Buarque de Holanda, *Raizes do Brasil,* 1936 (Rio de Janeiro: Editora José Olympio, 1969).

19. Do Salvador, op. cit., p. 61.

20. Nicolau Sevcenko, *Literatura Como Missão, Tensões e Criação Cultural Ma Primeira Republica,* 3d ed. (São Paulo: Editora Brasiliense, 1989), p. 205.

21. William H. Goetzmann, *New Lands, New Men: America and the Second Great Age of Discovery* (New York: Viking, 1986), p. 13.

22. Treadgold, op. cit., pp. 32–35.

23. Richard Van Alstyne, *The Rising American Empire* (New York: W. W. Norton, 1960), p. 106.

24. Joel Colton and R. R. Palmer, *A History of the Modern World since 1815,* 3d ed. (New York: Knopf, 1972), p. 670.

25. David H. Stauffer, "The Origins and Establishment of Brazil's Indian Service, 1889–1910," dissertation for the University of Texas at Austin history department, August 1955, p. 22.

26. Burns, op. cit., p. 353.

27. Oswald de Andrade, "Manifesto da Poesia Pau-Brazil," *A Utopia Antropofágica* (São Paulo: Editora Globo/Secretaria de Estado da Cultura de São Paulo, 1990), p. 43.

28. Burns, op. cit., p. 274.

29. Mário de Andrade, "Dois Poemas Acreanos," *Poesias Completas* (São Paulo: Editora Martins, 1980), p. 151.

3. ORDER AND PROGRESS

1. Edgar Roquette-Pinto, *Rondônia* (Rio de Janeiro: Brasiliana Editora, 1935), p. 5.

2. Sevcenko, op. cit., p. 152. This chapter draws heavily from this excellent comparison of da Cunha with author Lima Barreto.

3. José Murilo de Carvalho, "Um Bolschevismo da Classe Média," *A*

Revista do Brasil, Edição Especial, vol. 4, no. 8 (1990), p. 50 ff.

4. Euclydes da Cunha, *A Márgem da Historia,* vol. I (1905), pp. 652–53, cited in Sevcenko.

5. Aluísio Azevedo, cited in Mario da Silva Brito, *Historia do Modernismo Brasileiro: Antecedentes da Semana de Arte Moderna* (Rio de Janeiro: Editora Civilizacao Brasileira, 1964), p. 15.

6. José Murilo de Carvalho, "O Libelo de Luiz Felipe," *Jornal do Brasil,* caderno de *Idéias* (April 28, 1991), p. 8.

7. Edilberto Coutinho, "Rondon and the Brazilian Indian Policy in the Twentieth Century," lecture delivered at City University of New York, New York City, May 5, 1978.

8. Donald F. O'Reilly, "Rondon: Biography of a Brazilian Republican Army Commander," Ph.D. dissertation, New York University, 1969.

9. Ibid., p. 16.

10. José Mauro Gagliardi, *O Indígena e a Republica* (São Paulo: Editora Hucitec, 1989), pp. 44–46.

11. All the figures on this statue are characters from Brazilian literature or history. The white man is Caramaru, one of the first Portuguese conquistadors in Brazil. The Indian is Y-Juca Pirama, the noble savage of Gonçalves Dias's romantic poem of the same name. The black is the slave from Castro Alves's poem *A Cachoeira de Paulo Afonso,* an allegory about slavery in Brazil. The priest is Father Anchieta, a Jesuit evangelist. According to historian José Murilo de Carvalho, the woman holding a rose symbolizes the mixture of all these elements of the Brazilian "race."

12. From interview with José Murilo de Carvalho, April 1990, as well as selections of Carvalho's extensive writings on positivism.

13. Christopher Hibbert, *Africa Explored: Europeans in the Dark Continent, 1769–1889* (New York and London: Penguin, 1984), p. 260.

14. The cult of the Indian ran deep, from the first days of the colony through the second monarchy. Afonso Arinos de Mello Franco has written of the proud Portuguese who took back full-blooded Indian chieftains to the French court as though they were badges of savage reverence. (Many died on the way or in Europe.) Roger Debret, the French-born naturalized Brazilian painter, devoted thousands of canvases to the Indians he encountered—each, however, with remarkably white features.

15. Claude Lévi-Strauss, *Tristes Tropiques* (New York: Atheneum, 1973), p. 134.

16. Antônio Carlos de Souza Lima, "O Santo Soldado: Pacificador, Bandeirante, Amansador de Índios, Civilizador do Sertão, Apôstolo de Humanidade. Uma Leitura de *Rondon Conta Sua Vida,* de Esther de Viveiros," Museu Nacional & Universidade Federal de Rio de Janeiro, communicação #21, 1990.

17. Stauffer, op. cit., pp. 52–55.

18. Ibid., pp. 31–33.

19. John Hemming, *Amazon Frontier: The Defeat of the Brazilian Indians* (Oxford: Oxford University Press, 1987), p. 74.

20. Gagliardi, op. cit., p. 123.

21. Stauffer, op. cit., p. 310, cited in Souza Lima, *Sociedade e Indigenismo no Brasil* (Rio de Janeiro: Editora Marca Zero, 1987), p. 161.

22. Stauffer, op. cit., p. 21.

23. Cândido Rondon, in interview with *Jornal do Comércio,* Rio de Janeiro, April 7, 1922.

24. O'Reilly, op. cit., pp. 79, 189, and 272.

25. In some cases, such as in the territory of the Yanomami, a Stone Age forest tribe in north-central Amazonia, the military unapologetically set about to reduce the vast domain of their reservation. The idea was to crumble the 9.4 million hectares (23.4 million acres) of Yanomami lands into indigenous "colonies" within a sea of national park and forestland, whose mineral and timber wealth could be exploited for the benefit of dominant society. That is something their proponents said would amount to an Indian gulag archipelago.

26. Coutinho, op. cit. Thanks to vaccinations and better medical care, the Indian population of Brazil has climbed to about 230,000.

4. FRONTIER OUT OF SEASON

1. See Warren Dean, *Brazil and the Struggle for Rubber: A Study in Environmental History* (Cambridge, England: University of Cambridge Press, 1987).

2. Roderick Nash, *Wilderness and the American Mind,* 3d ed. (New Haven: Yale University Press, 1982), p. 143.

3. Lévi-Strauss, op. cit., p. 78.

4. Crosby, op. cit., p. 135.

5. FORGING CONTROVERSY

1. Cited in John Perlin, *A Forest Journey: The Role of Wood in the Development of Civilization* (New York: W. W. Norton, 1989), p. 168.

2. Data are from the Brazilian Institute of Geography and Statistics, IBGE, 1990 precensus estimates.

3. Bertha K. Becker, "Estudo Geopolítico Contemporâneo da Amazônia," unpublished study for the *Macrocenários, Amazônia 2010,* series

for Sudam, Superintendência do Desenvolvimento da Amazônia, 1989.

4. Skidmore, op. cit., p. 145.

5. Braudel, op. cit., vol. I, *The Structures of Everyday Life,* p. 362.

6. Michael Williams, *Americans and Their Forests: A Historical Geography* (New York: Columbia University Press, 1989), p. 147.

7. Frederick J. Turner, *The Significance of the Frontier in American History* (New York: Holt, Rinehart, and Winston, 1962), p. 313.

8. Braudel, op. cit., vol. I, *The Structures of Everyday Life,* pp. 362–71.

9. This information was culled from personal interviews in October 1990 with energy consultant Mauro de Almedia, then of Itaminas, and Luís Carlos Cardoso Vale, a forestry consultant for the steel industry, and from Ibama reports on reforestation and the steel industry.

6. FROM FORESTS TO TIMBER

1. Perlin, op. cit., p. 25.

2. Norman Myers, in his book *The Primary Source: Tropical Forests and Our Future* (New York: W. W. Norton, 1984), estimated that exports of tropical timber generated eight billion dollars a year for producer countries in 1984.

3. Alfred Russel Wallace, *A Narrative of Travels on the Amazon and Rio Negro, and Other Observations on the Climate, Geology, and Natural History of the Amazon Valley,* 1853 (New York: Hackell House, 1969), p. 32.

4. Christopher Uhl and Ima Célia G. Vieira, "Ecological Impacts of Selective Logging in the Brazilian Amazon: A Case Study from the Paragominas Region," *Biotrópica,* vol. 21, no. 2 (1989), pp. 96–98.

5. Christopher Uhl et al., "Wood as a Catalyst to Ecological Change in Amazonia," University of Florida Working Papers series, 1990.

6. Braudel, op. cit., vol. I, *The Structures of Everyday Life,* p. 362.

7. Perlin, op. cit., p. 105.

8. Braudel, op. cit., vol. I, *The Structures of Everyday Life,* pp. 363–65.

9. Williams, op. cit., p. 127.

10. Perlin, op. cit., p. 213.

11. Uhl et al., op. cit., p. 6.

12. Uhl and Vieira, op. cit., p. 99.

13. Perlin, op. cit., p. 108.

14. This seminal study is by N. R. de Graff, "Sustainable Timber Production in the Tropical Rainforest of Suriname," and was presented at a

workshop on management of soils in the humid tropics, San José, Costa Rica, 1982.

7. STRANGE FRUIT

1. From personal interview with Paraná state secretary of agriculture, Osmar Dias, Curitiba, Paraná, July 1990.

2. Of Paraná's emigrants, 54 percent went to São Paulo, 19.9 percent to Mato Grosso, and 10.6 percent to Acre, Rondônia, Amapá, and Roraima. Source: Paraná State Agriculture Department.

3. Much of the reigning wisdom on the Amazon settlers says that the frontier was a safety valve, the wastebasket, in the description of others, for the disinherited from the south. In fact, the Amazon's poor and desperate hail mostly from the northeast, where the most skewed landownership patterns persist until this day. The southerners who became pioneers in Mato Grosso and Rondônia were generally among the more fortunate and capitalized of the *colonos*. As sociologists put it, most were "pulled" more by cheaper land and the notion of betterment than they were "pushed" by big agribusiness or enclosure of public lands. As much as despair, a spirit of adventure helped open the way.

4. Van Alstyne, op. cit., p. 117.

5. José Murilo de Carvalho, *Teatro de Sombras: A Política Imperial* (Rio de Janeiro: Edições Vértice/Iuperj, 1988), pp. 84–105.

6. Ibid.

7. Francisco Graziano Neto, "Latifúndios e Verdades: Crítica ao Distributivismo Agrário," Rascunho no. 9, Faculdade de Ciências e Letras, Unesp/Araraquara, São Paulo, June 1990.

8. William H. Nicholls, "The Agricultural Frontier in Modern Brazilian History: The State of Paraná, 1920–1965," *Revista Brasileira de Economia* (October–December 1975), as cited by Martin Katzman, "Colonialization as an Approach to Regional Development: Northern Paraná, Brazil," *American Journal of Agricultural Economics* (May 1978).

9. In 1963, on the eve of the push toward modernization, São Paulo, the heart of Brazil's bread basket, had 6.3 million workers in the countryside. Not a quarter of a century later, in 1986, there were only 1.2 million farm workers in a state of 32 million. They represented only 6 percent of the state's work force but produced fully a fifth of Brazil's agricultural produce.

10. Lévi-Strauss, op. cit., p. 98.

11. Philip Fearnside, Meira Filho, Luiz Gylvan, and Antônio Tebaldi Tardin, "Deforestation Rate in Brazilian Amazon," joint report by the Bra-

zilian Space Institute (Inpe), and the Institute for Amazonian Studies (Inpa), August 1990, p. 5.

8. "ADVENTURERS, MADMEN, AND STARVELINGS"

1. Van Alstyne, op. cit., pp. 118–19.
2. *Columbus,* loc. cit., pp. 29–30.
3. Burns, op. cit., pp. 60–63.
4. Lévi-Strauss, op. cit., p. 263.
5. David Cleary, *Anatomy of the Amazon Gold Rush* (Iowa City: University of Iowa Press, 1990), pp. 24–26.
6. Ibid., p. 126.
7. Ibid., pp. 125–26.
8. Investors might be charier still after Goldmine's row with the Central Bank in early 1992 over "irregular" (though not illegal) exchange operations. Taking advantage of Brazil's two-tiered dollar-cruzeiro exchange rate, Goldmine aggressively bought and sold dollars, raking in more than five million dollars in 1991. Though many banks played the same game, Goldmine and another bank were charged with violating the spirit, if not the letter, of the law. Charges were dropped when both banks agreed to give back to the Central Bank the profits they made through such speculation. Though its reputation may have been tarnished, the foundation's *garimpo* clean-up campaign still seemed a worthy effort.
9. Not far from here the Brazilian Army had a top security base where it had dug a great cylindrical hole in the ground, apparently for nuclear testing. Collor, in a showy move, flew to Cachimbo to throw lime in that hole, a symbolic gesture meant to show Brasília's firm commitment against nuclear weapons. Doubts remained, however, about the fate of the shadowy parallel nuclear program run by the Brazilian military.

9. REPAIRING RONDÔNIA

1. George Martine, "Rondônia and the Fate of Small Producers," in *The Future of Amazonia: Destruction or Sustainable Development?,* ed. David Goodman and Anthony Hall (London: Macmillan Publishers, 1989).
2. *Diário do Congresso Nacional,* Brasília, June 1990, pp. 3124–25.
3. Buarque de Holanda, *Visões do Paraíso,* pp. 15–17.
4. Martine, op. cit.

10. Tempering the Tropics

1. Buarque de Holanda, *Moncões,* p. 104.
2. Sharp, op. cit., p. 371.
3. Ibid., p. 377.
4. Bryce, op. cit., p. 560.

11. Japanese in the Amazon

1. Roberto Santos, *A História Econômica da Amazônia, 1880–1920* (São Paulo: Editora T. A. Queiroz, 1980), pp. 105–6.
2. Christopher Uhl and Scott Subler, "Farming in the Amazon—Japanese Style," unpublished manuscript, Belém, 1990.
3. "The sight of grumbling Japanese farmers dumping loads of produce in the river at the end of the market day must have seemed even more odd," write Christopher Uhl and Scott Subler, Pennsylvania State University biologists who have long tracked developments in Tomé Açu. See Uhl and Subler, "Japanese Agroforestry in Amazonia: A Case Study in Tomé Açu, Brazil," research paper for Pennsylvania State University, Agriculture Department, 1989, p. 4.
4. Braudel, op. cit., vol. III, *The Perspective of the World,* p. 149.

12. Of Cattle and Kudzu

1. These data are taken from studies by Brazilian agronomist Adilson Serrão, of Embrapa's Humid Tropics Center, Cpatu, in Belém, and "Pecuária na Amazonia: A Evolucão da Sustentabilidade das Pastagens Substituindo Florestas," a presentation on ranching in the Amazon for a Brazilian Senate committee seminar: "O Futuro Econômico da Amazônia: Agricultura," held in Brasília, May 1990.
2. Crosby, op. cit., p. 162.
3. Judson Ferreira Valentim, "Impacto Ambiental da Pecuária no Acre," unpublished report for Embrapa-Acre, December 8, 1989, p. 21.
4. Ibid., p. 24.
5. Alfredo Kingo Oyama Homma, "Será Possivel a Agricultura Sustentada na Amazônia?," paper presented at the International Seminar on Agricultural Policy—DER/UFV, Viçosa, Minas Gerais, November 20–22, 1990.
6. Serrão, op. cit., p. 10.
7. The asphalt would not reach Rio Branco until early 1992.

13. The Death and Life of Chico Mendes

1. Author's translation of "Panela de Pressão." Original: *"Vamos dar valor ao seringueiro/ Vamos dar valor à esta nação/Pois é com o trabalho deste povo/ que se faz pneu de carro/e pneu de caminhão. . . . Tanta coisa da borracha que/ não sei explicar, não/ Encontrei pedaço dela em panela de pressão."*

2. In Brazilian law a judge may determine a longer sentence, but that would give the defendants the right to an automatic appeal.

3. In a startling ruling, however, in late February 1992 the jury's decision against Darly was overturned by a panel of three judges, who decided by a two to one vote that the evidence did not sustain a guilty verdict against the father. The decision gave Darly the right to a new trial, though the Mendes family lawyers promply appealed to the Supreme Court to maintain the original verdict. Darci's sentence was not altered, and Darly, convicted on several other murder cases, remained in jail.

4. Cunha, quoted in Santos, op. cit., p. 204.

5. Ibid.

6. Coagulation can be delayed by mixing the liquid latex with ammonia, an alkaline compound, but that requires hauling another heavy liquid through the forest.

7. Charles Peters, Alwyn H. Gentry, and Robert O. Mendelsohn, "Valuation of an Amazon Rainforest," *Nature* (June 29, 1989).

8. Fundação de Tecnologia do Estado do Acre (Funtac), *Monitoramento da Cobertura Florestal do Estado do Acre, Desmatamento e Uso Atual da Terra* (Rio Branco: 1990), p. 178.

9. Júnia Rodrigues de Alencar, "O Desafio Agrícola do Acre," *A Gazeta* (May 27, 1990), p. 13. Rodrigues, director of the Acre branch of Embrapa, cites state tax data showing that in 1983 rubber and nuts supplied 23 percent of total tax revenues, but only 12.8 percent in 1988. In the same period the contribution of meat and dairy products rose from a negligible 2 to 7.1 percent. In the agricultural sector alone, nuts and rubber accounted for 90 percent of tax revenues in 1983, but only 60.7 percent in 1988. During the same time cattle ranching increased its share almost fivefold, from 7.1 to 33.7 percent. (Cattle's share might even have been far higher; Acre officials admit that clandestine butcher shops escape the tax inspectors' net, and a good deal of meat, milk, and cheese routinely left the state untaxed.)

10. Funtac, op. cit., p. 177.

11. Warren Dean's *Brazil and the Struggle for Rubber,* loc. cit., is the best account of the Brazilian rubber economy.

12. Wallace, op. cit., p. 20.

13. Braudel, op. cit., vol. III, *The Perspective of the World,* p. 64.

14. Braudel, op. cit., vol. I, *The Structures of Everyday Life,* p. 364.

15. Felisberto Cardoso de Camargo, transcript of his lecture, "Nossa Crise de Borracha," at Higher War College (Rio de Janeiro, undated month/day, 1951), p. 3.

14. THE JUNGLE OF POLICY

1. Author's translation of poem by Prado, in *Retratos do Brasil.* Herewith the original: *São desgraças do Brasil/ Um patriotismo fôfo/ Leis com parolas/ Preguiça/ Ferrugem/ Formiga/e Môfo.*

2. Such programs of fiscal incentives did not begin with the military government or in the Amazon. They were, in fact, a preferred tool of Brazilian governments—be they democratic, populist, or dictatorial—since the beginning of the republic. Kubitschek, who wanted to yank Brazil out of the torpor of third world agriculturalism, was a champion of fiscal incentives—distributing favors, public works, and patronage throughout Brazil, especially in the interior. The military followed suit and upped the ante. Eventually some seven hundred million dollars were lavished on businesses, cattle ranches, and industries. Until 1988 Brasília blessed 674 such projects (mostly cattle ranches) with fifteen-year tax exemptions, cheap credits, and outright concessions or subsidies.

Such incentives, it was argued, were necessary to attract people to the forbidding frontier zone. And there are some things to show for all the money spent. One monument is the Zona Franca, the Free Zone of Manaus, which built an industrial park, with dozens of electronics industries and assembly plants, and created sixty thousand jobs. The Zona Franca operated thanks to concessions from the government, which exempted industries, especially electronics firms, from import duties to build high-tech equipment and sell it to the rest of Brazil. The policy did build a formidable industrial park, where Honda motorcycles, Panasonic VCRs, and Mitsubishi television sets are assembled. But twenty years after its creation, in 1970, the Zona Franca still owed its survival to government protection that made it more an economic greenhouse than a vigorous market. By 1991 the government, on a liberal trader binge, had threatened to pull the plug by lifting import restrictions on the rest of Brazil and so rudely yanking Manaus's special privileges. However, by May 1991 the gutsy economy minister, Zélia Cardoso de Mello, fell from grace and then from power. Persistent inflation and government infighting were largely to blame, but a good part of her downfall was her losing battle with the encrusted crony system of the Zona Franca. She clashed directly with the cronies' public godfather, President Collor's regional development secretary, Egberto Baptista, who fought, and won, the extension of import credits to the Manaus elite. Those credits, amounting to $1.6 billion, guaranteed the maintenance of the Amazon's industrial greenhouse. Baptista's brother was a partner in one of the companies blessed with new credits.

The best study on fiscal incentives is still the "Resultados de 20 Anos de Incentivos Fiscais na Agropecuária da Amazônia," a 1988 report for the government economy ministry by José Garcia Gasques and Clando Yokimozo. They reported that much of the money that was distributed under the rubric of fiscal incentives was simply squandered. An inspection team found a scandalous situation in the Amazon. The worst offenders were the 631 cattle ranchers who got fifteen years of tax breaks to plant pastures that barely supported cattle for five, before turning into brown, useless stubble. Of thirty-five projects bequeathed incentives after 1967, inspectors found that only one had reached "satisfactory" output, according to the rules of their contracts. Fully 30 percent of the projects had been totally abandoned. Of ninety-four ranches visited, only three were making profits. And fully thirty-nine of fifty-nine projects had been set up in forested regions, thus breaking the official rules on the books at Sudam.

Sudam, the government agency that administered and approved these projects, was all but paralyzed in 1990. "Sudam had become a counter for passing out money," Alcyr Meira, the new agency chief, told me in an interview. The counter had shut down in 1989, and through much of the next two years it was closed for inventory. However, many agencies were pursuing money on their own. Acre, which had never been favored in the Belém-dominated Sudam financing schemes, went directly abroad for money. It managed grants, loans, and consultancy contracts with organizations such as the IDB, the International Tropical Timber Organization, and the government of Canada.

3. H. Blair Neatby, *The Canadians, 1867–1967* (New York: St. Martin's Press, 1967), pp. 142–43.

4. Treadgold, op. cit., p. 246.

5. Each state had its own environmental agenda and policy. The result: In the Grande Carajás one major steelmaker in Maranhão State, Vale do Pindaré, was allowed to extract timber for charcoal under a state-sanctioned forest management plan, while a few miles down the tracks, in the state of Pará, Cosipar's plan was vetoed by that state's environmental agency.

6. Actually the numbers are slightly better than Lutz's. Samuel's reservoir covered 56,000 hectares (138,320 acres), and its capacity, in 1990, was 86,000 kilowatts. Still, that works out to a mediocre output of 1.5 kilowatts per hectare of flooded land.

7. Goldemberg was later promoted to education minister.

8. In late 1991 Collor at last issued a decree in favor of demarcating Yanomami lands, but as of March 1992 surveying work had not yet begun.

9. Lutzenberger finally got his reprieve in March 1992. In a broad brush accusation, Lutz charged that Ibama, the agency he commanded, was corrupt and had sold out to the timber industry. That sparked a loud public clash with Ibama president, Eduardo Martins, who threatened to quit and take 27 top echelon staffers with him. For several days Brazil's two top environmental authorities volleyed insults and accusations back and forth in the headlines, until Collor fired them both. The Education Minister, José Goldemberg, who was already encroaching on Lutzenberger's neglected terrain, was named interim environmental secretary.

10. Alberto Setzer and Marcos Pereira, "Amazonia Biomass Burnings in 1987 and an Estimate of Their Tropospheric Emissions," *Ambio*, Swedish Academy of Sciences (February 1991).

11. Data are from interviews with Brazil's former science and technology secretary, José Goldemberg, and with Gylvan Meira Filho, director of Brazil's Institute of Space Research. Meira Filho notes that Brazil is the only major country whose forest burnings contribute far more air pollution (a 3.5 to 1.5 ratio) than do its automobiles.

15. CALL OF THE WILD

1. Wallace, op. cit., p. 3.

2. Ibid., p. 47.

3. H. M. Tomlinson, *The Sea and the Jungle*, 1912 (New York: Time-Life Books, 1964), p. 10.

4. Lévi-Strauss, op. cit., p. 335.

5. Wayne Hage, *Storm over the Rangelands: Private Rights in Federal Lands* (Bellevue, Wash.: Free Enterprise Press, 1989), p. 159.

6. Turner, op. cit., pp. 269–71.

7. *Beyond Geography, the Western Spirit against the Wilderness* (New York: Viking, 1980), by Frederick Turner (no relation to his antithetical namesake, Frederick Jackson Turner), is a compelling, and condemning, book about the Western obsession with global conquest.

8. Dubos, op. cit., p. 5.

9. Ibid., p. 15, from Aldous Huxley, "Wordsworth and the Tropics," in *Do What You Will* (New York: Doubleday, 1929).

10. Nash, op. cit., p. 348.

11. Ibid., p. 23.

12. Earl Pomeroy, quoted in Brian W. Dippie, "The Winning of the West Reconsidered," *Wilson Quarterly* (Summer 1990), pp. 82–83.

13. Nash, op. cit., p. 369.

14. Slotkin, op. cit.

15. Lévi-Strauss, op. cit., p. 392.

INDEX